Economic Direct Democracy

Economic Direct Democracy:

A Framework to End Poverty and Maximize Well-Being

John C. Boik, Ph.D.

Economic Direct Democracy: A Framework to End Poverty and Maximize Well-Being

Library of Congress Control Number: 2014909756

Published in the United States of America by SiteForChange, at CreateSpace Independent Publishing Platform, North Charleston, SC

Contact via website: http://www.PrincipledSocietiesProject.org.

ISBN-13: 978-1499640595
ISBN-10: 1499640595

Cover design by Chris Mohler.

Version 1.1.0, May 30, 2014.
This manuscript may be periodically updated with corrections and small improvements. Revised versions may be posted to the Principled Societies Project website. If you find errors or have a suggested improvement, please contact us through our website.

The terms *LEDDA*, *Local Economic Direct Democracy Association*, *Certified LEDDA*, *Principled Business*, *Certified Principled Business*, and *Token Exchange System* are trademarks of John C. Boik.

Warning and Disclaimer
Every effort has been made to make this book as accurate as possible, but information is provided on an "as is" basis with no warranty implied. SiteForChange holds no responsibility for the persistence, accuracy, or appropriateness of URL links or the content of linked websites.

Bulk Sales
SiteForChange offers favorable discounts on this title when ordered in quantity. We invite nonprofits, social entrepreneurs, and others to use this book as part of their fundraising programs. And we invite instructors to use it in schools. For information, contact us through the Principled Societies Project website.

For Johanna, who has loved me through all the challenges.

Praise for *Economic Direct Democracy*

The first decade of the 21st century witnessed the global financial crisis, the Occupy and Arab Spring movements, skyrocketing income inequality, geopolitical shakeups, and irrefutable evidence that the planet can no longer sustain the destructive capacities of unfettered markets. In this book-length proposal for a new, local approach to economic organization—one steeped in transparency and democratic processes—John Boik asks us to envision a future beyond crisis. Rather than replacing dominant systems, his proposal seeks to harnesses them, in part by rethinking money itself. His aims are to sustain and enrich the public good by building the infrastructures necessary for cooperation and, ultimately, for human and planetary survival. This provocative book is a signpost for where we as a species enter the new millennium. Its viewpoint challenges us to imagine what we might become.

Bill Maurer, Ph.D.
Dean, School of Social Sciences
Professor, Anthropology, Law, and Criminology
Director, Institute for Money, Technology and Financial Inclusion
Co-Director, Intel Science and Technology Center for Social Computing
University of California, Irvine

Economic Direct Democracy offers an important and pragmatic roadmap for advancing a new economic paradigm based on well-being and happiness. Going further than Thomas Piketty (*Capital in the Twenty-First Century*), who proposed tax-based solutions to capitalism's fatal flaws, Boik aims at foundations of capitalism by questioning the meaning of money and the purpose of an economy. The result is a rational and compelling proposal for building a supra-capitalism economy atop the structure of the old one. It is the most complete and well-reasoned plan for addressing society's crises that I have read to date. We can do better than capitalism as usual. We can meet material needs, enjoy meaningful jobs, pay good wages, provide quality health care, and protect the environment. But we can't get there from here without asking who we are, what an economy is, and what makes us happy. I recommend *Economic Direct Democracy* to anyone interested in community well-being.

Mark Anielski
Adjunct Professor, School of Business
University of Alberta
Author, The Economics of Happiness
Co-founder, Genuine Wealth Inc.

John Boik's *Economic Direct Democracy* is a blueprint for achieving Occupy Wall Street's goals of social equality and sustainability, and the Tea Party's goals of more effective, more responsive, and more local self-governance. By proposing new tools to organize and turbocharge local economies, Boik offers a viable path to greater economic security, greater equality, and enhanced well-being. His bold, imaginative, and thought-provoking book offers a fundamentally new, exciting way to think about community and economic development.

Michael Shuman
Director of Community Portals, Mission Markets
Author, Local Dollars, Local Sense

In *Economic Direct Democracy*, John Boik accomplishes what few critics of existing economic systems have dared attempt. He offers a specific, systematic, reasoned plan for an improved structure. His proposal aims to transform business as usual into business as sustainable, maximization of profit into maximization of well-being, too-big-to-fail into locally owned diversity, and financial crisis into financial flourishing. The specificity of his proposal invites critique—and critical, open-minded consideration is exactly what it deserves.

Helen Scharber, Ph.D.
Assistant Professor of Economics
Hampshire College

Thought-provoking and revealing, *Economic Direct Democracy* fills the gap between the ideals of economic democracy and its concrete, feasible implementations. The book addresses concerns held by local-currency skeptics who question the potential of community currencies to act as tools for local economic development and social regeneration. And it provides concerned citizens, who might have minimal previous knowledge of economics, a framework for understanding. Boik delivers a novel synthesis that promises to empower community leaders in achieving meaningful social progress.

Georgina Gomez, Ph.D.
International Institute of Social Studies
Erasmus University, Rotterdam

The possibility of utopia—that is, of a radically improved world—has been thrashed by the press in the neoliberal period, especially after Margaret Thatcher's famous quip about capitalism, "There is no alternative." Yet steering the course over recent decades has only made the failings of capitalism more transparent. Sweeping change is needed, and it starts with imagination. Moving from TINA to TAPAS ("there are plenty of alternatives") is essential if we want to pass on a livable world to our children. In this context, *Economic Direct Democracy* is essential. Boik's work makes clear that hopes for a greener, happier, healthier, and more secure world are not ephemeral wisps of wishful thinking, never to see fulfillment. Rather, they are sane, necessary, and, with publication of this book, increasingly grounded and ready to ignite action. Through concrete designs and thoughtful analysis, Boik offers practical solutions to the myriad problems that arise when political democracies are weak and control over economic decisions resembles a feudal hierarchy.

Michel Bauwens
Founder, The Foundation for Peer-to-Peer Alternatives
Primavera Research Fellow, University of Amsterdam
Research Director, FLOK Society Transition Program, Ecuador

Economic Direct Democracy offers original and intriguing ideas for addressing a number of deep-seated and seemingly intractable social and economic problems. As threats mount, we must be willing to consider new approaches. Would his ideas work? One of the intriguing aspects of John's proposal is its focus on trial and implementation at the local scale, building on existing economies. This practical approach might allow us to find out. If he's right, it could help point a way forward.

Andrew Heintzman
President and CEO, Investeco Capital Corp.
Board of Directors, Tides Canada Foundation
Author, The New Entrepreneurs

Economic Direct Democracy is an important and powerful contribution to the evolving and urgently needed discussion about how to stop our slide—both political and economic—toward oligarchy, and the means to implement democratic policies that benefit all.

Thom Hartmann
Host, "The Thom Hartmann Program"
Author, The Crash of 2016

Contents

Foreword

Each generation has its visionaries. No real progress is possible without some individuals seeing beyond the day-to-day complacency of conventional wisdom to help us imagine a better world. In ages past, the insights of visionaries might have taken decades or centuries to influence change. But in the modern, wired, technological era, change can come blindingly fast, even if it starts slowly and in small groups. More than ever before, innovative ideas can be impossible to arrest.

John Boik has a few to share. He is among a new cohort of original thinkers who dare to push boundaries and challenge accepted truths. A biologist trained to think in terms of systems, he sees our economic woes from the fresh perspective of a scholar and outsider. These days, the discipline of economics is marred by conflicts of interests and a disheartening level of complacency, so it is not surprising that the most promising innovations may come from non-economists. We must encourage out-of-the-box thinking among ourselves, our students, and civil society.

As an academic unburdened by "economics as usual," John is a passionate advocate for social change. I read his 2012 book, *Creating Sustainable Societies*, and am excited to see this expanded version, which, like the first, is published under a Creative Commons license— a fitting approach for sharing ideas about how cooperation can change the world.

Economic Direct Democracy is a radical manifesto for change that is, above all, sensible. It merges theoretical reflections, systems thinking, and the results from computer modeling to generate a scientifically sound, captivating narrative. John's views complement those of several political and ecological economists, including myself, who have discussed at length the inadequacy of the current development model to deliver equity, social justice, and sustainability.

Hard as it may be for some to accept, our economic institutions are largely outdated. Neoclassical views of economic growth—and the use of GDP as *the* guide for policy—are ripe for replacement. They have been proved unsatisfactory, and new approaches are available to supplant them. Yet neoclassical views continue to influence our decisions, permeating university textbooks, politics, investment strategies, and corporate boardrooms.

Neoclassical views may be consistent within their own frameworks, but they lead down the wrong path. They fail to take into account that humans are inherently social, motivated by empathy as well as self-interest, and that an economy is a human-designed system of governance. More so than political institutions, the economic "rules of the game" define how we act in day-to-day life, what we can attain, and the type of society in which we live. Although we are taught to believe that economies are neutral or indifferent, just "attached" to a society, the reality is that they are systems of interrelations and institutions that spring from a society, for good or ill.

Indeed, the best way to think of an economy is as a web of rules that describe and define human interactions. And money—the quintessential element of economic interaction—is nothing other than a governance tool. Rather than viewing the functions of money as a measure of value or medium of exchange (as is taught in university courses), we are better off thinking of money primarily as a mechanism to register preferences—in John's words, as a "voting tool."

When viewed as such, money becomes a powerful adjunct to conventional tools of politics. This is not money undermining politics, but rather money creating new opportunities for the "common" person to express social power, including expression of empathy, support, environmental concern, and preference to cooperate. If we want real change—if we want a world that is actually fair, functional, healthy, and sustainable—we may very well start by rethinking money itself.

By reducing inequalities and empowering all peopl[e]
meaningful role in economic decision-making, we w[ill]
the trajectory of self-destruction induced by our curr[ent]
models. If our economic "rules of the game" remain [for the]
ultra-wealthy and ultra-powerful, there is little hope t[hat our]
institutions will break free of their influence sufficientl[y]
about needed radical transformation.

For some years now, many of us have been critiquing the cu[rrent]
economic model for its flaws and the deep injustices it perpetua[tes.]
Economic Direct Democracy will help us move from "critique" t[o]
"action." Through a series of compelling arguments, analyses, and
proposals, John makes a crucial contribution to the global debate
occurring among civil society, academics, governments, and progressive thinkers about innovative approaches to new, more sustainable
social systems.

Unlike conventional approaches that view challenges as discrete
problems to be addressed by partial reforms and technological inter-
ventions, the arguments in this book make clear that the challenges
we face are profoundly interrelated. Success depends on adopting
a holistic, systems viewpoint, and reorganizing societies so that our
methods and policies align with our values.

By taking the wide view and connecting the dots, we can reframe our
seemingly intractable societal problems into ones that readily express
solutions—we can imagine new ways forward.

The insights and approaches advanced in this book have far-reaching
implications. Even though its analysis is restricted to the United
States, its findings may very well apply elsewhere in the world. In
fact, the transformative potential of local currencies and economic
democracy is even greater in societies that still retain important
features of solidaristic economic development, social cohesion, and
a strong sense of community responsibility—something that many
"developed" societies seem to have lost.

Most important, *Economic Direct Democracy* delivers a powerful
message: change is not only possible, it is within reach. Politicians
and technology gurus will not fix the world for us. But we can,
through a steady process of regaining control over our economies.

asserting the importance of democratic control over economic cisions, we may very well trigger the most powerful revolution f all times: a calm, bloodless revolution led by millions of women and men of common sense who are dedicated to building a more equitable, safer, fairer, and happier world.

Lorenzo Fioramonti
Professor of Political Economy
Director, Centre for the Study of Governance Innovation
University of Pretoria, South Africa
Author, *Gross Domestic Problem: The Politics Behind the World's Most Powerful Number*

Preface

One might wonder why a cancer biologist is writing a book on economic systems. The reason is simple: I read the national news, and it's frightening. I read science papers in a range of fields, including environmental and climate science, and economics—and many of them are frightening. I watch as too many friends and family members suffer from unemployment, inadequate health care, low wages, and job dissatisfaction. I smell foul air and see filthy water. And I wonder why life is like this, and even more, what can be done. But every simple solution that I hear of, or can think of, falls short.

Our problems are like the proverbial skein of tangled yarn—if we pull one loop in an attempt to straighten the mess, the tangle tightens elsewhere. My mother, an excellent knitter, and pragmatist, reaches for a new skein when an old one has become too jumbled to repair. It's apparent to me that if we are to solve our intractable, intertwined socioeconomic and environmental problems, truly solve them, we will need to do something similar.

Our problems—indeed, economies themselves—are, to a substantial degree, outward expressions of inwardly held ideas and beliefs. If we are to fix our problems, then we will need to examine—and replace as necessary—root concepts. Who are we, as social creatures? And what is our relationship to other beings on this planet? What makes people happy, in the deepest sense? What is democracy? What is an economy? What is money? A good portion of *Economic Direct*

Democracy describes new mechanisms for a better economy, but new mechanisms are useful only to the degree that they are supported by a change in understanding. Policies, institutions, and economies shift when consciousness shifts. Ideas matter more than mechanisms themselves.

In replacing established beliefs, our own biology offers a source of inspiration.

There are nearly 7 billion people on the planet today—an almost incomprehensible number. It's amazing that a global society with so many members somehow manages to feed itself, or at least mostly feed itself. Yet the number of humans on the planet is tiny compared with the roughly 10 trillion cells that make up the human body. In some meaningful sense, these trillions of cells do a better job of cooperating with one another than we humans do.

Despite the layered dynamics inherent within the complex society of cells we call a person, each cell receives what it needs. Cells in the legs do not starve, for example, while cells in the thumbs receive excessive resources. Wastes do not pile up to dangerous levels. And the body doesn't prematurely self-destruct if given modest care. All cells benefit the whole, and growth occurs only when and where it is needed.

The perfection and harmony manifest in this inner cellular society are nothing short of awe-inspiring, especially when contrasted with the injustices and cruelties observed in human history and in current society. Biology has much to teach about how we might organize ourselves to cooperate more fully, support others inhabiting the shared global environment, and enjoy deeper wellness.

Biology also teaches us what to avoid. Sometimes things go wrong within a cell. Its DNA can become so damaged that the cell no longer responds to the restraining signals produced by its neighbors and environment. When this cell passes on its faulty DNA to daughter cells, and they in turn pass it on to their descendants, a cancer is born. Harmony is disrupted. Anthropomorphically speaking, the new tumor displays greed. It devours the resources other cells need. In growing without restraint, it destroys everything in its path. Eventually, it destroys the very body that gives it life. Our own biology is proof that cooperation secures well-being and greed destroys it.

Fortunately, the imperative to cooperate that is genetically programmed into our cells also expresses itself in the person as a whole. Like the cells of which we are composed, we instinctively seek cooperation. This is the good news that somehow always seems underreported. The large, perhaps vast majority of us long to cooperate and help others, and want others to cooperate and offer help in return. This crucial notion—too often missing in the public discourse—could by itself bring about rapid, positive social change. Once it is fully grasped, the misconception that humans are predominantly selfish—and deserve a dirty, dog-eat-dog world—falls away. So too does the trance-inducing power that dysfunctional systems hold over us. To the degree that a system thwarts cooperation, allows poverty, or harms the shared environment, it is understood to act against human nature and is viewed as a failure.

To paraphrase Gandhi, the best way to bring about change is to "be the change." Then it is immediate and real. Cooperation becomes more powerful when more join in. Much can be accomplished when two people choose to help one another, but far greater achievements are possible when 2,000 or 200,000 do so. This is the size where new beginnings are possible—where change can most easily and most rapidly begin. While it is important to demand better leadership from state and federal governments, it is not necessary, or wise, to wait for them to act. We can "be the change" now, as communities. Communities define the front lines of social, environmental, and economic stress. A community knows its problems firsthand and, with the right tools, is positioned and motivated to make rapid, even sweeping progress.

The goal of this book is to help unleash the power of communities by offering a useful toolbox. The vision behind it is of human societies in the not-too-distant future displaying a harmony and beauty that rival the remarkable society of cells within us.

* * *

As a note to the reader, the format used here for literature citation follows a style commonly used in scientific writing. In the text, citations appear as numbers in brackets, for example [1], and refer to entries in the "References" section at the end of the book. Standard footnotes with superscript numbers refer to explanatory entries that appear on the same page.

Economic Direct Democracy is a major revision of my 2012 book, *Creating Sustainable Societies*, which is out of print. Clarity has been improved, new chapters and references added, and more focus placed on the local currency system and other elements as mechanisms of democracy. In short, the presentation has matured.

Thanks to Steven Kim for editorial assistance on preliminary drafts. Thanks to James Gien Varney-Wong for his encouragement and comments. Thanks to Lorenzo Fioramonti for his support and interest in writing the foreword. And special thanks to Dinah McNichols, my primary editor for both books; without her suggestions and prodding, neither book would be worthy of your attention. I take full responsibility for the content of both books—any mistakes or omissions are due alone to my lack of understanding.

John Boik
Houston, May 2014

Abbreviations and Glossary

Note: Words in italics denote first reference and are defined later in the glossary.

CBFS: Crowd-Based Financial System. The crowdfunding system that *members* use to fund for-profit businesses, *nonprofit organizations*, and *nurture engagements*. The four major arms are: lending, subsidy, donation, and nurture.

CGS: Collaborative Governance System. The hybrid direct democracy system that members use to deliberate and vote on *LEDDA* rules and policy. The three arms are: administrative, legislative, and judicial.

Earmarks: A fraction of total income or token *incentive bonus* that members pay into the CBFS. One or more earmarks exist for each arm of the CBFS.

Engagements: The positions that the CBFS funds. The three types are: *market*, *service*, and *nurture*.

Growth period: In the *LEDDA Microsimulation Model*, the first 15 years in which member incomes and the *token share of income* rise.

Incentive bonus: A bonus paid in *tokens* to those individuals who choose *Wage Option* 2. In the LEDDA Microsimulation Model, the incentive was 3,000 tokens per year.

Income target: A series of annual incomes, to be paid in tokens plus dollars, to those individuals who choose Wage Option 1. Like the incentive, the income target is decided upon by the LEDDA membership.

IP Pool: Intellectual Property Pool. A collection of IP rights for works or inventions developed by the *Principled Businesses* of a LEDDA or group of LEDDAs.

LEDDA: Local Economic Direct Democracy Association. A membership-based, community-benefit association that implements the LEDDA framework.

LEDDA Microsimulation Model: The simulation model of a county-level token–dollar economy submitted for journal publication.

LFNJ: LEDDA-funded new job. A job that is created via CBFS funding.

Market engagement: An engagement funded by the CBFS within the for-profit sector. It is similar to a normal job in the for-profit sector.

Member: A person, business, nonprofit, or other organization that chooses to join a LEDDA and thus is eligible to receive tokens.

NIWF: Not in workforce. Reference to a person or persons who are not in the workforce and so are neither employed nor unemployed.

Nonprofit organizations: Charitable organizations that apply for and receive IRS 501(c)(3) tax exemption, and other organizations that receive tax exemption by default or under a different section of IRS Code. In this book, nonprofit organizations can include schools and colleges, research institutes, charities serving households, public service agencies, churches, and government agencies.

Nurture engagement: An engagement funded by the CBFS that provides income assistance to unemployed and NIWF members. Nurture engagements similar to commissions might also be offered to artists.

Post-CBFS income: Pre-tax income after CBFS contributions have been made. It can be thought of as pre-tax, take-home income.

Principled Business: A business that conforms to a hybrid model unique to the LEDDA framework. The model is a cross between nonprofit and for-profit business models.

Service engagement: An engagement funded by the CBFS within the nonprofit sector. It is similar to a normal job in the nonprofit sector.

Standard business: A for-profit business that is not a Principled Business.

T&D: Tokens plus dollars, or if either is zero, tokens or dollars. The purchasing power of the token is assumed equal to that of the inflation-adjusted dollar.

Target population: In the LEDDA Microsimulation Model, the population of local families that have incomes initially below the 90th percentile (about $101,000 per year).

TES: Token Exchange System. The system that defines token–dollar flow. It consists of the CBFS and *TMS*.

TMS: Token Monetary System. The system that creates and destroys tokens.

Token: The local electronic currency that a LEDDA issues.

TSI: Token share of income. The fraction of a member's income that is paid in tokens.

TSI target: A series of annual TSI values that apply to incomes of individuals who choose Wage Option 1.

Wage Option: An annual choice given to members regarding how their CBFS contributions are calculated. In Wage Option 1, contributions are calculated based on the income target. In Wage Option 2, they are calculated based on the incentive bonus.

Chapter 1

Getting There From Here

"Change is the law of life. And those who look only to the past or the present are certain to miss the future."
—John F. Kennedy (1917–1963)

Imagine for a moment that it is April 1994. David Filo and Jerry Yang have just released the Yahoo! directory, and as yet there is no Internet search engine as we now know it. The Yahoo! directory is not much more than a hand-compiled list of websites. In that same month, Brian Pinkerton releases WebCrawler, the first Internet bot that automatically travels the World Wide Web to index entire pages. AOL is only a year old, and most Americans have never heard of, and don't understand, the concept of email.

Now imagine someone tells you that within 20 years there will be 3 billion email accounts worldwide, more than 15 billion indexed web pages, and $260 billion per year in e-commerce conducted in the United States alone. Suppose someone says you will be able to retrieve driving directions and road maps, complete with satellite and street-view photographs, to almost any destination you desire—all with a click of a mouse. And that you can watch TV and movies, trade stocks, and make international phone calls over the Internet. Would you be skeptical? Intrigued?

Now suppose I say that within the next 25 years local economies will diversify and boom. Cities and counties, small and large, will flourish and lead the way forward in culture, politics, education, and environmental protection and reclamation. The middle class will dramatically expand and poverty will be reduced. Schools and nonprofits will be funded, and quality of life will markedly rise. Corporations will become smaller, on average, and more will be locally owned and financed. The jobs they offer will be more meaningful and satisfying. Transparency and trust will increase, and a cooperative, hopeful spirit will prevail. Would you be skeptical? Intrigued?

Such a future is possible, and this book describes an innovative economic and financial framework (hereafter, economic framework) that can bring it to life. The framework infuses a local economy with democracy. It empowers cities and counties to take more control over their social, economic, and environmental destinies, and acts, in essence, as a local layer of organization on top of the dollar economy. The framework injects a new currency into a region as a complement to the dollar, boosting economic activity and creating jobs. And it helps communities balance their trade with other regions. No one is forced to participate, but every person who does receives a direct economic gain.

In short, by offering deeper democratic control over the local creation and flow of currency, the framework gives individuals a chance to remake their economy into one that optimally serves their needs. The framework can help cities and counties to accomplish bold goals that might otherwise be difficult, if not impossible, to achieve. While the focus of this book is on U.S. cities and counties, and the U.S. economy, its ideas are applicable to cities and regions around the world.

The framework is novel, as a whole, but its components are not. It synthesizes multiple approaches already in use in some cities around the country and the world into a coherent, consistent, integrated whole. The framework builds on ideas from buy-local, invest-local, local-currency, local-food, local-sharing, open-source, open-government, open-data, participatory democracy, and related community development, knowledge transfer, and decision-making initiatives. Each of these shows merit. Each is already helping society to move in a better direction. Used alone, they are powerful, but intelligently combined, they could be even more so. An integrated approach could help us move forward quickly and efficiently, and with relative ease. No legislative action of any kind is required.

1.1 A Confluence of Crises

Modern geologists have yet to perfect the science of earthquake prediction, but the accuracy of their models is steadily improving. We can now estimate, for example, that the chance of a magnitude 7.0 or greater quake hitting Southern California between 2014 and 2036 stands at 87 percent.[1] To put the risk in perspective, a 7.0 magnitude quake is considered "major," large enough to damage most buildings, even those designed to withstand seismic shaking. Moreover, there is a 3 percent chance that a magnitude 8.0 or greater quake will strike. This would be a "great" quake, large enough to cause massive damage and loss of life. One would think that individuals who live in earthquake zones would take precautions, given the substantial and increasingly well-defined risk, but often they don't. The majority of people do little to reduce their vulnerability.[2]

This example sums up the current environmental, social, and economic conditions in the United States and most other countries. (It also sums up the political conditions, but politics is not a focus of this book.) We face a high risk for major damage, and smaller, but not inconsequential risk for catastrophic damage. Yet our response to the dangers has been underwhelming. If we wish to achieve a bright future, of the kind described in the opening to this chapter, we will need to pay attention to the warnings and rumblings beneath our feet. The hope is that unlike geological quakes, environmental, social, and economic disasters can be prevented or at least mitigated, if we act in time.

There is growing consensus that we must somehow restructure our societies in a fundamentally new way if we are to avoid these risks. The most concrete way to achieve the many necessary changes is by developing economic systems whose salient features are already suggested by the limitations confronting our current one.

Six Challenges

In proposing such an economic system, this book highlights six challenges bearing down on us: (1) climate change; (2) resource depletion, habitat destruction, and pollution; (3) debt and financial crises; (4) income and wealth disparities; (5) decaying infrastructure; and (6) rising health-care costs and rising rates of preventable disease. The proposed framework offers a practical means to address each issue. Each has, at its root, an economic component.

Of the six challenges, two are introduced briefly here: climate change—because of the severity of risk—and disparities of income and wealth—because of their central, insidious, and corrosive nature.

In its 2012 report *Turn Down the Heat: Climate Extremes, Regional Impacts, and the Case for Resilience*, the World Bank gave this dire warning:

> *Even with the current mitigation commitments and pledges fully implemented, there is roughly a 20 percent likelihood of exceeding 4°C by 2100. If they are not met, a warming of 4°C could occur as early as the 2060s.*[3]

A 4-degree Celsius rise in average temperature (about 7 degrees Fahrenheit) would far exceed the 2-degree rise that has long been viewed as a threshold we dare not cross. To put the risk in perspective, a 4-degree rise could result in the extinction of more than 40 percent of all species.[4] Anticipated impacts include more frequent and intense droughts, hurricanes, floods, heat waves, forest fires, hail, wind, and tornadoes. Agricultural productivity is expected to drop, and sea levels are expected to rise. The secondary social impacts are likely to be immense. According to the World Bank, they could include widespread hunger, mass migrations, economic crises, and rising poverty.

The latest report from the United Nations Intergovernmental Panel on Climate Change (IPCC), titled *Climate Change 2014: Impacts, Adaptation, and Vulnerability*, expressed similar dire warnings.[5] Climate models for the "high emissions" (i.e., business-as-usual) scenario estimate that global temperatures will rise more than 4.5 degrees Celsius over preindustrial levels by 2100. In summarizing all data, the report warns of "severe, pervasive, and irreversible impacts," and states with high confidence that "a large fraction of both terrestrial and freshwater species faces increased extinction risk." "Unless we act dramatically and quickly," said U.S. Secretary of State John Kerry in response to the report's publication, "science tells us our climate and our way of life are literally in jeopardy."[6]

The gap between the wealthy and poor is greater in the United States than in almost every other developed nation.[7] The richest 400 individuals own nearly as much wealth as is owned by the poorest 50 percent of Americans.[8] Globally, conditions are worse; just 85 people own as much wealth as is owned by the poorest 50 percent of the human race.[9] One-third of all Americans either live in poverty or earn incomes marginally above the poverty level. Almost half of Americans live in poverty or are low-income.[1][11]

Because financial and political power are deeply entwined, income and wealth disparities skew the democratic process and threaten the capacity of Congress to govern. Political gridlock and dysfunction abound, in part due to the influence of big money.[12] The 2012 Congress was the least productive in two decades, and the 2011 Congress was not far behind it.[13] Seventy percent of likely U.S. voters believe that big business and Congress are on the same team, working against the interests of common citizens.[14] The public's trust in Congress, big business, and banks is at or near historic lows.[15] Robert Shiller, winner of the Nobel Prize in economics, has called rising inequality the most important economic problem facing society today.[16]

Local Problems

Climate change, income and wealth disparities, and the four other challenges identified make our current trajectory unsustainable. The question is, what can we do to change course? The first step is to recognize that these challenges are not superficial. All involve complex economic, social, and political issues. Nor are they transient. Most have been with us for decades, and in some cases much longer.

---

[1] "Low income" refers to incomes of 100 percent to 200 percent of the poverty level. The low-income threshold is roughly $45,000 a year for a family of four. One-third of Americans live either in poverty or are near-poor, meaning they have incomes of 100 percent to 150 percent of the poverty level.[10]

Not only have we been unable to solve them, most are growing worse. Apart from some progress to contain health-care costs, there is little indication that real solutions are on the horizon.

It appears that we might be incapable of solving our problems without a dramatic change in approach. Yet dramatic change seems unlikely, given Washington's political gridlock and dysfunction. While our situation is sobering, if not frightening, there is a glimmer of hope. Dramatic change is possible if we shift some attention to the local level. Although all the challenges identified are national (if not global) in scope, each can be addressed effectively at the level of cities, counties, and multi-county regions. If a majority of local regions act, national and global impacts will follow.

State and federal governments have shown sporadic and isolated leadership, and any progress should be praised and encouraged. But in the meantime, cities and counties face the brunt of social, environmental, economic, and financial stresses. Because they can't afford to wait for higher levels of government to act, many are starting to take the initiative. In their article "How Cities Are Fixing America," Katz and Bradley of the Brookings Institution summarize the situation:

> *Cities and metropolitan areas are on their own. The cavalry is not coming. Mired in partisan division and rancor, the federal government appears incapable of taking bold action to restructure our economy and grapple with changing demography and rising inequality. With each illustration of partisan gridlock and each indication of federal, and also state, unreliability, metros are becoming more ambitious in their design, more assertive in their advocacy, more expansive in their reach and remit.*[17]

This is the milieu in which the new economic framework is proposed. It represents a fresh, more democratic, and more transparent approach to economic organization. It is designed to help cities and counties lead the way in meeting their challenges, and in transforming local economies into ones that are sustainable, resilient, and fair.

1.2 Purpose

Even if higher levels of government are currently unable to solve pressing challenges, is a new local economic framework necessary? Can't we make progress at the state and federal levels through legislative reform?

We can, and must put pressure on state and federal governments. But reform isn't enough. For one thing, it is too slow, given the urgency of our needs and the inertia holding back change. Nor should we be satisfied with incremental change, as we have the capacity and resources to take bold steps. Further, reform is not sufficient if we want an economy that maximally improves the public good.

To see this, consider the question, what is an economic system? The answer can be approached from several angles, one of which is function. Paraphrasing from the *International Encyclopedia of the Social Sciences*, the four functions of any economic system are to determine: (1) what products will be produced; (2) how they will be produced; (3) for whom they will be produced and to whom income will flow; and (4) what portion of resources and products will be consumed now, or saved as investment for future production.[18] In other words, an economic system is, at its core, a decision-making system.

But is our economic decision-making system democratic, in the sense that every person has an equal influence over aggregate outcomes? Clearly, this is not the case. Nor is it intended to be. The United States has a political democracy, not an economic one. Billionaire investors and large corporations have far more influence over economic decisions—say, millions of times more influence—than does the typical family or the typical small business.

There is a saying in modern architecture that "form follows function." When it comes to economic systems, the equivalent saying might be "design follows purpose." Arguably, no amount of reform can change our economic system into one that maximally improves conditions for the public—because to achieve this outcome, its design and purpose would need to change. The result would be an entirely new economic system, one that is highly transparent, infused with democracy, and geared to maximize the public good.

As an analogy, the purpose of a tractor is to help farmers till the soil and perform other such duties. Tractors are designed with these functions in mind. No amount of refinement (or reform) will turn a tractor into a race car. Racing is a different function altogether and thus requires a different mechanical design. A tractor might be modified to move rapidly, relative to other tractors, but it can never compete with cars built from the ground up for speed. If we want an economic system that maximizes the public good, we will have to design one from the ground up so that its every element is in service to its purpose.

What does it mean to maximize the public good? It means building wealth, but not just of the financial kind, and not just for a few. In 1898, the American writer and political economist Henry George put it this way:

> *The original meaning of the word "wealth" is that of plenty or abundance; that of the possession of things conducive to a certain kind of weal or well-being. ... In the economy of individuals or social units, everything is regarded as wealth the possession of which tends to give wealthiness, or the command of external things that satisfy desire, to its individual possessor, even though it may involve the taking of such things from other individuals. But in the other economy, that of social wholes, or the social organism, nothing can be regarded as wealth that does not add to the wealthiness of the whole.*[19]

We are concerned with the common good, the public well-being, or as George puts it, the "wealthiness of the whole." In this book, public well-being is broadly defined as consisting of three components. The first is the well-being of every individual. Every person is unique, but in general we wish to live fulfilling and meaningful lives, to express our full potential for happiness, health, creativity, knowledge, wisdom, and love. Conditions conducive to this include access to food, shelter, clothing, health care, and other basic goods and services. In addition, they include strong communities and friendships, education, skill development, ample leisure time for family and friends, opportunities for recreation and exercise, creative outlets, and meaningful work.

The second component of public well-being consists of the quality and volume of tangible and intangible assets held in common that can be transferred from generation to generation. These include art, science, teachable skills, and culture. They also include a clean environment and healthy ecosystems that support life and provide resources, as well as natural beauty, recreation, and inspiration. A central component of healthy ecosystems is a stable climate.

The third component consists of liberty, justice, and freedom, which together offer capacity to both choose and affect personal and collective destinies, without coercion or manipulation.

Local well-being is defined accordingly, only with focus shifted to a local region. The central effort of this book is to develop a new, more democratic economic system that serves to maximize local well-being, and by extension, national and global well-being. As we shall see, a design that follows from this goal produces a local economic system that looks very different from our national one.

1.3 Strategy

While reform efforts are well directed at state and national governments, implementation of new systems is best undertaken at the local level, where there is more flexibility and greater potential for support. Costs are lower, and for the design presented here, no legislative changes are necessary. This book proposes a local economic framework that acts as an overlay to the local dollar economy. The scale is county or metropolitan/micropolitan statistical area.[2] In general, think city, suburbs, towns, and surrounding farming and rural regions. Throughout this book, the residents and organizations of local areas are referred to as *communities*.

City and county governments should be excited by the proposal. After all, the framework should boost local economies, reduce unemployment and poverty, and generate funds for schools, colleges, nonprofits, and public service agencies. The ample funds it generates could also be used for infrastructure repair, social services,

---

[2] There are 374 metropolitan statistical areas identified by the U.S. Census. If smaller, micropolitan statistical areas are included, there are more than 955 areas in total.[20]

health care, environmental reclamation, and climate change action. But implementation and management do not occur through local governments. Rather, users of the system are in charge.

Individuals, businesses, schools, nonprofits, local governments, and others who voluntarily choose to participate form a membership-based community-benefit corporation, called a *Local Economic Direct Democracy Association* (LEDDA, pronounced lee-dah). The members of a LEDDA implement and democratically manage their local system. Hereafter, the term *member* refers to an individual who joins a LEDDA, unless otherwise specified. That organizations are also members is implied.

The strategy is straightforward. Once the framework is fully developed and tested using computer simulations, the first implementation will occur as part of a scientific pilot trial in a host city or county. After this, necessary improvements will be made and other communities will be encouraged to form their own LEDDAs.

Note that the initial participation rate does not need to be high in order for an implementation to occur; a small percentage of a local population can start a LEDDA. If the framework functions as intended—if members experience a direct economic gain and well-being begins to improve—then more people will naturally be attracted, participation rates will rise over time, and new LEDDAs will form. As these occur, impacts will grow.

Taking a closer look, the development roadmap can be divided into three phases. In Phase I, the preliminary work is conducted. The framework is developed, computer simulation models are created to assess design and examine potential impacts, and the software necessary to support use of the framework is constructed.

Some early results from this work are already available, this book being one example. Others include articles referencing an earlier version of this book, which have appeared in *The Guardian*, as well as on blogs such as *Sharable* and *Stanford Social Innovation Review*.[21, 22, 23] Another example is development of the first simulation model of a LEDDA economy. Results are scattered throughout this book and the study itself is available for free download.[3] For convenience,

---

[3] A paper describing the model has been submitted for journal publication. A pre-publication version is available for download.[24]

the model is referred to hereafter as the *LEDDA Microsimulation Model*.

In Phase II, the first scientific pilot trial is conducted. That trial is likely to last about two years. Once completed, the software code that implements the LEDDA framework will be made available to the public via an open-source license (if this has not already occurred). As such, the public will be able to examine, change, and use the code, free of charge, as desired. After results of the pilot trial have been assessed, and necessary improvements to the framework and code completed, other communities will be encouraged to implement their own LEDDAs.

As the LEDDA framework spreads to new communities, further refinements will be made. Considering that the framework allows flexibility and could coexist with and gain from other local-currency, buy-local, share-local, invest-local, and related community development initiatives, each LEDDA will likely develop its own unique flavor.

Should success continue as anticipated, Phase II could turn into Phase III—spread of the framework to many, perhaps even most communities. As the numbers of LEDDAs increase over time, so too should their collective impacts on society. At some point in Phase II or III, an association of LEDDAs would likely form in order to set standards and encourage cooperation in trade and other matters. Refinement of the LEDDA framework would continue in Phase III, but the growing pains of the early years would begin to recede.

To be clear, the intent is not that LEDDAs spread until a single large LEDDA exists across the nation or globe. Quite the contrary. The intent is that LEDDAs remain local and that their economies complement the national one. By staying local, they remain sensitive to local conditions and allow communities to express their own unique flavors. Further, a local scale facilitates transparency and offers agility; wait times are shorter between the recognition of a need and initiation of action. A local scale also engenders a sense of familiarity and belonging, which encourages friendships and other social ties to form.

Nor does a LEDDA replace city or county governments. It complements them, and makes the jobs of local officials easier. To the degree that a LEDDA boosts local economic activity, local governments benefit. Tax revenues increase, unemployment drops, and social services and schools receive greater funding. Indeed, a LEDDA might even help fund some local government services. In these and other ways, LEDDAs can complement and assist local governments and, in so doing, indirectly help state and federal governments.

1.4 Cooperation

A LEDDA is an organization that helps its members to cooperate. There are various types of cooperation—collusion and racketeering among them. In this book, the word *cooperation* refers to fair, transparent, and widely beneficial engagement among individuals and groups. Cooperation is the defining aspect of any successful society. For example, the Great Seal of the United States contains the phrase *e pluribus unum*, which translates to "out of many, one." It is through cooperation, not selfishness, that we achieve shared goals.

A design goal of the LEDDA framework is to make cooperation so easy that it becomes the default behavior. Thus, cooperation is hard-wired into the mechanics of a LEDDA as much as possible.

Some readers might question whether people are too selfish to cooperate any more than they already do. And it is not difficult to understand why some would view humans as inherently selfish. After all, news headlines regularly tell of executives, corporations, officials, and ordinary individuals who act out of greed and even criminal self-interest. Even standard economic models are constructed on the assumption that narrow self-interest drives decision-making. Many believe that the first laws of human behavior are "looking out for number one" and "survival of the fittest," but a great deal of science says otherwise.

Clearly, humans have the capacity to behave in selfish, even violent ways. But we also act in benevolent and self-sacrificing ways. New evidence from a variety of fields, including psychology, sociology, behavioral economics, neuroeconomics, evolutionary biology, and game theory suggests that humans are hard-wired to cooperate. In fact, our tendency to cooperate might be responsible for our success as a species. We are by nature highly social animals. Further, we inherited it from our ancient ancestors; social organization, cooperation, and seemingly altruistic behavior can be seen throughout the animal, insect, and even microbial world.[25, 26, 27] From early humans onward, we displayed a predisposition to seek cooperation from others and to penalize those who fail to cooperate (see box).

A Genetic Predisposition to Cooperate

From an evolutionary standpoint, our genetic makeup is much more attuned to clan and tribal life than it is to life as modern consumers. Anatomically modern humans developed about 200,000 years ago, and full behavioral modernity developed around 50,000 years ago. Clan and tribal societies slowly expanded into larger social structures, eventually resulting in the first proto-states about 6,000 years ago in what is now Egypt. Greek civilization, which laid the philosophical foundations for Western society, began its rise about 3,000 years ago.

The last 200 years of steady economic growth, an anomaly in human history, account for only about 0.4 percent of the period since behaviorally modern humans developed. If this book contained the history of behaviorally modern humans, the last 200 years of economic growth would not even fill a single page. The history of human civilization from classical antiquity onward would not even fill the reference list.

During our long evolution as clan and tribal members, humans benefited from a predisposition to cooperate. By cooperating in hunting and gathering, we obtained more food. By cooperating in child care, we better protected vulnerable youth. As a complement to cooperation, humans also developed a tendency to penalize selfish behavior. If one member of a tribe took more than his fair share or failed to contribute, the risks to or burden on every member increased.

In modern game theory, the strategy to reward cooperation and punish selfishness is called *tit for tat*. It is among the most successful strategies in game competitions. Several variants exist. In *reciprocal altruism* an individual helps another at some cost to himself with the expectation that help will later be reciprocated. Research suggests that genes are passed down from generation to generation that confer behavior for tit for tat, as well as for altruism, empathy, and sympathy, which supports cooperation.[28] That humans owe success as a species in part to these qualities has been called "survival of the kindest" by some investigators.[29]

Today, as suggested by a multitude of social experiments conducted in populations around the globe, we understand that the success of human social organizations is largely dependent on meeting three conditions: (1) rules should not discourage cooperation; (2) actions should be transparent; and (3) participants should have the ability to punish freeloaders (persons who benefit from the cooperation of others, but who do not cooperate themselves). When these three conditions are met, social organizations tend to thrive. When they are not met, organizations tend to move toward dysfunction.

To emphasize the point, it is not that humans begrudgingly agree to cooperate because logic tells us that doing so brings advantages. Although this certainly can happen, there is a deeper force driving us, one built into our DNA. We *long* to cooperate, to help each other, and to express love in all possible ways. Helping others makes us feel good. It stimulates the pleasure centers of our brain and improves psychological well-being.[30] It even improves our immune response.[31] We are hard-wired to cooperate, and we feel stress when cooperation is thwarted. Our gut tells us that selfish behavior is unhealthy.

In his book *The Good, the Bad, and the Economy*, Louis Putterman provides an extensive examination of the human nature question. He concludes with this warning:

> *One of the worst mistakes our society could make would be to adopt measures and institutions that would work well for angels but that fail to account for the pernicious sides of human nature. But an equally bad mistake would be to adopt policies and institutions that assume self-interest to be all that people are capable of. The human inclination to think and act socially is real. There's much evidence that it's innate. When wisely summoned into use, it flourishes. And we dismiss it at our peril.[32]*

Humans are not angels. Under certain circumstances we can be selfish, destructive, and brutal. The LEDDA framework is designed to avoid these circumstances, and instead create those that favor cooperation. Taking a cue from modern research, its design encourages cooperation, makes actions transparent, and gives participants the ability to discourage and penalize selfish behavior.

While this chapter has covered several topics, perhaps none is more important than the notion that humans are hard-wired for cooperation. To grasp it is both liberating and empowering. It allows our current national economic system to be seen as an aberration, a dysfunctional expression of true human nature. Not only does the system reward, and therefore encourage, selfish behavior, it lacks the transparency needed to publicly expose selfish acts. Once we accept that humans prefer cooperation, action naturally follows. We have motivation to press for national reform and to transform our local economies into systems that faithfully reflect who we are.

Chapter 2

The LEDDA Framework and Notions of Justice

"A new type of thinking is essential if mankind is to survive and move toward higher levels."

—Albert Einstein (1879–1955)

As the name *Local Economic Direct Democracy Association* implies, the heart of the framework is economic direct democracy. In this book, *LEDDA economic direct democracy* refers to the specific system of decision-making used within a LEDDA that offers all participants roughly equal and direct opportunity to influence their local economy.[1] LEDDA economic direct democracy gains strength and endurance by emphasizing the triad of democracy, transparency, and education. Without transparency, democracy is blind and easily corrupted. Without education, it is easily misunderstood and mismanaged. Thus, we see already that LEDDA economic direct democracy is not just about voting.

---

[1] The term *economic direct democracy* also has a generic meaning. It refers to grassroots efforts to organize the purchasing and investing actions of the public in order to accomplish economic, social, environmental, and/or political goals.

Nor are its voting components just about casting ballots, although this is one part. A good portion of the LEDDA framework implements a different type of voting: *voting with money*. A LEDDA issues a local electronic currency—called the *token*—and uses it in combination with the dollar. Together, the two currencies define a *token–dollar* economy. In LEDDA economic direct democracy, the token and, by extension, the dollar function in part as voting tools. It is helpful to think of the token primarily as a voting tool, although it exhibits several characteristics typical of money.

While the LEDDA framework includes a formal system of voting based on direct democracy principals, token–dollar voting occurs semiformally in two arenas: purchasing decisions in the local marketplace and funding decisions in the LEDDA financial system, called the Crowd-Based Financial System (CBFS). In both arenas, transparency, data collection, and education inform members and provide feedback of voting results.

The concept of LEDDA economic direct democracy, and the design of the LEDDA framework, are deeply entwined with notions of justice. Justice is a component of well-being, as defined in Chapter 1. A great many luminaries within political philosophy, economics, ethics, mathematics, and other fields have made profound contributions to theories of justice. In this chapter, we examine ideas from three of them: Adam Smith, John Rawls, and Amartya Sen. But first, an outline of the complete LEDDA framework is needed to provide context.

2.1 Elements of the LEDDA Framework

As mentioned in Chapter 1, an economic system is, in essence, a decision-making system. For our purposes, an economic system consists of eight components: (1) a monetary system that creates money and regulates its volume, value, and (interest) cost; (2) a financial system that uses savings or other sources of money to fund business and other organizations; (3) a market system that provides goods and services to consumers; (4) a property rights system that assigns ownership and use rights for physical, intellectual, and other types of property; (5) an incentive system that encourages desired behavior; (6) a governance system that regulates the preceding five components;

(7) a conceptual model that describes how the economy functions; and (8) a purpose that gives meaning and direction to the preceding seven components. Not every economic system consists of these eight components, and some components are not normally considered parts of an economic system. This is, however, an organization that is useful for the discussions that follow.

Mirroring this outline, the LEDDA framework has eight elements (references to chapters indicate where the topics receive the most detailed discussions):

1. **Monetary system.** The monetary system is called the *Token Monetary System* (TMS). A TMS creates tokens by fiat (by regulation) via a debt-free process, and destroys them as needed (Chapter 6).

2. **Financial system.** The financial system is called the *Crowd-Based Financial System* (CBFS). The CBFS engages the entire membership in funding decisions. It consists of four major arms: loan, subsidy, donation, and nurture. The first three provide funding to for-profit businesses and nonprofit organizations (which can include schools, colleges, and public service agencies). The nurture arm provides funds for membership assistance. A minor arm funds operations of the Collaborative Governance System. Funding occurs using a combination of tokens and dollars. The integrated monetary/financial system is called the *Token Exchange System*, or TES (Chapters 3 and 6).

3. **Market system.** For-profit businesses and nonprofit organizations provide members with goods and services though the local marketplace. For-profit businesses can be *standard businesses* or *Principled Businesses*. A Principled Business is formed according to a socially responsible business model that is unique to the LEDDA framework. It blends characteristics of nonprofit and for-profit models. A standard business is a for-profit business that is not a Principled Business (Chapter 7).

4. **Property rights system.** Property rights in a LEDDA follow national norms but differ in at least three ways:

    a) Principled Businesses participate in an intellectual property (IP) pool or similar program designed to increase access to information, stimulate creativity, and speed scientific discovery (Chapter 7).

    b) Restrictions apply on the sale of Principled Businesses and transfer of their assets, not unlike current restrictions that apply to nonprofits (Chapter 7).

    c) The LEDDA framework and the TES and Principled Business models, in particular, are highly transparent (Chapter 8).

5. **Incentive system.** A multicomponent incentive system is used to encourage cooperative behavior:

    a) A reputation system makes public the accomplishments and contributions of members in the context of a LEDDA, and can report disciplinary actions. It provides a type of social transparency that promotes responsible action and recognizes reputation as a form of currency (later this chapter).

    b) Social norms arise out of the shared desire by members to create an organization that is cooperative, fair, efficient, transparent, effective, and guided by science and reason. A LEDDA encourages and supports beneficial social norms (later this chapter and Chapter 9).

    c) One or more well-being indexes act as score cards to assess the effectiveness of a LEDDA in improving conditions. The indexes span a variety of concerns, including public health, education, economic security, food quality, environmental quality, public infrastructure, governance, leisure time, recreation, job satisfaction, and housing (later this chapter).

6. **Governance system.** Each LEDDA is governed by its members via an online system of direct democracy called the *Collaborative Governance System* (CGS). The CGS engages the entire membership in creating and amending rules, and setting policy. Members have the opportunity to draft, deliberate, and vote on proposals (Chapter 9).

7. **Conceptual models.** Theoretical, computer simulation, and mathematical models of token and dollar flows, human capital, energy and waste flow, decision-making, and other social, economic, and environmental states and events serve as tools, helping members to improve systems, assess conditions, and make projections and plan for the future. Transparency and data collection programs support modeling efforts (Chapter 8).

8. **Purpose.** The purpose of a LEDDA is to maximize member well-being and benefit the global public (later this chapter and Chapter 1).

This outline provides a cheat-sheet overview of the LEDDA framework. The remainder of the book fleshes out details and discusses motivations and meanings for the design.

2.2 Notions of Justice

To set the tone for discussions in later chapters, it is useful to consider ideas of justice offered by Adam Smith, John Rawls, and Amartya Sen. This section examines how LEDDA elements support or reflect notions of justice, and highlights some nuances of framework design.

Adam Smith

Adam Smith is considered by many to be the father of modern economics. His two major works, *The Theory of Moral Sentiments* (1759) and *An Inquiry into the Nature and Causes of the Wealth of Nations* (1776), are classics.[33, 34] Indeed, Smith's notion of an "invisible hand" that guides the market is still widely celebrated in neoclassical economics and the popular press. Smith also gave us a popular dictum, often used by economists to help justify the view that strict self-interest is *the* motivator of human behavior:

> *It is not from the benevolence of the butcher, the brewer, or the baker, that we expect our dinner, but from their regard to their own interest.*

Economists often disregard, however, the extensive attention that Smith placed on morality, the central concern of *The Theory of Moral Sentiments*. Smith based his theory of morality on the concept of "sympathy," a natural tendency to care about the well-being of others for no other reason than the pleasure of seeing them happy. He argued that even "the greatest ruffian, the most hardened violator of the laws of society" is not immune to sympathy. Moral behavior, he wrote, arises from an "impartial spectator," an internal voice of reason and objectivity, that informs our decisions and engages our sympathy. The impartial spectator is able to consider how our actions might affect the lives of others, near and far.

In current terms, we can view Smith's full work as describing "emergent" order, in which interactions between individual actors, who each behave according to a simple set of rules, produce collective social patterns of organization. Between his two works, Smith embraced ideas of a free market, as well as ideas of morality, trust, public welfare, virtue, and responsibility. The order that stems from these, he wrote, is one of social harmony and wise use of resources.

It turns out, however, that Smith's concept of an efficient market is missing an important ingredient: information. Nobel laureate Joseph Stiglitz, together with Bruce Greenwald, has shown that due to information asymmetries, markets are efficient only under exceptional circumstances.[35] George Akerlof, who jointly won the 2001 Nobel Prize in Economics with Stiglitz, illustrates the problem by way of the used-car market. The potential buyer of a used car might not know the full history of car damage and repair. As such, the buyer is at a disadvantage and so is willing to pay only an average price. But this reduces the incentive for an owner of a high-quality car to sell hers in the market; she will not be able to obtain the car's true value.

As per Smith, the LEDDA framework relies on a free market in which organizations compete for customer support. But consistent with insights from Stiglitz and Greenwald, the LEDDA market is information-rich. While consumers would not necessarily know the full history of each product, they would know far more about a firm and its products than is common today. This is especially true of Principled Businesses, element No. 3 in the framework.

Because the token–dollar combination is used as a voting tool, and because a LEDDA seeks to maximize member well-being, the framework is designed to achieve a high degree of income equality, which could be full equality. In a political democracy, allowing one person to cast millions of votes, while others cast only one, would undermine stability and conflict with purpose. So, too, allowing one member to cast (spend or make funding decisions with) a large number of token–dollar votes, while others cast far fewer, would undermine LEDDA stability and conflict with the stated purpose. Said another way, because money is used for voting in the LEDDA framework, income inequality is, essentially, a form of voter exclusion for those at the lower end of the income spectrum.

It is acknowledged that income equality is a charged political issue. In the LEDDA framework, it serves several purposes, one of which is to make voting via purchasing and CBFS funding decisions inclusive and fair. But apart from the LEDDA framework, one can reasonably argue on economic, social, and ethical grounds that a high degree of income equality is justified. Several such arguments are touched upon in Chapter 5.

It is important to understand, however, that a LEDDA increases income equality while at the same time increasing member incomes. The power of members to direct their token–dollar economy grows and is shared more equally as incomes grow. Roughly speaking, one can say that a LEDDA "pays" people to become members and attain equality in voting power.

In the LEDDA framework, Smith's "invisible hand" is seen from a wider perspective. It is not the drive for personal fortune that fuels business activity—this is nullified for members under conditions of income equality. Rather, the fuel for business is the desire for greater well-being, both personal and public. Harmonious social order arises because the butcher, the brewer, and the baker act to make themselves happy, in the broadest sense of the term. Perhaps they enjoy interacting with customers, take pleasure in their co-workers, like the creative challenge of running a business, take pride in their work, feel they are useful, or have other reasons why they chose these jobs over others. In the LEDDA framework, higher incomes are achieved—a degree of fortune is gained—but it is gained more or less equally for all members, through cooperation.

John Rawls

John Rawls was an American philosopher who revived the field of political philosophy with his groundbreaking work, *A Theory of Justice* (1971).[36] In it, Rawls set out to resolve apparent ethical contradictions between freedom and equality. His approach was to integrate both under the notion of justice, and to subsume justice under "fairness." Fairness can be roughly interpreted as a demand for impartiality, for unbiased reasoning.

Rawls's argument centered on the "original position," a thought experiment in which a group of individuals are asked to reach agreement on the social and economic institutions that govern a society—the social contracts of a society. But each individual in the group is ignorant of his own personal identity, and so must choose institutions that he would want no matter what his actual position in society might be.

Rawls's intention was to identify unique principles of justice that would lead to the choice of just institutions. In a his multistep process, principles lead to choices, choices lead to just institutions, just institutions lead to reasonable behavior by individuals, and reasonable behavior leads to a just society. Once just institutions exist, the rest falls into place; people willingly agree to honor their institutional choices because it is in their mutual best interest to do so.

Rawls argued that two fundamental principles exist, the first of which trumps the second:[37]

1. Each person has an equal right to a fully adequate scheme of equal basic liberties, which is compatible with a similar scheme of liberties for all.

2. Social and economic inequalities are to satisfy two conditions:

   a) They must be attached to offices and positions open to all under conditions of fair equality and opportunity.

   b) They must be to the greatest benefit of the least advantaged members of society.

Amartya Sen

Amartya Sen, an Indian economist and Nobel laureate, was deeply influenced by Rawls's work and has extended it in new directions.[38] Whereas Rawls placed almost exclusive attention on a transcendental social contract from which a just society follows, Sen argues that justice should be evaluated along a continuum, based on actual behavior. One society can be more or less just than another, for example. And even if group consensus is reached on the form of just institutions, reasonable behavior on the part of individuals might not necessarily follow.

Second, Sen argues that Rawls's focus on the social contract as a prelude to justice excludes other possibilities, including the more flexible "impartial spectator" offered by Smith. Behavior informed by an impartial spectator can accommodate actual social relationships; it is more flexible than the black-and-white rules that a just institution might produce.

Third, Rawls's focus was exclusively on a group setting. But every sizable group interacts with and affects the outside world. Sen sees the need for a theory of justice that is more global in nature, that can invite perspectives and input from other groups. He argues that local parochialism and vested group interests can hinder justice if concerns from the outside world are not taken into account.

Sen received the Nobel Prize for his work on social choice theory, which unifies elements of welfare economics and voting theory. Social choice theory provides a theoretical framework for the question "Can we aggregate information on individual preferences/welfare in order to reach a decision/summary that is faithful to true conditions?"

The importance of this question to the LEDDA framework is obvious. For example, what formal voting method (for the Collaborative

Governance System) is most fair? And what index or indexes of well-being best reflect the conditions that members actually experience?

The underpinnings of social choice theory originated during the Enlightenment due to efforts of the French mathematician and political scientist Nicolas de Condorcet and others. Condorcet, an intellectual leader of the French Revolution, did not survive the wave of bloodshed that followed in the revolution's wake. As a result, little progress was made until his ideas were revived in the 1950s by American economist and Nobel laureate Kenneth Arrow, famous for Arrow's impossibility theorem.[39]

The theorem states that given at least three distinct choices, no rank-order voting system can be designed that fulfills a set of minimal "fairness" criteria. For a time, Arrow's impossibility theorem acted as a wet blanket in academic circles, squashing hopes of identifying fair methods to aggregate individual preferences/welfare. Over time, however, Sen and others made progress by offering reformulations of the problem in which "information broadening"—consideration of multiple data sources and types—overcomes limitations.

Sen has applied social choice theory to a variety of issues, including famine and poverty. He argues that public welfare is best measured not by counting commodities (food, income, etc.), as has been typical in welfare economics, but by identifying "functionings" and assessing "capabilities." In Sen's terminology a functioning is what an individual chooses to do or to be. A capability, in contrast, is the freedom to choose functionings that matter from the set of feasible functionings.

The Human Development Index (HDI), in use by the United Nations for the past two and a half decades, is an outgrowth of Sen's collaboration with Pakistani economist Mahbub ul Haq and others in the 1990s. They conceived the HDI as a composite index of capabilities, a means to evaluate development not just by economic measures (commodity counts), but also by the ability of individuals in a society to develop alternative meaningful life plans. The current HDI encompasses measures of education, life expectancy, and income, with an adjustment for income inequality.[40]

Rawls, Sen, Arrow, and the LEDDA Framework

Results from the LEDDA Microsimulation Model, to be discussed in Chapter 4, suggest a pathway by which a LEDDA could increase incomes, achieve income equality, and produce full employment, for members. If the simulation results approximate what is achievable in practice, if people are interested in achieving these results, and if adequate funding for developing the LEDDA framework can be secured, then income equality for many could be a reality within the next 25 years, a period mentioned in the first few paragraphs of this book. Not to detract from the importance that such an achievement would represent, the goal is not income equality per se. The goal—the purpose of the framework—is to maximize member well-being and benefit the global public. That is, income equality is not as important as what income equality is used to achieve.

The purpose statement, element No. 8 of the framework, gives meaning and direction to all other elements. It is useful to examine it in more detail. The statement contains two distinct parts: maximize member well-being and benefit the global public. The first part requires that member well-being be defined and quantified; maximization necessitates quantification, or at least the ability to compare alternative states.

Defining and quantifying well-being are not small tasks, however, and this book does not attempt to complete them. A broad definition of well-being is given in Chapter 1, and the need for indexes to measure it is identified in element No. 5(c) of the framework. More effort is needed to develop precise definitions of well-being and its indexes. Fortunately, work done by Sen, Stiglitz, and others provides an excellent starting point (see box "GDP and Well-Being").

Likewise, more effort is needed to develop voting methods within the Collaborative Governance System (element No. 6 of the framework). Some general suggestions are provided in Chapter 9, but much like well-being and its indexes, an exact definition is not given. The work of Arrow, Sen, and others in social choice theory can serve as a starting point.

GDP and Well-Being

It is difficult to plan without first measuring. In 1937, with the Great Depression lingering, Simon Kuznets, an economist at the National Bureau of Economic Research, proposed to Congress the concept of gross domestic product (GDP).[41] GDP was intended as a measure of economic progress. It summarizes the net economic output of a nation, the total value of all new goods and services produced in a given time period. It was a bold proposal, requiring greater transparency, coordination, and accounting of national economic data. Congress acted, and by 1944, following the Bretton Woods conference, the GDP was enshrined internationally as the yardstick to measure a nation's economic welfare. Lorenzo Fioramonti provides a full political history.[42]

The GDP and its cousin, gross national product, do not measure economic development (which, like well-being, is concerned with economic, social, political, and environmental health and sustainability). Prominent economists had already begun to question use of the GDP as a measure of welfare by 1968, when Bobby Kennedy made his now-famous speech at the University of Kansas:

> *Yet the gross national product does not allow for the health of our children, the quality of their education, or the joy of their play. It does not include the beauty of our poetry or the strength of our marriages; the intelligence of our public debate or the integrity of our public officials. It measures neither our wit nor our courage; neither our wisdom nor our learning; neither our compassion nor our devotion to our country; it measures everything, in short, except that which makes life worthwhile.*

Since then, numerous alternatives and complements to the GDP have been proposed.[43, 44] One group consists of GDP adjustments, in which economic, social, and environmental factors translate into dollar values. An example is the Maryland Genuine Progress Indicator (GPI), which considers 26 factors. Vermont is working on its own GPI and is the first state to include it within legislation. Another group consists of composite indexes, like the Human Development Index, that do not translate factors into dollar values but instead normalize them in other ways. A third group consists of subjective approaches, where people are asked about well-being, happiness, satisfaction, and other topics.

Progress in these areas will occur as development of the LEDDA framework continues. However, the ultimate arbitrator will be the membership itself, both of a single LEDDA and of the association of LEDDAs. Recall from Chapter 1 that if and when the LEDDA framework begins to spread, an association of LEDDAs would likely form to set standards and encourage cooperation. While the initial framework, software, and templates for LEDDA rules and procedures will likely be developed by a core group, this effort would impact the pilot trial more so than subsequent LEDDAs. Any specific approaches implemented for the pilot trial would and should be modified by the membership over time. Trade-offs exist between different approaches, and their meaning cannot be divorced from the values that members hold. Further, the values that members hold can be expected to change over time. As mentioned in Chapter 1, the software code that runs the LEDDA framework will be made available to the public under an open-source license. The membership can change the code as it sees fit, and can alter rules and procedures through the Collaborative Governance System (element No. 6 of the framework) and/or through its equivalent within the association of LEDDAs.

The phrase "benefit the global public" within the purpose statement also deserves attention. Sen warned that as local parochialism and vested group interests develop, justice can be harmed. One way to reduce that danger is to consider concerns of the outside world. While the LEDDA framework empowers a community to manage its token–dollar economy, this should not be seen as a throwback to mercantilism, the promotion of local economic power at the expense of other groups. A stated purpose of the LEDDA framework is to benefit the global public, and it cannot do this through a mercantilist approach. To take a cue from Rawls, LEDDAs should maximize member well-being compatible with a similar plan of well-being for all. Perspectives of the outside world can be invited into the dialogue that occurs informally among members and formally within the Collaborative Governance System, and within its equivalent in the association of LEDDAs.

The LEDDA engagement system, to be discussed in Chapter 5, is consistent with Sen's concepts of functionings and capabilities. In brief, the jobs that a LEDDA helps fund in the for-profit and nonprofit sectors, and the income assistance given to unemployed and not-in-workforce members, are called "engagements." Every member has an engagement (which can change over time, just as jobs change). As such, every member is cared for. Not only does each member have an engagement, and so have a "doing," each also has the capability to choose from among those engagements that are feasible. The engagement system is designed to be dynamic, continually producing new opportunities for members to secure meaningful and agreeable positions, with obvious consideration of community needs.

The framework provides members the tools to exert a profound influence over their token–dollar economy. Not only do members use the CBFS (element No. 2 of the framework) to fund the types of jobs (engagements) that they would like to hold, they also use it to balance different sectors of the economy to best suit their needs. For instance, members can influence the percentage of the workforce that holds jobs in the standard business, Principled Business, and nonprofit sectors.

Looking at the big picture, the framework is in fact more true to the ideas of Sen than Rawls. First, an increasing degree of justice is gained over time. In each year, more jobs are created, more choices become available to members, incomes rise, and income equality increases.

Second, the framework has a global perspective, as established by the purpose statement.

Third, the framework is not the direct result of membership consensus, reached though impartial reasoning based on principles of justice. Actually, much of the development will likely occur before a membership exists. But once a LEDDA is established, members can change the framework as they see fit.

Finally, although individuals choose to become members knowing the purpose of a LEDDA, it is expected that they will need incentives to cooperate. While a LEDDA would retain some capacity for punitive action against members who violate rules in the extreme, the focus is on encouragement; incentives for achieving social compliance and cooperation are built into the framework. For example, transparency can identify cheaters, and education can highlight the benefits that cooperation can bring. Deliberation, the basis of direct democracy, can help shape membership mood and direction. But in addition to these, a LEDDA has an incentive system (element No. 5 of the framework) aimed at providing encouragement. It consists of well-being indexes, a reputation system, and a set of social norms.

Well-being indexes act as feedback systems, or report cards. Members can watch their collective well-being rise or fall over time in response to their choices. Eventually, computer models will allow members to examine alternative actions and policies by projecting well-being indexes into the future. The reputation system provides public recognition for worthwhile deeds. Most individuals want to gain the respect and appreciation of others for generous behavior or jobs well done, and will alter their behavior accordingly. The reputation system provides transparency of action; it recognizes reputation as a form of social currency. Last, most people desire to fit in with others by following established rules of social conduct, as long as the rules are viewed as helpful. While a LEDDA cannot "dictate" social norms, it can create conditions under which beneficial norms are likely to arise.

Finally, the token–dollar economy is seen as a type of participatory economic system. Members actively guide their economy via formal deliberation and ballots, and via semiformal voting with token–dollars. Participation is emphasized in the chapters to follow. But, as per Sen, the framework allows for actual human behavior. Some members will want to participate less than others, for example. Indeed, some might join a LEDDA primarily because of income gains, caring little for its participatory aspect.

Multiple approaches are used to encourage participation, while allowing for variable levels of interest. The incentive system (element No. 5 of the framework) encourages participation, as do user-friendly interfaces of the LEDDA software applications. And much of the deliberation and voting within the Collaborative Governance System occurs online via applications streamlined for efficiency.

Information gathering is also efficient. As just one example, an easy-to-navigate online database provides information on member businesses and products. And when making decisions, members can request information, assessments, and guidance from nonprofits funded to offer this service, from Collaborative Governance System committees, and from individuals and other groups who choose to offer assistance.

Members can also delegate any portion of their decision-making power to proxies. Proxies can be friends, committees, nonprofits, paid consultants, or other persons or groups. Proxy power is revocable on demand and can be granted for specific decisions or types of decisions, and for limited scope. For instance, a member might give proxy power to a committee regarding some issue that is being deliberated by the Collaborative Governance System. At any point, she could switch proxies, if desired, or make decisions on the issue herself. Further, she might give proxy power over CBFS lending decisions to a consultant, but only up to a certain amount of tokens and dollars, and only in a particular economic sector. This flexible encouragement–recommendation–delegation system reflects a synthesis of ideas seen within direct democracy, participatory democracy, and delegative democracy (liquid democracy).[45, 46, 47, 48]

The point is, the LEDDA framework incorporates a realistic view of human behavior. Cooperation is incentivized, and made easy. While democratic participation is encouraged, only minimal participation is required. Freedom lies in the ability to choose the intensity, timing, topic, and means of participation that one has reason to desire.

Chapter 3

Economic Direct Democracy

"Money has to serve, not to rule."

—Pope Francis (1936–)

Having established that an economic system is essentially a decision-making system, this chapter examines how decisions are made in a LEDDA. It introduces the mechanics by which members guide their token–dollar economy. LEDDA economic direct democracy, made possible by advances in technology, forms the heart and soul of the framework.

It is a form of democracy geared for the 21st century that maximally distributes decision-making power among participants. The concept springs from the notion that an economy is a decision-making system that belongs to the people who participate in it. An economy is considered a "common good," a set of agreements shared by participants for mutual benefit. LEDDA economic direct democracy involves online deliberation and voting, as one might expect, but democratic participation is embedded deeper than this. It is evident in each element of the LEDDA framework.

As introduced in Chapter 2, decision-making in LEDDA economic direct democracy occurs formally through deliberation and voting, and semiformally though purchasing and funding decisions. By name alone, these processes do not appear unique to the LEDDA framework. People decide every day what they will purchase using dollars. But as we shall see, the way these processes are integrated into a comprehensive form of democracy is unique. The complete system offers participants an unprecedented level of control over economic decisions.

Before discussing the mechanics of decision-making, it is useful to say a few words about democracy itself.

3.1 What Is Democracy?

Democracy is generally defined as government in which supreme power is vested in the people and exercised by them directly or indirectly through a system of elected representatives. The term *government*, for our purposes, might refer to that of a nation, state, city, corporation, club, or any other group—a LEDDA itself is a membership-based association, not a public body. The definition of democracy might seem straightforward, but in fact, democracy is a matter of degree.

The United States is recognized as a representative democracy, but is supreme power vested in the people? Is it vested equally in all people? Certainly, power was not equally vested prior to the civil rights era or before women's suffrage. But even today, one could argue, power is not equally vested. For example, hyper-wealthy citizens have greater opportunity to affect campaigns and elections than do ordinary people. In the primaries leading up to the 2012 presidential election (the most expensive election in U.S. history), 25 percent of all Super PAC donations came from just five wealthy donors.[49] These individuals had an enormous influence over who might become the final candidates.

Further, big corporations can hire expensive lobbyist firms to influence legislation and even craft the very wording of new laws.[50] And big corporations can sway politicians with post-term job offers.[51, 52, 53] The latter practice is referred to as Washington's revolving door.

In a 2014 analysis that examined nearly 2,000 policy issues for the period 1981–2002, Gilens and Page conclude that:

> *... economic elites and organized groups representing busi-*
> *ness interests have substantial independent impacts on U.S.*
> *government policy, while average citizens and mass-based*
> *interest groups have little or no independent influence.*[54]

In effect, they argue that for the period they examined, the United States was a plutocracy with regard to policy-making. If recent record-breaking election spending is any indication, then the influence of the elite over policy has only grown stronger. William Domhoff, too, has argued that wealthy elites in the United States dominate key issues in policy-making, despite elections.[55]

One can also question whether voter sentiment is effectively communicated. During a typical two-year session, thousands of bills are introduced to congressional committees.[56] A remarkable amount of activity occurs in each session, yet the only formal mechanism that allows voters to influence legislation is the biannual election system; every other year voters can give a thumbs up or thumbs down to candidates on the ballot. Informal mechanisms, such as writing letters and signing petitions, are available, but their impact is often questionable.

Taking a top-level view, democracy comes in three forms, representative, direct, and hybrid. U.S. voters are familiar with the first of these; we elect a small group of representatives to draft and enact bills on our behalf. By contrast, voters in a direct democracy control the political process; they enact bills themselves. One form of direct democracy is the referendum system used by many states. Another example, which will be mentioned again in Chapter 9, is the city-state of Athens in the years 507–338 BCE. Hybrid democracy combines elements of representative and direct democracy. One example is delegative democracy, developed by Bryan Ford.[46] For convenience, direct and hybrid forms are both considered as "direct" in this book.[1]

---

[1] LEDDA economic direct democracy is a hybrid form of democracy. It encourages participation in direct democracy mechanisms but also incorporates a recommendation–delegation system, as discussed in Chapter 2. Further, it acts in the economic sphere using money as a voting tool, so by definition it is a nonstandard approach.

Advances in technology and expansion of education make direct democracy ever more practical for decision-making. As education expands, so does the capacity of people to offer meaningful guidance to their governments. And as technology advances, governments are held to ever higher standards of transparency and accountability. Matt Leighninger, executive director of the Washington, D.C.-based Deliberative Democracy Consortium, puts it this way:

> *In the 20th century, public life revolved around government; in the 21st century, it will center on citizens. Beneath the national radar, the relationship between citizens and government is undergoing a dramatic shift. More than ever before, citizens are educated, skeptical, and capable of bringing the decision-making process to a sudden halt.*[57]

Of course, educated, empowered citizens can also facilitate the decision-making process, not just bring it to a halt. The point is, the relationships are rapidly changing and people want a louder voice. A host of new organizations have sprung up that reflect public demands for greater transparency, accountability, and opportunities for input. These include the Deliberative Democracy Consortium, Open Secrets, Open Plans, and the Sunlight Foundation.[58, 59, 60] And cities are using new online technologies to engage residents in solving local problems. For example, New York City is experimenting with participatory budgeting. So far, residents of ten districts have decided how to spend $14 million of public money on projects involving schools and education, housing, parks and recreation, public health and the environment, public safety, and other issues.[61, 62]

To the degree that a government lags behind advancing technology— to the degree that transparency, accountability, and opportunities for input do not keep pace with possibilities—its legitimacy weakens in the public eye. On a sobering note, a 2012 poll suggests that 60 percent of likely U.S. voters believe that the federal government does not have the consent of the governed.[63] Only 25 percent of respondents disagreed with the statement. And confidence in Congress is now at a historic low.[15] To maintain legitimacy, governments must evolve with the times. If technology is advancing at an exponential rate, so too should government responsiveness.

Similar forces are at play in the economic sphere. People are seeking greater influence in the realms of business and finance, and they desire greater transparency and accountability. And why not? The business and finance worlds directly and indirectly affect us all. As one sign of the times, the number of social and environmental shareholder resolutions filed in the 2014 proxy season set an all-time record, surpassing the already high number in 2013.[64, 65] In this smartphone-savvy age, new apps for consumer activism are popping up. One, called Buycott, lets consumers scan the barcode on any product to trace ownership of the company all the way back to its top corporate parent. Consumers can boycott single companies and/or join user-created campaigns to boycott whole groups of business that violate stated principles.[66]

The economic system is ripe for transformation through greater transparency, accountability, and public input. Indeed, while one can argue that power over the federal government is not vested equally in all citizens, it is even easier to make this case for the economic system. Recall that the richest 400 Americans control nearly as much wealth as the poorest 50 percent combined.[8]

Most hyper-wealthy individuals obtain the bulk of their income through investments, and the investment decisions they make have far greater impact than those of ordinary Americans. Wealthy investors and big banks decide, in large part, which businesses receive funding and which do not. Further, by hiring top-line lobbyists, big corporations exert enormous influence over who receives business tax breaks and government subsidies. Indeed, many Fortune 500 firms pay more in lobbyist fees than they do in taxes.[67] Last, by amassing patents and other intellectual property, big businesses and wealthy investors have a profound influence over who has access to new technologies and how innovation will proceed.

The influence of the wealthy over the economy is deeper still, as the purchasing decisions they make convey more information to the market than do those of ordinary families. Wealthy individuals can afford to make choices based on a wide range of criteria, including price, quality, safety, impact on social status, and social and environmental concerns. In contrast, the criteria for most Americans are more skewed; low wages force them to emphasize price. A mother, for example, might choose not to feed her children fresh, organically grown vegetables, even if she believes they are safer, easier on the environment, and more nutritious. Instead, she might choose canned vegetables because of their lower cost. Or if hers is among the nearly 50 percent of families that live in poverty or are low-income (Chapter 1), she might skip the vegetables entirely and serve cheap but less nutritious fast food. In fact, fresh vegetables might not even be sold in some poor neighborhoods.[68] The point is, markets react to information. The information conveyed through the purchasing decisions of most Americans is limited; it does not convey with fidelity the full spectrum of reasonable desires and needs.

Given that economic issues are consistently front and center of the public's mind, why would people target only governments for greater transparency, accountability, and opportunity for input when they could aim for the same within the economic sphere? Transparency, accountability, and impact are exactly what LEDDA economic direct democracy offers.

3.2   Decision-Making Processes

Decision-making in LEDDA economic direct democracy occurs through three processes: formal deliberation and voting, purchasing decisions, and funding decisions. The first process, deliberation and voting, will not be discussed in detail here. It receives full treatment in Chapter 9. But a few comments are in order. Deliberation and voting occur via an online system of direct democracy called the Collaborative Governance System. The CGS is not a "referendum-based" form of direct democracy, where proposals are put before a group for an up/down vote. Rather, it engages members in the full decision-making process. Members have the opportunity to create, deliberate, and decide on the rules and policies that their LEDDA will follow.

The majority of democratic decisions that members make do not occur through the Collaborative Governance System, however. They occur through the other two processes: purchasing and funding decisions. That is, they occur through use of tokens and dollars.

Although the token is called a currency, it is unlike any other. The classic functions of a currency are to act as a medium of exchange (to buy and sell products), as a unit of account (to compare the relative worth of products), and as a store of value (as a means to store wealth). While the token fulfills the first two of these, it also serves a different function: to convey preference. That is, the token and, by association of use, the dollar serve as voting tools. The rest of this chapter focuses on how voting occurs via purchasing and funding decisions.

Purchasing Decisions

Consider the purchasing decisions made by a typical U.S. family. The median household income in 2011 was $47,198, when adjusted to a two-adult household.[2][69] Given that this is only about 250 percent higher than the poverty threshold, the median family struggles to keep food on the table and a roof overhead. After paying for housing, utilities, food, health care, and other expenses, a typical family has only about $100 left at the end of each month, which leaves little room for unexpected costs.[70] Indeed, nearly half of American families would have a difficult time raising $2,000 in an emergency.[71] As already mentioned, these constraints force most families to place a priority on price when making purchasing decisions.

But what would happen if families had higher incomes? Further, what would happen if consumer education programs encouraged families to consider price, quality, safety, and social and environmental impacts when making purchasing decisions? And what if families viewed shopping as an act of direct democracy—as a viable means to shape their local economy? What if transparency in the marketplace allowed families to monitor the aggregate effects of purchasing decisions? What would occur is that purchasing decisions would strongly impact what is produced, how it is produced, where it is produced, who benefits, and how workers and the environment are treated.

Bakery Example

A simplified example may be helpful to illustrate some of the concepts of LEDDA economic direct democracy. Suppose that three bakeries participate in a LEDDA, meaning that they become members

---

[2] If all families were to stand in a line ordered by income, the median income would be that of the family halfway through the line, the 50th percentile. This differs from the mean family income, which is the average income over all families.

and accept payment in both tokens and dollars. One produces healthy whole-wheat bread, one produces healthy rice bread (for those with gluten allergies), and one produces not-so-healthy bread made with processed white flour. Further, suppose that if members buy bread, they buy it from one or more of these three bakeries. Non-members also buy bread from the bakeries.

Every time a member buys bread, he "votes" for one of the bakeries. Each sale, each token and dollar received, helps the bakery to meet or exceed its operating costs. The purchasing decisions of a member might be influenced by many factors, just as they would be for non-members. These factors might include taste preferences, health concerns, location, price, friendship with owners, and bakery ambiance. But LEDDA members might take into account other factors, as well.

First, because incomes rise, LEDDA members have more freedom to focus on quality and other concerns besides price. Second, members might be influenced by education programs. Suppose a LEDDA is trying to improve the health of its members by promoting healthy food choices. Perhaps it decides to fund cooking classes, community cook-offs, and support groups. The education campaign might have other aims, too. For example, it might be designed to strengthen community ties, create a sense of shared purpose, reduce medical costs, and increase revenues for local fruit and vegetable farmers. Armed with new health information and greater social support, LEDDA members might purchase more products from the bakeries that produce the healthier breads.

Third, members might base their purchasing decisions in part on how the bakeries are organized and/or operated. They might prefer to support bakeries that are Principled Businesses (element No. 3 of the LEDDA framework, Chapter 2). Environmental concerns could also affect decisions. Members might want to support bakeries that use organically grown grains, or green energy. Finally, members might prefer to support bakeries that buy from local supply chains. When a local business buys from other local businesses, dollars circulate longer in the community. Tokens flow more smoothly, too. Thus, it is in the best interests of each member to strengthen and expand circulation by supporting local businesses that support other local businesses.

Transparency and data collection help members assess the quality and quantity of token and dollar flows. But flows can be complex. Perhaps one of the three bakeries purchases grain from local farmers, electricity from a local wind generator, and equipment from a local manufacturer, all of whom are LEDDA members. Perhaps the other two bakeries purchase a different set of goods from other local suppliers. The impact on token and dollar circulation gained by supporting one bakery over another would not necessarily be intuitive. Some local supply chains may have a larger impact on circulation than do others. To untangle the complexity of token and dollar flows and supply-chain links, a sophisticated analysis is needed. That's one role of the computer simulation models (element No. 7 of the LEDDA framework).

To continue the bakery example, suppose that at the end of a given year the whole-wheat bakery has received tokens and dollars in excess of its operating costs. This means the whole-wheat bakery will have received enough token and dollar "votes" to continue on for another year. It could use tokens and dollars to pay staff, purchase supplies, meet other obligations, and grow its business. The other two bakeries weren't so successful and are operating at a deficit. Their fates are more uncertain, but outcomes could be influenced through the other LEDDA voting mechanism: funding decisions.

The Crowd-Based Financial System

As already mentioned, funding decisions occur through the Crowd-Based Financial System. For-profit member businesses can apply for subsidies and interest-free loans, and member nonprofits can apply for donations and interest-free loans.[3] An entrepreneur might apply to the CBFS for token-and-dollar loans to help start a new business, for example, or an existing business might seek a token-and-dollar subsidy to expand a research program.

---

[3] The term *donation* is used two ways in this book. First, the CBFS has a donation arm, which accepts token-and-dollar contributions from members. Members use the donation arm to fund nonprofits. Second, members can voluntarily donate dollars (and tokens) to favored nonprofits, as usual, apart from the CBFS. The term *contribution* in this book refers to mandatory CBFS payments. Contributions differ from a typical tax in that existing income is not affected; contributions are designed to share *increases* in income created by the LEDDA with the membership as a whole. Further, members retain decision-making power over use of their contributions.

Each member who receives tokens must contribute some amount of tokens and dollars to the CBFS. Once those contributions enter the CBFS, the member chooses which applicants to support, and at what amount. In combination with transparency, data collection, and education, this design helps to ensure that tokens and dollars are channeled toward those businesses and nonprofits that best serve members and the public. Because the CBFS funding system is profit-neutral, opportunities for private gain are limited. As such, community concerns naturally rise to the forefront.

The interest-free quality of CBFS loans is unusual relative to typical forms of lending (exceptions include microloan services like Kiva.org). Interest-free lending has some advantages. Among these, it improves the efficiency of a local economy in that it reduces "overhead" costs paid to the financial sector. As will be discussed in Chapter 8, the financial sector has grown rapidly in recent years. Currently it accounts for about 13 percent of corporate business output (measured as gross value added), and about 8 percent of consumer spending.[4] Interest-free CBFS lending gives member businesses a big advantage. Money otherwise spent on financial services can be spent on wages, supplies, improvements, and expansion.

The CBFS consists of four major arms: lending, subsidy, donation, and nurture. The first three provide funding for local nonprofit and for-profit organizations, and the last provides income assistance to members who are unemployed or not in the workforce.[5] Lending also acts as a form of storage; each member stores tokens and dollars by building up a lending portfolio. Contributions made to the lending arm can later be recovered for personal use, given certain restrictions, and minus losses caused by loan default.

Only members—individuals or organizations—receive or spend tokens. Thus, only member organizations can apply for CBFS funding. All member organizations offer their employees an option to receive

---

[4] Gross domestic product (GDP) is equal to gross value added plus taxes on products minus subsidies on products.

[5] The CBFS is described in this book as a means to fund organizations and provide income support to members. It would be possible to add an additional CBFS arm to provide consumer loans to individuals. Like loans to organizations, token–dollar loans to individuals would be offered at zero interest. In addition to benefits already mentioned, zero-interest lending is not subject to securities regulations, as discussed in Chapter 6.

wages paid in a combination of tokens and dollars. New businesses or other organizations created through CBFS funding are member organizations by default.

The rate of CBFS contributions to be paid by members is determined by a set of *earmarks* (fractions of income or income gain), democratically chosen by members via the Collaborative Governance System. One or more earmarks is assigned to each arm of the CBFS. By setting the relative values of earmarks, members influence the overall makeup of their economy. For example, by increasing the earmarks associated with nonprofits, members can create more jobs within the nonprofit sector. The CBFS and its earmark system give members a great deal of flexibility in deciding the overall tone of their economy, as well as in deciding the amount of support they will give to any particular applicant.

Earmarks also influence the quality and rate of token and dollar circulation. They are among the leverage points, or control dials, that allow a LEDDA to fine-tune its token–dollar economy. Another leverage point is the negative interest rate that is placed on tokens. Tokens left in an account for too long—past a grace period—incur a negative charge, which increases the *demurrage*, the cost of holding money over a period of time. Demurrage encourages members to keep tokens in circulation, where they can be of use.

Bakery Example, Continued

To continue the simplified bakery example, recall that two of the three member bakeries were now operating at a deficit. As with any business, these two bakeries could apply for bank loans or seek other types of conventional financing. But for a variety of reasons, they might want to apply for CBFS funding. Perhaps the zero-cost financing attracts them, or they view the CBFS as a means to engage new customers.

If the two bakeries are organized as for-profits, they could apply for CBFS loans and/or subsidies. If they are organized as nonprofits, they could apply for loans and/or donations. Members may, for example, want to support the bakery that makes rice bread, even if few shop there themselves. Perhaps they recognize that the bakery serves the needs of a subset of the population with gluten allergies. Without such a bakery, quality of life for people in this subset might suffer.

Suppose the rice-bread bakery is organized as a for-profit business. If members believe its revenues would increase, they might be willing to extend CBFS loans. In reviewing the loan application, they might suggest that the bakery produce an additional kind of bread, one more popular in the membership and/or general population. Or they might suggest that the bakery engage local independent grocers to help sell their breads, or that it extend its market to include outlets elsewhere in the country.

If members do not believe that the rice-bread bakery's revenues would increase, they might be willing to offer CBFS subsidies. Here again, members might suggest ways that the bakery could make its application more appealing. Members might also suggest that the bakery re-form as a nonprofit, which would allow them to support it via tax-deductible CBFS donations.

The bakery example shows the different ways that purchasing and funding decisions can influence economic outcomes. Recall from Chapter 1 that the functions of an economic system are to determine what products will be produced, how they will be produced, for whom they will be produced and to whom income will flow, and what portion of resources and products will be consumed now or saved as investment for future production. In the bakery example, all four of the functions were affected. Members influenced what products the bakeries produced, how the businesses were organized, to whom they sold products, from whom they bought supplies, and how much investment money they received. By infusing each function of an economic system with democracy, the LEDDA framework helps individuals in a community to communicate their needs, and helps businesses and other organizations to understand those needs and act as attentive partners.

Chapter 4

LEDDA Impact

"The good we secure for ourselves is precarious and uncertain until it is secured for all of us and incorporated into our common life."

—Jane Addams (1860–1935)
First American woman awarded the Nobel Peace Prize

In Chapter 1, the LEDDA framework was described as a system that can help communities take action on pressing social, economic, and environmental challenges. If it is to be useful in this way, it must have the capacity to raise a substantial volume of funds. In this chapter we start to examine potential impact. But first, a more complete description is needed of how a LEDDA expands a local economy.

4.1 Integrated Approach

As noted in Chapter 1, the LEDDA framework reflects a synthesis of numerous community development, participatory democracy, and other initiatives. These were made more concrete in Chapter 2, in the list of framework elements. The role of purchasing and CBFS funding decisions was discussed in Chapter 3. This chapter begins to explain how the framework's elements work together to effect the token–dollar economy. For the moment, it will be helpful to think of the framework primarily as a combination of local-currency, fund-local, and buy-local initiatives.

When money circulates longer within a community, the community experiences greater economic power. This is the idea behind buy-local programs. Interest in these programs has surged, driven in part by Institute for Local Self-Reliance surveys that indicate buy-local programs can help independent businesses and their communities achieve substantial gains. The 2014 survey reported that annual revenue growth was 7.0 percent for independent businesses in communities with buy-local campaigns, compared to 2.3 percent for those in communities without such campaigns.[72]

Whereas buy-local programs are proliferating, most fund-local programs are still young. Some fund-local strategies are based on investing. The basic idea is that rather than investing in Wall Street companies that may not be sensitive to community concerns, individuals could divert some investment funds toward community-responsive local businesses.[73] Some progress has been made. For example, groups such as Slow Money are working to connect investors with small farms, food-processing, and food-distribution businesses. Since 2010 Slow Money has raised $30 million in donations, loans, and equity funds for 221 different businesses around the United States.[74]

Another example of progress in this area is the 2012 federal JOBS (Jumpstart Our Business Startups) Act, which contains provisions to encourage crowdfunding as a means to raise equity capital. Under the law, companies can receive up to $1 million in equity funding from crowds without engaging certain securities regulations. The amount each person can invest is capped, based on his or her income.[75] The Securities and Exchange Commission is still in the process of writing rules to implement the law.

The LEDDA framework takes a different approach. It raises funds for local businesses, nonprofits, and member assistance through the CBFS, as outlined in Chapter 3. The CBFS is not, however, an invest-for-profit system; it is a profit-neutral mechanism used to fund the organizations that members favor.

The CBFS is part of the Token Exchange System (TES)—the local currency system at the heart of the LEDDA framework. Local currency systems, also known as *community*, or *complementary* currency systems (sometimes with regard to geographic extent), are gaining in popularity. One database lists hundreds in the United States and elsewhere around the globe, over half of which were started after 2009.[76] Lietaer and Dunne suggest that the actual number is far higher, approximately 4,000 systems worldwide.[77] Nearly all of these are small, with just a few hundred to perhaps a few thousand participants. But in rare cases they grow quite large. For example, in 2002 more than 2 million Brazilians were using the Red de Trueque system as a complement to the Brazilian national currency.[78] As another example, the WIR Bank, founded in 1934, now services about 80,000 Swiss businesses.[79]

A LEDDA boosts a local economy via its integrated local-currency, fund-local, and buy-local programs by: (1) introducing tokens; (2) reducing the flow of dollars out of a community; and (3) using the gain in tokens and dollars to increase incomes, fund jobs, and provide member assistance. The three steps repeat themselves in a virtuous cycle, each year building the economy further.

4.2 LEDDA Microsimulation Model

With this background, it is possible to examine the results of the first simulation model of a LEDDA economy, the LEDDA Microsimulation Model. The model emulates token–dollar flow in a virtual U.S. county. The aims are to introduce the LEDDA framework, describe general concepts of token–dollar flow, and demonstrate that a set of parameters exists that results in increased mean family income, full income equality, and full employment, for the simulated member population. The model, while hypothetical, is semi-realistic in the sense that dollar flows at the start of the simulation resemble those of a real county economy, and conditions evolve from this base. For example, starting income levels resemble real income levels, and tax rates resemble real tax rates.

The model is concerned only with a limited set of events and flows within the token–dollar economy. The dollar economy and demographics serve primarily as a static backdrop. Thus, for example, inflation, normal economic growth, personal savings and investment, birth and death of individuals, and income changes for non-members are not modeled. While such variables might be important for a model intended to describe the dollar economy or make forecasts about it, neither of these is an aim. The model describes a token–dollar economy, and is not predictive.

Although the model is elementary in many respects, it represents a milestone; it is the first simulation model to examine semi-realistic flows of community and national currency within a local economy. It sets the stage for future studies that will expand the model, assess its assumptions, and examine whether such results can be practically achieved in a real LEDDA.

For simplicity, it is assumed that all adults in the county are married, two to a household. By construction, the LEDDA participation rate starts at 5 percent of county residents in Year 1 and then climbs to 90 percent in Year 15. This interval is called the *growth period*. Also by construction, the income target and token share of income (TSI) target steadily rise during this period.

The income target is a series of annual token-plus-dollar (T&D) incomes that some members receive. Likewise, the TSI target is a series of TSI values that apply to the income target. (TSI is the the fraction of a member's income that is paid in tokens.) In the simulation, both targets are constructed using a linear growth formula. The TSI target starts at 5 percent in Year 1 and grows to 35 percent in Year 15. By construction, no new members join after the growth period ends, and both the income and TSI targets remain steady until the simulation ends in Year 28. Only minor further changes would be seen in most of the variables tracked if the simulation were to continue past Year 28.

In a real LEDDA, income and TSI targets, and CBFS earmarks, would be chosen by members using the Collaborative Governance System before operations begin. Members would also use the CGS to amend these parameters over time as necessary.

In short, the model describes how the participation rate, income and TSI targets, CBFS earmarks, and other more minor parameters affect the income, TSI, and job status of individual members.

As noted, 90 percent of the county population joins the LEDDA by the end of the growth period. Some might join because they are forward-thinking and understand that cooperation can help them accomplish goals that would otherwise be difficult or impossible to achieve alone. Others might join for the social or business aspects, such as introductions to new friends and business relationships. While members might be attracted for multiple reasons, it is assumed in the simulation that they join due to income gain.

Every person who joins and who receives tokens obtains an income increase. (Some non-working members do not receive tokens right away.) Persons who have low starting incomes see proportionally greater income gains. The 90 percent who join all come from families with starting incomes below the 90th percentile (below about $101,000 per year). This group is called the *target population*. Gains for persons who come from higher-earning families are modest, and might not be enough to motivate membership. In a real LEDDA, however, members would likely come from all income brackets because all families could gain in well-being, even if they gain little in income.

Figure 4.1 shows the gain in member mean family income over the simulation period for a county population of 100,000 adults. Mean income starts at about $40,000 annually in Year 0 (based on U.S. Census microdata) and rises to about 104,000 T&D in Year 28. This is *post-CBFS income*—pretax income after contributions to the CBFS have been made. One can think of post-CBFS income as pre-tax, take-home income. Throughout this book, it is assumed that one token equals one inflation-adjusted dollar in purchasing power. As such, mean family income increased by 267 percent in the simulation. Every member family experiences an increase relative to Year 0. Figure 4.1 also shows mean post-CBFS income plus accumulated savings stored in the lending arm of the CBFS.

Note that because of the simulation design, income gain is due only to activities of the LEDDA. In a real LEDDA, additional economic expansion and income gain might occur through non-modeled processes, including population growth and inflation. However, as will be discussed in Chapter 8, average real incomes for the U.S. working class and poor have remained almost stagnant for the past 40 years.

While Figure 4.1 shows post-CBFS mean family income, pre-CBFS family income is actually much higher. For many members, it is about twice as large. The large volume of CBFS contributions is what enables job growth, effective democratic control over funding

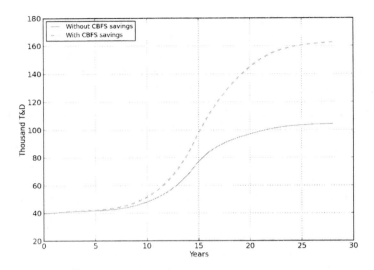

Figure 4.1: Mean post-CBFS family income with and without accumulated CBFS savings.

decisions, and member assistance. (Member assistance is discussed in Chapter 5.)

As a direct result of funding and job creation stemming from CBFS contributions, the unemployment rate drops. As shown in Figure 4.2, full employment is reached in Year 10 for members. That is, the unemployment rate falls to the structural unemployment rate, which for the simulation is assumed to be 1 percent.[1] Full employment is reached for the county as a whole in Year 15.

Finally, Figure 4.3 shows the volume of CBFS funding received by local for-profit and nonprofit organizations. By Year 28, CBFS funding reaches a plateau of over 2.6 billion T&D annually.

An annual funding pool of 2.6 billion T&D is a large amount of money for a county of population 100,000. It is roughly on par with total outstanding loans at U.S. commercial banks, which in 2011 was

[1] Structural unemployment is caused by fundamental long-term trends in the economy and a mismatch between jobs offered and workers available to fill them. For example, some people will always lose jobs through changes in technology.

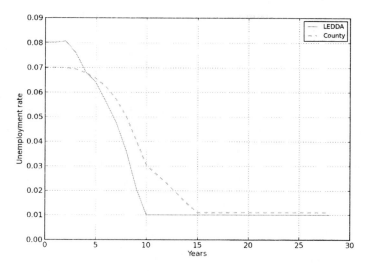

Figure 4.2: LEDDA and LEDDA county unemployment rates, as fractions.

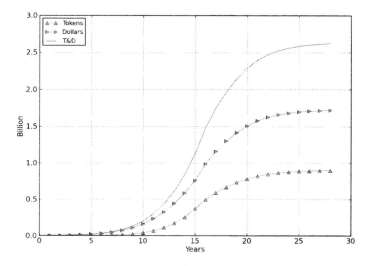

Figure 4.3: CBFS funding of local organizations.

about \$2.3 billion on average for a county.[2][80] In the simulation, it is enough to reduce unemployment to near-zero. If similar results were seen for a real LEDDA, conceivably it would be enough to allow residents to reshape the county economy into one that they most want.

To provide just a few examples of how CBFS funds might be used, members could help upgrade schools and colleges, hire teachers, construct research and development facilities, repair and improve infrastructure, pursue climate change action, provide health care, expand park systems, hire firefighters, fund small farms and farmers markets, expand recycling programs, develop green energy facilities and green manufacturing firms, support arts programs, and help fund other amenities, services, projects, and production that they view as important.

To give some idea of how far 2.6 billion T&D might stretch in a county, the American Society for Civil Engineers gives U.S. infrastructure (roads, bridges, dams, airports, sewers, water mains, etc.) a failing grade of D+. The estimated cost to make needed repairs across the United States is \$3.6 trillion over the next six years (by 2020), or an average of \$190 million per county per year.[81] Expected costs for climate change action—both for mitigating impact and slowing temperature rise—are expected to run about 4 percent of GDP.[82] For the United States, this would be about \$680 billion annually in current dollars, or an average per-county cost of about \$216 million. Even added together, these costs for infrastructure repair and climate change action are less than 16 percent of 2.6 billion T&D.

The upshot is, if results similar to those of the simulation are achievable in practice, then communities would have ample funds to address infrastructure decay, climate change, and other major challenges, at the local level, while maintaining full employment.

---

[2] In 2011, outstanding commercial bank loans totaled about \$7.3 trillion nationally, or about \$2.3 billion per county. The average U.S. county size is roughly 100,000 adults, the same size as the population in the simulation. The United States has 3,144 county and county-equivalent regions.

Chapter 5

Income Equality

"We can have democracy in this country, or we can have great wealth concentrated in the hands of a few, but we can't have both."

—Louis D. Brandeis (1856–1941)
U.S. Supreme Court Justice

The quote by Justice Brandeis captures the notion that extreme disparities in wealth threaten a political democracy. Financial power and political power are deeply entwined: a concentration of one favors a concentration of the other. This might explain, for example, why more than half of all benefits from tax breaks accrue to households in the top 20th percentile of income and why 17 percent of benefits go to the top 1 percent.[83] As noted in Chapter 3, at least one comprehensive study suggests that the United States might already be a plutocracy with regard to policy-making. But if political democracy is put at risk by income and wealth disparities, then LEDDA economic direct democracy could be even more susceptible to abuse; it uses money itself as a voting tool.

As discussed in Chapter 3, LEDDA economic direct democracy is expressed partly through purchasing and funding decisions, where members "vote" with their tokens and dollars. Thus, the more tokens and dollars a member has, the more power she has to affect her economy. Allowing large disparities of token-and-dollar income—and by extension, token-and-dollar wealth—would be like allowing a few people to cast thousands, or even millions of votes in a presidential election, while others only cast one. Such unfairness would undermine the heart and soul of a political democracy. The same is true of income inequality in LEDDA economic direct democracy. As mentioned in Chapter 2, income inequality would be a form of voter exclusion for those at the lower end of the income spectrum.

This chapter focuses on how a LEDDA achieves a high degree of income equality. It is useful to start by looking at the degree of inequality present in the United States dollar economy.

5.1 Income and Wealth Distributions

Figure 5.1 illustrates the distribution of 2010 U.S. family income, based on Federal Reserve data. A "normal" distribution (a bell-shaped curve) is shown for contrast.[1] An income distribution, such as shown in Figure 5.1, is a picture showing the "spread" of income values in a population. When looking at an income distribution, the key point to remember is that wherever the curve (or bar) is relatively high on the vertical axis, the probability of a random person having the respective income shown on the horizontal axis is also relatively high.[2]

The normal distribution (dotted line) in Figure 5.1 is centered at $78,300, the average family income in 2010. The peak at $78,300

---

[1] Dollar income and wealth distributions shown in this section are produced using microdata provided by the Federal Reserve Board's Survey of Consumer Finances. Note that different federal agencies use different definitions of income, and some report family income while others report household income. In particular, the Federal Reserve definition of income does not exactly match that provided by the U.S. Census. The LEDDA Microsimulation Model uses U.S. Census income data because it is available at the county level. The bell curve rises higher than the actual income distribution in Figure 5.1 because of the wide spread of income data.

[2] More formally, a distribution shows the probability of a person randomly selected from a population having an income less than or equal to a particular value. The area under a distribution curve is normalized to 1. That is, the Y-axis, density, is scaled so that the area under the curve is 1. Actual values of density are not important to understand the general meaning of the distributions.

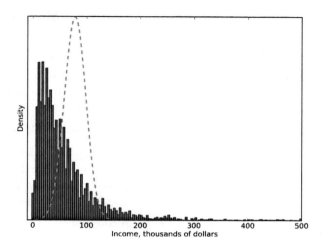

Figure 5.1: 2010 U.S. family income distribution (bars) and normal curve (dotted).[84]

indicates that for this imaginary population, more families had an income of about $78,300 than any other level. As one looks left or right from the peak, the curve only slopes downward.[3] Some might consider a normal distribution to be "fair"—not too many poor, not too many rich, and most families earning near the average. Indeed, most Americans mistakenly believe that the true U.S. income distribution has a shape of this type.[85] But they would be wrong, as the figure demonstrates.

Actual income levels are severely skewed—most families have low incomes; a few families have high ones. As can be seen from the peak in the figure, more families have an income of roughly $20,000 than any other income value. The average income might be $78,300, but not so many families actually earn it. The average is bumped up by a very few families that have extremely high incomes. Figure 5.1 only shows incomes up to $500,000, but in 2010 they ranged all the way up to $361 million. If the full distribution were shown, the highest income would be located about 192 feet (roughly two-thirds

---

[3] If the variance, or "spread" of the normal curve had been higher or lower, the curve would have sloped downward slower or faster, respectively.

of a football field) off the page to the right. In contrast, the typical (median) family income was $45,700, or nearly 8,000 times lower than the highest one.

All other things being equal, if 2010 incomes had actually followed a normal distribution, the median and mean family income would be the same, $78,300. That is, income for the typical family would have increased by 71 percent, from $45,700 to $78,300. Moreover, about 73 percent of all families would have received an income gain.[4]

Even a modest reduction in income inequality would make a substantial difference for those at the bottom. A 2013 report for the State of Maryland concluded that a return to the 1968 income inequality gap—which was less severe than seen today—would double the average income of the poorest households from roughly $15,000 to nearly $30,000.[86]

Income for top earners continues to rise, and the inequality gap continues to widen. The average adjusted gross income for the top 400 earners nearly tripled between 1992 and 2009, after adjustment for inflation.[87] Meanwhile, incomes for the poor and middle class remained nearly flat. Income disparity is now greater in the United States than in almost every other developed nation. Based on CIA data of 140 countries, Sweden enjoys the most equitable income distribution. The U.S. ranks 94th in the list, just behind Cameroon and the Ivory Coast, and just in front of Uruguay and Jamaica.[88] Risks to society increase with rising inequality. Motesharrei, Rivas, and Kalnay warn that the collapse of advanced civilizations is a recurrent theme throughout human history, and the driving force is typically a toxic combination of resource depletion and economic inequality.[89]

If the skew in income distribution is bad, the skew in wealth distribution is even worse.[5] This is as expected, of course, because accumulated (saved) income is a component of wealth. Also, families who have incomes greater than their base expenses can increase their wealth further via investments and other opportunities.

---

[4] The average income, $78,300, was located at the 73rd percentile.

[5] *Wealth* (or *net worth*) refers to the value of a person's financial assets minus liabilities. A subset of this, *financial wealth,* refers to "liquid" wealth that is immediately available for consumption or investment. It is defined as wealth excluding home mortgages.

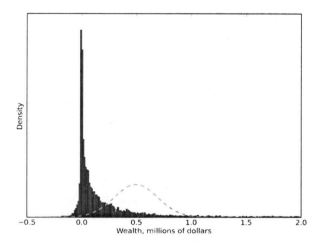

Figure 5.2: 2010 U.S. family wealth distribution (bars) and normal curve (dotted).[84]

Figure 5.2 shows the 2010 distribution of U.S. family wealth (net worth), again compared with a normal distribution. The normal distribution (dotted line) is centered at $500,000, roughly the average family wealth in 2010.[84] Relatively few families have average wealth, and the skew in the wealth curve is quite apparent. The median is $77,000, less than one-sixth the average. The intensely high peak near zero indicates that more people had near-zero wealth in 2010 than any other value. To put things in perspective, the wealthiest American in 2010 was Bill Gates, with $54 billion.[90] If Figure 5.2 were to include his wealth, it would have to extend off the page about 1.4 miles to the right. The wealth of the typical family was over 700,000 times lower than his.

The distributions of U.S. income and wealth are pictures of extreme inequality. In contrast, the normal distributions shown are pictures of less extreme inequality. If the ends of the normal distributions were squeezed together bit by bit (i.e., if the variances, or spreads, of the distributions were reduced), they would be pictures of increasingly less inequality. If their ends were squeezed completely together, making single vertical lines, the distributions would be pictures of full equality.

A LEDDA does not have to choose income targets that lead to full income equality, although there are good reasons for doing so. For simplicity, the income targets used in the LEDDA Microsimulation Model are based on full equality. Countywide results from the study are shown in Figure 5.3 for Year 0, prior to the introduction of tokens, and Year 28, the end of the simulation. By Year 28, all families in the target population (90 percent of the county population) have become members and receive an income of about 104,000 tokens plus dollars (T&D). As noted in Chapter 4, mean family income increased by 267 percent in the simulation.[6]

Income changes for non-members families (those above the 90th income percentile) were not modeled and so in the simulation do not change. For non-member families, income and post-CBFS income are identical.

5.2   Issues of Income Equality

It is anticipated that some will object to the idea of full income equality. Even for those working on poverty issues, a reduction in the severity of inequality is a more commonly stated goal. One reason for this might be practicality; as yet, no widely accepted means has been proposed to achieve full income equality. In contrast, reduction of income inequality via redistribution of income by progressive taxation, combined with needs-based government assistance, is widely accepted.

More recently, the concept of *basic income* as a means to reduce income inequality has been gaining in popularity. A basic income is a subsistence-level government payment guaranteed to all citizens, without needs-based testing. Proponents claim that basic income programs are less expensive to administer than needs-based welfare programs.[91, 92] Neither needs-based welfare nor basic income programs would be suitable for LEDDA economic direct democracy, however, as neither would result in roughly equal sharing of power over economic decisions.

---

[6] An animated version of the year-to-year change in distribution is available at the Principled Societies Project website http://www.PrincipledSocietiesProject.org.

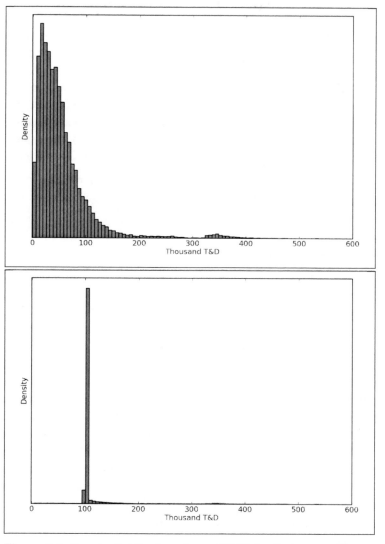

Figure 5.3: County distribution of post-CBFS family income. Top panel: Year 0; Bottom panel: Year 28.

The LEDDA framework takes a novel approach. Rather than a government program, which applies to all residents of a state or nation, LEDDA programs apply only to people and organizations that volunteer to become members. Further, a LEDDA does not rely on outside grants or other types of conventional funding to reduce poverty. Nor does it redistribute *existing* income through a tax policy. It increases income, and the gains from this are shared (via the CBFS). As the membership grows, and as incomes increase, a larger percentage of the local population achieves income equality. One can say that a LEDDA uses a market-based approach; it offers a product (increased income and improved well-being), the price for which is membership, income equality, and deeper cooperation.

Besides the means to alter incomes, numerous other issues arise in arguments for or against income equality and reduced inequality. A few of these are discussed below.

Americans want greater equality, and half see full equality as ideal.

In a 2010 study, Harvard and Duke researchers showed three un-labeled pie charts depicting wealth distributions to a representative sample of more than 5,000 U.S. residents. One chart illustrated full equality, and the others illustrated actual wealth distributions in the U.S. and Sweden. Wealth is distributed far more equally in Sweden than in the United States. For all pairs of charts, individuals were asked to choose the one that they felt was most ideal, given a Rawlsian "original position" stance (Chapter 2). By overwhelming majority— 92 percent versus 8 percent—respondents indicated that the Swedish distribution was more ideal than the U.S. distribution.[85] This choice held true over all subgroups of the experimental population, including women, men, Democratic voters, Republican voters, wealthy persons, and poor persons. Moreover, when asked to choose between full equality and the Swedish distribution of wealth, roughly half chose full equality.

Next, the researchers asked respondents to drop the Rawlsian "veil of ignorance" and create a distribution that best represented current conditions in the United States. Respondents vastly underestimated the actual level of inequality. Finally, respondents were asked to indicate their preferred distribution of wealth. All subdivisions preferred a more equal distribution of wealth than what is currently the case, and one more equal than what they estimated the current distribution to be.

In the American Dream, anyone who works hard can become rich. People want the opportunity that the American Dream provides.

The American Dream offers hope of success to those who work hard. But as comedian George Carlin quipped, "It's called the American Dream because you have to be asleep to believe it." If your parents struggle economically, there is a good chance that you will struggle too. In the United States, the level of income a person attains is strongly associated with the income level attained by his parents. The probability of changing income brackets—the degree of economic mobility—is lower in America than in almost all other developed nations.[93]

Income inequality and generational economic mobility are at odds with each other. Inequality shapes opportunity. And it polarizes society, heightening income-dependent differences. It changes incentives and institutions, and shifts power to the wealthy, who can then affect policies, make influential connections, and otherwise improve the chances of success for their children.[94]

As Figure 5.2 suggests, almost all Americans have little to modest wealth—most have little. In contrast, and in reference to income rather than wealth, the bottom panel of Figure 5.3 shows what might be possible under the LEDDA framework. Members benefit in multiple ways. They obtain a higher family income, relative to today's median, and strike it rich by becoming wealthy in well-being.

People do not necessarily work harder when they see a promise of financial reward.

People already work hard for low salaries and scant promise of raises, bonuses, or other income gains. As will be discussed in Chapter 8, inflation-adjusted incomes have remained almost stagnant for the poor and middle class for the past 40 years. Moreover, plenty of people work hard for no remuneration at all. Most popular open-source software development projects owe their success in part to the efforts of volunteers who contribute time and expertise. Indeed, 62 million Americans volunteered through an organization in 2008. Eight billion hours of service were donated, worth an estimated $162 billion.[95]

While no study has examined work motivation under LEDDA conditions, a few have examined motivation under basic income settings. The most comprehensive study so far is the Namibia Basic Income Pilot Project, 2008–2009.[96] Although the Namibia project was small in size and duration—it was funded by a church charity rather than a government—results suggest that basic income can reduce poverty, improve education, reduce crime, increase food security, and increase motivation due to new entrepreneurial opportunities.

Moreover, money is not the strong motivator of human behavior it is assumed to be. Modern social science research suggests that numerous factors, in addition to money, influence human behavior.[97] As discussed in Chapter 1, humans are social creatures. We are driven by creative impulses, curiosity, and playfulness. We want work that is meaningful, and we want to earn the respect of peers and maintain self-respect. We like learning and developing skills. And we dislike situations that compromise our reputation or integrity, waste our time or talents, are unfair, or cause harm to other people or our environment. Although income can act as an incentive to behavior, it often takes a back seat to these other factors. Indeed, in some circumstances, offering rewards of higher income can actually reduce work effort.[98]

Two theories of human motivation are worth mentioning here. The first, Ryan and Deci's self-determination theory, holds that people are motivated by a combination of extrinsic and intrinsic factors. Extrinsic factors can include reward systems, money, evaluations, and punishment. Intrinsic ones can include interests, curiosities, and values. Of all motivators, the most potent appear to be mastery of skills, autonomy, and relatedness (social engagement, caring, etc.).[99]

The second theory is Abraham Maslow's hierarchy of needs. In this theory, needs motivate behavior. Needs are arranged and tend to be satisfied according to five hierarchic classes: (1) physiological needs, including food, water, and sleep; (2) security, including safety, shelter, and health; (3) relationship, including friendship, love, and community; (4) self-esteem, including respect, recognition, and achievement; and (5) self-actualization, including wisdom, knowledge, and creativity.[100] Money tends to affect the lower portions of the needs hierarchy, suggesting that once a modest income threshold is reached, other concerns often take precedence.

U.S. and cross-country studies back this up. Personal happiness and emotional well-being tend to rise little, if at all, with income in the United States once a modest threshold of about $75,000 is reached; but low incomes are associated with less happiness.[101, 102] Further, the promise of higher pay tends to be useful as a motivator only in limited circumstances, where tasks are highly repetitive and not creative. In common work settings, mastery of skills, autonomy, and social engagement tend to be stronger motivators.[98]

In short, people desire and benefit greatly from incomes that are high enough to provide a reasonable level of comfort and security. But as incomes rise (higher than about the U.S. average), money affects happiness to a lesser and lesser degree. Other needs, including social and creative needs, tend to move to the forefront.

These observations help put income levels in perspective. If the goal of a LEDDA is to improve well-being, then it must increase incomes that are low, while creating conditions that help members fulfill their basic and higher needs. Discussions throughout this book suggest that by adopting a balanced approach toward human needs, consistent with findings from modern social science, LEDDAs can help create a happier, more creative, healthier, and more secure society.

Income is not a fair measure of social contribution.

Some might argue that income equality is unfair. If all incomes are equal, the people who contribute the most to society would not receive their due reward. But income levels do not faithfully reflect the degree of social contribution. The notion that the two are related stems in part from marginal productivity theory, developed in the late 1800s.[103]

The theory holds that if competition is perfect, the social contribution of each worker is exactly equal to her compensation. Intended as an explanatory theory, it has since been transformed into a normative one: people who contribute more *ought* to receive higher pay. Going one step further, if markets determine that different people receive different incomes, then the differences can be taken as ethically justified.

The trouble is, the requirements of marginal productivity theory are not met in practice, and its logic is unsound, if not circular.[104] It requires perfect competition and separation of factors (such as capital and labor) that contribute to total production. But these requirements are not met in the real economy.

Rather than reflecting social contribution, incomes in the real economy tend to reflect differences in resources, bargaining power, and other factors.[94, 105] Bargaining power itself is affected by unemployment rates, discrimination, the capacity of workers to organize, and the concentration of financial power in the hands of employers and their skill in exploiting it. Further, income inequalities affect opportunities, education, medical care, and cultural participation. These in turn affect income gain in a circular feedback loop. As a result, those near the top—and their children—tend to rise higher, and those near the bottom tend to stay at the bottom.

A case in point: CEO salaries. In 2012, CEO compensation at top firms averaged about 354 times higher than compensation for rank-and-file workers.[106] Yet a 2013 study on 500 corporate executive positions using 20 years of data found that 38 percent of CEOs were fired, had to pay massive settlements or fines related to fraud, led firms that failed, or led firms that had to be bailed out by government funds. As an aside, those who were fired received an average golden parachute of $48 million.[107]

Why do CEOs, attorneys, doctors, and investment fund managers tend to make far higher incomes than say, teachers, family farmers, and police officers? Are the social contributions of the former group really that much larger than those of the latter? For that matter, why are there small differences in wages between some professions? For example, why do court reporters tend to make 5 percent lower salaries than librarians?[108] Do court reporters contribute 5 percent less to society? And why are incomes for new female graduates 7 percent lower than their male counterparts, after controlling for work hours and graduation subject?[109] Do women contribute 7 percent less to society?

The idea that income inequality is inherently ethical and representative of social contribution is difficult to support. Indeed, it is difficult, if not impossible, to analytically separate and rationally quantify the contributions that each person makes. The main metric available is income itself, but that leads to circular logic: a political consultant is worthy of a massive salary because that is what she makes. A librarian is worthy of a higher salary than a court reporter because that is what historic wage data show.

Of course, the entry cost to some professions (medicine, for example) is high, and quantifiable. Student debt must be paid off. But the spread of income data cannot be explained by entry costs alone. Further, this is more an argument for free education than an argument against income equality.

Quantifying contribution is made all the more difficult if we consider non-economic factors. Almost every reader can think of a person whose benefit to society is in excess of his or her income. A grandmother active in her community might have a profound influence as its moral center, even if her income is close to zero. If we can't reliably measure the social contribution a person makes, how can we justify incomes that are very high or very low, or slightly higher or lower than others?

In short, inequalities in income are ethically arbitrary and to a large extent a reflection of power distributions and circumstances of birth, upbringing, access to education, and luck. A person who works hard can, on rare occasion, rise from humble beginnings to extreme wealth. But a meteoric rise to success is usually due to a host of factors, of which but one is hard work. And besides, the concern here is not with the exceptions.

In contrast, the idea that income equality is ethical can be supported on multiple fronts. It is consistent with concepts of compassion, fairness, and equality. Income equality is also consistent with ideals of freedom; those from poor and low-income backgrounds—nearly half the U.S. population—do not enjoy the same freedoms to make purchases, travel, attend school, relocate, select medical care, and so on, compared to high-earners. Last, and of critical importance in this book, income equality is consistent with economic democracy. As we have seen, an economic system functions as a decision-making system. If an economy is to reflect democratic ideals—if all participants are to have a more or less equal say over broad economic decisions—then incomes must be more or less equal.

Inequalities reduce economic growth and well-being.

International data suggest that income inequality is strongly associated with lower sustained growth.[110] Some experts believe income disparity in the United States could be limiting economic growth by as much as a third.[111] Further, poverty not only reduces the subjective well-being of low-income families, it also reduces well-being for higher-income families.[112] Living in an unequal society is detrimental to everyone's life-satisfaction level.

5.3 Engagements

"I am now convinced that the simplest approach will prove to be the most effective—the solution to poverty is to abolish it directly by a now widely discussed measure: the guaranteed income."
—The Reverend Martin Luther King Jr. (1929–1968)

We will now address in more detail how a high degree of income equality is achieved for members. For the sake of argument, and for simplicity of exposition, suppose that members choose an income target (Chapter 4) to produce full equality over time.

If every member of a LEDDA were able-bodied, properly trained, and of working age, and if there were at least one job or job offer for each, then the income target—and income equality—could largely be pursued by means already discussed. That is, members could use the CBFS to fund jobs that offer wages in keeping with the target.

But real-world conditions are much more complex. Some adults are ill, mentally or physically. Some are elderly or disabled. Some are in full-time school or training programs. And some stay home to take care of children or elderly family members. In this book, individuals who are unemployed and not seeking jobs are termed not-in-workforce (NIWF). Nationally, about 37 percent of the adult population is NIWF.[113] Under conditions of full employment, however, the percentage would likely fall a bit; about 7 percent of NIWF persons desire work.[114] One can reasonably expect that between 30 percent and 40 percent of LEDDA members will be NIWF.

A LEDDA uses the CBFS to achieve equal income for essentially all adult members, including those who are unemployed and NIWF.[7] Previously, the CBFS was described primarily as a mechanism to fund nonprofit organizations and for-profit businesses, but members use it in a broader sense. They fund *engagements*, which are classified as either *market*, *service*, or *nurture*. Market engagements are jobs that are typically offered for wages in the for-profit business sector. Service engagements are jobs that are typically offered for wages in the public and nonprofit sector. And nurture engagements are not jobs per se, but positions that people hold when they are not holding market or service engagements.

For example, members can use the CBFS to fund for-profit and non-profit organizations that employ farmers, nurses, bakers, carpenters, scientists, and so on. As part of the application for a loan, subsidy, or donation, an organization indicates how many and what types of market or service engagements the funding will support. Of course, organizations are always free to shift their employees internally as needed or to fire them. But in their CBFS application, they provide an estimate of the numbers and types of engagements that they intend to offer.

Members can use the CBFS to fund nurture engagements for individuals who are full-time college students, unemployed, or not working due to disability or age. It can also fund nurture engagements for artists (somewhat like an artist's commission for ongoing work). Nurture engagements can cover a parent who stays home to care for a child, or an adult child who stays home to care for a parent. The income assistance provided via nurture engagements would take into account other types of assistance a person might be receiving. For

---

[7] A LEDDA might have reason to exclude some members from full benefits. For example, a person who broke the rules of a LEDDA might have his or her benefits reduced as a penalty. In extreme cases, membership might be revoked. By using the phrase *essentially all*, the intent is to suggest that exclusions would be kept to a minimum.

example, some members who receive nurture engagements might also receive government disability payments.

Some nurture engagements would require no duties at all, while others might require full- or part-time duties. College students holding a nurture engagement, for example, might be required to attend classes and make satisfactory progress. On the other hand, an elderly person might be exempted from any duties. Further, some engagements might invite duties, in a non-obligatory fashion. For example, a retired but able-bodied member might be invited to mentor youths for a few hours per week, help in a community garden, or assist in some other way.

Together, market, service, and nurture engagements cover the full range of situations that members might encounter. All engagements benefit the community, some in the short term and some in the long term. Some engagements are obviously productive, in an economic sense, while others are obviously necessary, in a human sense. It is necessary, for example, to care for the elderly and sick. Doing so benefits the whole community in a multitude of ways.

The nurture engagement system would require administration. Administrative services could be provided by nonprofit organizations that apply for CBFS funding for this purpose. For example, a nonprofit focused on promoting access to college might apply to the nurture arm of the CBFS. It would distribute any nurture funds it receives to the students under its care and supervision. In fact, members might fund several nonprofits that serve the same purpose. As such, a diversity of administrative approaches could be tested.

Further, by using the CBFS to fund nonprofits as administrators, the membership retains full control over social program decisions. Members could change funding levels as they see fit, and encourage competition as appropriate. Said another way, the nurture engagement system puts the membership in charge of its own care.

The flow of token–dollars between organizations, individual members, and the CBFS is illustrated in Figure 5.4. This is an abbreviated picture of token–dollar flow (even more abbreviated than that used in the LEDDA Microsimulation Model), but it does capture the general notion that members receive income from organizations and from CBFS nurture funds, and they make CBFS contributions and spend

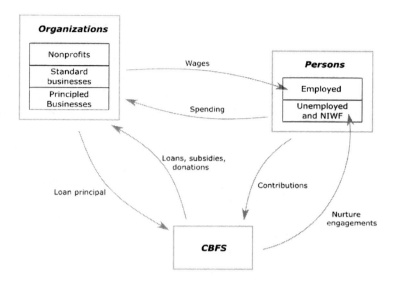

Figure 5.4: General features of token—dollar flow between organizations, persons, and the CBFS.

money at organizations. Further, members use the CBFS to fund organizations through loans, subsidies, and donations. For simplicity, the administrative role of nonprofits in distributing nurture funds is not shown in the figure. Rather, the nurture funds that members receive are depicted as coming directly from the CBFS.

Market and service engagements might simply have been called "jobs." For all practical purposes, businesses and nonprofits would apply for CBFS funding for these and, if funding is approved, hire applicants as normal. But both the "engagement" term and the concept of an organization as an "administrator" of engagements are useful. Just as nonprofits would administer nurture engagements, businesses and nonprofits would administer market and service engagements, respectively. The terminology reinforces the notion that members are "on loan" to businesses and other organizations at the membership's discretion. An organization is expected to provide benefit to the community, and to attend to and assist those members under its concern. Although on paper, members would use the CBFS to allocate funds, in actuality they would be allocating themselves; they would democratically decide how to contribute their time and energy to the local economy. They would fund their own jobs, and their own care.

The engagement system is dynamic. Most members would change engagements occasionally, just as is done in the dollar economy. For example, a student might graduate and move from a nurture engagement to a market engagement. Or an individual might switch service engagements to obtain one that is more aligned with her interests and skills. Also, a firm might fire an employee, or go out of business. And a person might retire, and switch from a market engagement to a nurture engagement. But at every moment, each member of a LEDDA would hold at least one engagement, and some might hold two or more part-time engagements. This system provides the mechanism by which the target income distribution is reached and every member is cared for.

To be clear, no member would be forced to accept an engagement, just as no person is forced to accept a job in the dollar economy. In general, members would compete for the engagements that are most popular. For example, a funded business might offer an attractive management job, or an arts-based nonprofit might offer attractive nurture engagements for musicians or actors. Attractive engagements would likely receive many applications.

The engagement system helps members address the big challenges facing society, such as climate change, resource depletion, infrastructure decay, rising health-care costs, and pollution. In choosing which engagements to fund, a LEDDA can favor those that help solve the big problems. As just one example, members might fund biologists via service engagements to better assess watershed health and water quality.

If results similar to those of the LEDDA Microsimulation Model can be achieved in practice, a mature LEDDA would not have difficulty raising enough money to fund an engagement for every member. The real challenge put before the membership is to decide what the needs of the LEDDA and greater community are. This entails public discussion and long-range planning.

If a LEDDA wants better health and lower health-care costs, for example, it might choose to fund organizations that offer engagements for doctors, nurses, and medical researchers. As well, it should consider the future, and fund organizations that support enough full-time students in these fields. Likewise, if it wishes to develop new technologies in energy, materials, communications, and robotics, it would fund organizations that administer the market, service, and nurture engagements appropriate for these. Planning can be complex, and computer models would help LEDDA members examine present and future needs.

A LEDDA would have many economic, scientific, social, artistic, public health, manufacturing, and environmental goals. In fact, it is likely to have more goals than it has members to implement them. Thus, human capital (rather than financial capital) is likely to play the limiting role. For this reason, a LEDDA would want to invest in each member and help each to reach full potential. Every member would be important.

Chapter 6

Token Exchange System

> *"The fact is that the work which improves the condition of mankind, the work which extends knowledge and increases power, and enriches literature, and elevates thought, is not done to secure a living. It is not the work of slaves, driven to their task either by the lash of a master or by animal necessities. It is the work of men who perform it for its own sake, and not that they may get more to eat or drink, or wear, or display. In a state of society where want was abolished, work of this sort would be enormously increased."*
>
> —Henry George (1839–1897)
> U.S. political economist

This chapter provides a more detailed look at the Token Exchange System that a LEDDA administers. A TES is composed of two parts, the Token Monetary System and the Crowd-Based Financial System. Together they form an integrated monetary/financial system that embodies the ideals of transparency, fairness, democracy, and cooperation.

The TMS provides a means to create new tokens, distribute them to members, and remove them from circulation when necessary. The CBFS provides a means to generate token-and-dollar loans, subsidies, and donations for nonprofit organizations and for-profit businesses. As discussed in Chapter 5, a deeper meaning of the CBFS is to fund market, service, and nurture engagements, and in so doing fulfill community needs and achieve income equality.

The TES acts as an overlay to the local dollar economy, creating a token–dollar economy. As such, dollars play an obvious role. For example, local, state, and federal taxes are paid in dollars, as usual. Purchases from or sales to non-members, local or distant, are also transacted using dollars, as usual. Member merchants accept a mix of dollars and tokens when they sell products to other members. And the CBFS uses both tokens and dollars to fund organizations. The main focus of this chapter, however, is the token itself.

The token is, in a real sense, a manifestation of a community's faith in itself and its desires for a better future. But the token holds value only to the degree that it is used in commerce and finance. That is, it gains utility only through circulation. Thus, much of the design of the TES is focused on meeting two primary objectives: to maintain a quality circulation, such that the token's value remains constant over time; and to implement LEDDA economic direct democracy.

The quality of circulation is defined in part by the smoothness and evenness with which tokens flow. Tokens are called a currency, and it might help to imagine token flow as an electric current. Consider a circuit board used within a battery-powered radio. Tiny metal strips embedded in the board connect numerous small electrical components. When the radio is turned on, electrons flow in a circle from the negative terminal of the battery through the different branching and cascading pathways, in and out of different components, and finally return to the battery again, at the positive terminal. The radio works only so long as the electrons continue to flow uninterrupted. If circulation stops, or if an excess builds up in any location, the radio either functions poorly or ceases to function.

And so it is with tokens. They flow through different branching and cascading pathways to reach all members at an appropriate rate. Neither excesses nor deficiencies should occur. When the different parts receive the right flow, each can play its role in fulfilling the purpose of the whole. But flow is dynamic, economies are dynamic. Because conditions constantly change, the circulation network must be designed for robust service. It must be capable of absorbing and smoothing out fluctuations, and righting itself when things go wrong. It must allow LEDDA members to easily adapt and adjust as bumps are encountered along the road, as new opportunities arise, and as new needs appear.

Although this chapter focuses on TES mechanics, flow actually depends upon much more. As mentioned in Chapter 2, LEDDA economic direct democracy gains strength and endurance within the triad of democracy, transparency, and education. Education can include workshops and trainings on how a TES functions and its role in LEDDA economic direct democracy. Social norms also play a role, as does the intellectual property pool. Each element of the framework listed in Chapter 2 influences the quality of token flow.

6.1 Overview of Local Currencies

The Token Exchange System is not the first local currency system to be proposed. Local currencies have a rich history, both in the United States and elsewhere. During the Great Depression, bank failures caused an acute demand for cash, and some businesses and organizations issued scrip as an alternative form of exchange. More than 3,000 different scrips were issued in the United States alone during that period.[115] A Depression-era example outside of the United States occurred in Wörgl, a small town in Austria.[116, 117] Unemployment rose and new construction stalled. The town's mayor suggested that the city print a set of labor certificates, each of which carried a negative 1 percent monthly interest rate (a form of demurrage). The experiment was apparently quite successful. The currency circulated faster than the national currency, unemployment dropped, and the city's revenue increased. The program met stiff opposition from the Austrian central bank, however, and was eventually shut down.

In recent decades, local currency systems have been implemented in a growing number of locations globally, including locations in the United States.[118, 119, 120, 121, 122, 123, 124] Systems occur at the municipal, regional, and national levels. In this book the term *complementary currency* is used to describe systems that might be local, regional, national, or international in scope.

Although there are exceptions, most complementary currency systems fall into just a handful of models: (1) commercial barter exchange systems, which allow business-to-business trade without use of national currency; (2) local exchange trading systems (LETS), in which individuals and businesses create currency backed by their own services and goods; (3) Time Bank (service exchange) systems, in which individuals create currency backed by their own labor; and (4) systems backed by national currency, where complementary currency is purchased using national currency and can usually be redeemed for national currency. Systems also exist in which complementary currency is backed by energy or other commodities. A typology for complementary currency systems captures some of these differences.[125]

Local and Regional Complementary Currencies

Notable local currency systems in the United States include the Ithaca Hours and BerkShares. The Hours, developed by Paul Glover for Ithaca, N.Y., is one of the largest local currency systems in the nation. Hours are currently accepted in more than 400 retail and service establishments. Over $100,000 worth of Hours are in circulation.[126]

BerkShares are a local currency for the Berkshire region of Massachusetts. As of 2014, more than 350 local businesses and 13 banks participate in the program. BerkShares are purchased using dollars and can be redeemed for dollars.[127]

New local currency systems continue to emerge. San Francisco alone has recently seen two new additions. The Bernal Buck acts like frequent-flyer miles, only for shopping in the Bernal Heights neighborhood. It might be the world's first local currency in which transactions occur via a debit card.[128] The Bay Buck, which serves the entire city, is San Francisco's first local barter exchange.[129]

Notable complementary currency systems outside of the United States include the Bristol Pound in the United Kingdom and the Red de Trueque in Argentina. The Bristol Pound, launched in 2012, is the U.K.'s first citywide local currency.[130] It is accepted by about 600 Bristol businesses and can be used to pay for rides on city buses and to pay some local taxes. The mayor has chosen to take his entire salary in the local currency.[131] A partnership with the Bristol

Credit Union allows for distribution of the paper money and management of electronic accounts. One popular feature is TXT2PAY, which allows shoppers to text the transaction, making purchases easier and faster.[132]

Red de Trueque was launched in 1995 by a small group of disenfranchised middle-class Buenos Aires environmentalists who were seeking relief from the nation's crippling economic depression. The initial system was based on mutual credit (LETS) but was later converted to fiat paper money as popularity grew. By 2002, buoyed by the meltdown of the Argentine economy, participation soared to more than 2.5 million users nationwide. Within just seven years of implementation, it had become the world's largest experiment in complementary currency. In aggregate, the system added about 0.6 percent of value to the national GDP.[133, 78]

By early 2003 the Argentinian economy was recovering and the government began to offer expanded unemployment insurance. Both factors reduced the demand for complementary currency. Moreover, Red de Trueque began to buckle under the strain of its own rapid growth—numerous design weaknesses posed problems. Counterfeiting and inflation were among the challenges. Popularity fell as dramatically as it rose. In just a few months, the user base collapsed to about 10 percent of peak size. Since 2003 it has stabilized at about 5 percent of its peak (roughly 120,000 users), still substantial by today's standards.

The example of Red de Trueque highlights both the potential of a complementary currency to spread rapidly and the necessity of careful, intelligent design prior to implementation. To reach and maintain a high level of success, a system must be scalable, secure, fair, transparent, user-friendly, and resilient. Circulation must be complete; bottlenecks and dead-ends in currency flow are recipes for disaster. The governance mechanism must be sound, efficient, and democratic. And the system must inspire confidence and be capable of producing tangible benefits, or few will want to use it. Indeed, all modern complementary currency systems face these challenges; they are the main obstacles to growth.

Global Complementary Currencies

Bitcoin, introduced in 2009, is an electronic cash system that operates via peer-to-peer technology, without a central authority.[134] Creation and management of coins follow rules defined at the system's inception. Coins are created through computational effort—solving a difficult computational problem results in issuance of a fixed number of new coins. As coins are produced, the computational effort needed to create additional coins increases. As such, the volume of coins follows a well-defined and inflexible trajectory. No more than 21 million coins will ever be produced. Because the volume is inflexible, it cannot grow or shrink in response to the needs of a dynamic Bitcoin economy. At the same time, the inability to create an unlimited numbers of coins instills confidence, in some users.

The value of the Bitcoin has skyrocketed since its inception. The total value of all available coins is now about $12 billion but fluctuates wildly.[135] Much of the meteoric rise and volatility have been due to speculators who have bet that, like gold, Bitcoin could act as a safe haven for wealth in turbulent times.[136] Although some people fear that Bitcoin is being used to move money illegally, so far federal authorities have not targeted Bitcoin or its uses. The exception is a large exchange system that failed to register as a money transmitter. In 2013, the European Banking Authority issued a warning about trading the currency, citing wide value swings, lack of regulation, and money-laundering risks.[137]

While Bitcoin has made a few investors wealthy, its chief economic value stems from its ability to offer zero- or near-zero transaction fees. Considering that credit card fees are costly to merchants, a business can save money by accepting payment in Bitcoin. Not surprisingly, the number of online and off-line businesses that accept Bitcoin has grown rapidly.[138]

Bitcoin has another value: it is a pioneer virtual currency, paving the way for greater acceptance of others. Indeed, during a recent congressional hearing, Obama administration officials generally had positive comments on the currency and recognized its legitimate role in innovation. Their main concerns focused on its potential for illicit use.[139]

Airline frequent-flyer miles represent another kind of complementary currency with international reach.[140] Frequent-flyer miles were created to promote customer loyalty in exchange for free travel. But now miles can be earned through credit card use and other activities, and redeemed for car rentals and other products and services. Two-thirds of all British Airways miles are redeemed for something other than airline tickets. Miles can even be traded for cash via PayPal.[141] As of 2005, 14 trillion airline miles had been issued. With an estimated value of $0.05 per mile, about $700 billion in miles have been created.[142]

The LEDDA token displays some similarities with other current or historical complementary currencies, but differences also exist. Foremost, the TES is but one element within a larger framework that implements LEDDA economic direct democracy. The framework as a whole is unique, as is the combination of ideas embodied within a TES: use of an electronic debt-free local currency; a mandatory crowd-based system to finance organizations; interest-free loans offered in both local and national currency; demurrage to control flow of local currency, and earmarks to control flows of both local and national currency.

The LEDDA framework allows flexibility and could coexist with and gain from other types of complementary currency systems. For example, a LEDDA, and especially a network of LEDDAs, might benefit from business-to-business barter exchange systems. Such systems could open new opportunities for inter-LEDDA trade, without exchange of dollars. Local exchange trading systems and Time Bank systems could also be integrated into a LEDDA or operate as complements to it.

6.2 Flow in the Token Exchange System

The flow of tokens among the four main components of a TES is illustrated in Figure 6.1. The four components are: member accounts; for-profit and nonprofit organizations; the TMS, which creates and destroys tokens; and the CBFS, which funds organizations. Connections to the Collaborative Governance System are also shown.

For simplicity, tokens targeted for destruction are depicted as originating from member accounts; in reality, they would likely come

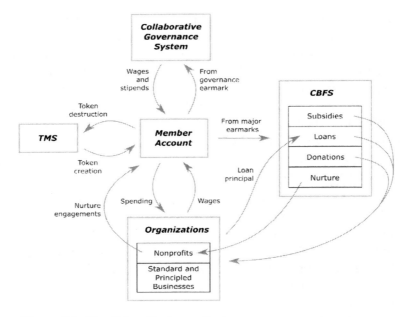

Figure 6.1: The Token Exchange System.

from tokens destined for CBFS contributions. Also, repayment of loan principal by organizations is shown as re-entering the CBFS loan arm. In reality, each member would manage lending and receipt of payments through a lending portfolio. Likewise, each would manage subsidies, donations, and nurture funds through corresponding subsidy, donation, and nurture portfolios.

A LEDDA operates its own token accounting system, which includes an online software application that allows members to access and manage their token accounts and portfolios, and view transaction histories. The electronic nature of the token facilitates accounting, transparency, and data collection. The token accounting system is part of the larger software system that allows online voting in the Collaborative Governance System and which implements other elements of the LEDDA framework.

The token accounting system is integrated with a dollar accounting system, which records dollar flow, including CBFS dollar loans, subsidies, donations, and nurture funds. But the dollar accounting system would likely be managed jointly by a LEDDA and willing credit union, local bank, or public bank partner.[143, 144] The Cyclos enterprise banking software, versions of which are open source, might act as an inspiration.[145]

Any individual or organization is welcome to apply for LEDDA membership. Members can include individuals, businesses, nonprofits, schools, colleges, public service agencies, government agencies, and local branches of national nonprofits and businesses. Figure 6.1 is drawn from the perspective of a member individual.

The token does not function as a means to store financial wealth, as most currencies do. As noted in Chapter 3, the demurrage rate ensures that tokens remain in circulation rather than in storage.[1] Instead, financial wealth is stored within loan portfolios, built up through the lending arm of the CBFS. As loans are repaid, members can use the incoming tokens and dollars to make additional loans (as further storage of financial wealth), or, given certain restrictions, can use the repaid principal for making purchases or for other uses. A loan certificate trading system, discussed later in this chapter, allows members to retrieve tokens and dollars from loan portfolios as needed. Thus, the notion of "circulation as wealth" is made explicit. Members store their financial wealth as circulation—they lend their excess to others who then keep tokens and dollars in movement.

The Token Monetary System

Tokens enter a member's account from various sources and exit to various destinations. One source/destination is the Token Monetary System, which manages the volume of tokens. It issues new tokens and destroys old ones, as needed. It can also recycle tokens received from demurrage or other payments. Tokens are issued via two pathways: addition and substitution.

The default pathway is "addition." Here, tokens are created debt-free by fiat and distributed to member accounts (which can include business accounts). This pathway has similarities to and differences from the way dollars are created. Both tokens and dollars are issued by fiat in a controlled process. Dollars, however, are created primarily by banks; banks loan dollars into existence via interest-bearing

---

[1] The flow of demurrage is not explicitly shown in Figure 6.1, but would be similar to the flow depicted for token destruction.

debt.[146] Tokens are created by a LEDDA, free of debt. More will be said about the dollar creation process in Chapter 8. Tokens issued via the "addition" pathway increase the local money supply (tokens plus dollars) that is available to members.[2]

The "substitution" pathway plays a secondary role. Here, tokens are also created by fiat, debt-free, but are sold for dollars. That is, tokens displace dollars. The dollars collected are (eventually) removed from the local economy. For example, they could be used to retire bank debts, spent in outside areas, or transferred to the U.S. Treasury in the form of taxes or other payments. The substitution pathway provides a means to increase token volume, and thus token impact, without increasing the local money supply (and inflationary pressure, Chapter 8).

Several types of restrictions on token creation or use could be developed, if necessary. For example, restrictions could prevent any single member from purchasing an excessive volume of tokens via the "substitution" pathway. This would limit the ability of wealthy persons to gain excessive power over aggregate token–dollar decisions. As another example, the bulk sale of tokens for dollars, or vice versa, could be restricted. This could help protect the integrity of a TES, stabilize the value of the token, invest members in building token circulation, and prevent speculative attacks. If restrictions on token/dollar exchanges were enacted, members could still sell tokens for dollars in certain circumstances, such as when an individual terminates membership.[3]

The TMS also destroys tokens when necessary. An excess of tokens could occur if too many are created, if the circulation rate slows too much, or if the membership shrinks.

For-Profit and Nonprofit Organizations

For-profit and nonprofit member organizations constitute a second source/destination for tokens, as shown in Figure 6.1. For-profit

---

[2] The formula for expansion of the money supply is $DollarSupply \times (1 + TSMS/(1-TSMS))$, where $TSMS$ is the token share of the money supply.

[3] A waiting period of perhaps several years might be required before a person can reapply for membership after choosing to terminate. This would prevent people from joining and terminating serially in order to gain advantages.

businesses include standard businesses and Principled Businesses. Members purchase goods and services from organizations, typically using a combination of tokens and dollars. Organizations, in turn, pay wages to LEDDA members using a combination of tokens and dollars. Thus, the token share of income is roughly similar to the token share of spending.

As discussed in Chapter 5, another source of tokens for some members is the nurture engagements administered by nonprofits. For instance, unemployed members might receive token-and-dollar income assistance through nurture engagements.

There are numerous reasons why a nonprofit organization would want to participate in a LEDDA. One is the possibility of obtaining zero-cost financing in the form of token-and-dollar donations and interest-free loans. Indeed, the CBFS donation arm funds 100 percent of ongoing employee wages for any LEDDA-funded new job (LFNJ) created in the nonprofit sector.[4] Said another way, nonprofits can hire employees at essentially no extra cost to the organization. Moreover, additional CBFS support can help cover operational expenses.

In these ways, LEDDAs can offer a new, substantial, and steady flow of funding to the nonprofit sector. In the LEDDA Microsimulation Model, the size of the nonprofit sector doubles from about 7 percent of the workforce to about 14 percent. Further, dollar donations apart from the CBFS more than double. If similar results are seen in practice, a LEDDA could provide a windfall of revenue to local schools, colleges, charities, public service agencies, and other nonprofit organizations.

For-profit businesses also benefit by participating in a LEDDA. Most businesses require loans from time to time, and many might be pleased to receive a subsidy. Small businesses, in particular, can have difficulty meeting cash-flow needs.

A 2014 survey reported that of those independent businesses that applied for bank loans, 42 percent either failed to obtain a loan or received a loan for less than the amount they requested.[72] Banks reject more than half of all applications for small-business loans; the approval rate from big banks is only 16 percent.[147] Further, when

---

[4] Such service engagements might require periodic review and renewal by the membership.

credit is offered to small businesses, it often comes in the form of a credit card, which is more expensive than a commercial loan.[148]

In addition to zero-cost financing, businesses might have numerous other reasons for joining a LEDDA (see box).

Why Businesses Join a LEDDA

In addition to the possibility of obtaining zero-cost financing in the form of loans and subsidies, a business might join a LEDDA for a variety of reasons:

- A business builds community goodwill by participating, and helps improve community well-being.

- Participation could generate new customers, and new advertising and marketing opportunities. Members must use their tokens at participating organizations and so will seek out organizations that accept tokens.

- Transaction fees are near-zero for token sales, but costly for credit card sales.

- Members might be drawn into a store to use tokens but spend extra dollars once there. Indeed, members would be encouraged to support participating businesses with dollar purchases.

- A business might receive valuable feedback from members, as well as introductions to job seekers. The online system allows businesses to communicate with the membership, and vice versa.

- A business might gain free access to a substantial pool of intellectual property, as discussed in Chapter 7.

Participating businesses would be able to manage the details of their token acceptance offers through the online software system. For example, a retail clothing store might offer to accept two tokens and $38 for a shirt that sells to non-members for $40. A store could make a token offer for one day only or make a standing offer for every

Tuesday, if it wanted. Further, a store could offer some products for tokens only, some for a combination of tokens and dollars, and some for dollars only. Sales transactions would occur via secure website, smartphone, and/or debit card systems.

Collaborative Governance System

A third source/destination for tokens is the Collaborative Governance System, which operates and manages a TES and LEDDA. The CGS uses its revenues to pay for staff and other expenses, which might include stipends paid to volunteers to encourage service on councils and committees. As noted in Chapter 2, a minor arm of the CBFS funds the CGS. It is minor in the sense that the governance earmark is small, relative to the others, and the governance staff lightweight. The budget authority of the CGS covers only immediate staff. The vast majority of funding decisions that a LEDDA makes occur through the CBFS.

The CGS can form various councils, one of which would likely consist of technical managers who oversee day-to-day management of the TES. Technical managers can be empowered to make noncontroversial decisions in accordance with policies set by the membership. These might include limited power to adjust the "dials" of the TES: rates of token creation and destruction, earmarks, and demurrage. Controversial issues would be decided by the membership itself, at its discretion. Again, computer simulation models would assist managers and members in making operational decisions.

Crowd-Based Financial System

The fourth and last source/destination for tokens is the CBFS, which members use to fund for-profit and nonprofit member organizations. These organizations, in turn, offer members jobs—or more broadly, administer LEDDA-funded market, service, and nurture engagements.

Even though members must contribute tokens and dollars to the CBFS, each member receives an income gain through participation. This is accomplished via the Wage Option system. The LEDDA Microsimulation Model uses a simple Wage Option system, but a real LEDDA would use a more sophisticated version.

In the simple version, each family that receives tokens (from employers, nurture engagements, or otherwise) annually makes a Wage Option choice. Two options exist, and a family chooses the one that most increases its post-CBFS income. Once the choice is made, the option applies to all adult family members.

In Wage Option 1, each person's income matches the current income target (Chapter 4), which increases each year until some final maximum value is reached. Each person's CBFS contribution is based on a fraction of income—that is, on a fraction of the income target. In the simulation, the total contribution rate (the sum of all earmarks) is about 0.5.

In Wage Option 2, each person's income is unchanged, except for an incentive bonus paid in tokens (an incentive of 3,000 tokens is used in the simulation). Each person's CBFS contribution for Wage Option 2 is based on the same fraction used in Wage Option 1, but applied only to the incentive. In the case where only one family member is receiving tokens, Option 2 is always chosen, and income for other family members is not affected.

To see how the Wage Option works, suppose that both persons in a two-adult family earn $40,000 in pre-tax wages, for a total family income of $80,000. This is called their *base income*. Neither person is a LEDDA member at this point. For simplicity, assume that all families have two adult members. Further, suppose that the current income target is 35,000 T&D per person (the purchasing power of the token is assumed equal to that of the inflation-adjusted dollar).

The couple joins a LEDDA and their employers, who are also LEDDA members, ask which Wage Option they will choose. If they choose Wage Option 1 (based on the income target), each person experiences a wage cut of 5,000 T&D. So instead they choose Wage Option 2 (based on the incentive), which provides each person a wage gain of 3,000 tokens. Each then contributes about half of their gain to the CBFS. In the end, post-CBFS income for this family increased by about 3,000 T&D.

Now suppose that some years later the income target has increased to 90,000 T&D per person. Again the couple is asked to choose a Wage Option. This time, however, they choose Wage Option 1. That way, each person receives 90,000 T&D, contributes about half to the CBFS, and obtains a post-CBFS income of about 45,000 T&D. As a family, they gain about 10,000 T&D over their combined base incomes. The income target continues to rise in subsequent years, and the family continues to choose Wage Option 1.

In order for the simulated LEDDA to function properly, essentially all members in the target population must eventually choose Wage Option 1. By so doing, all members receive about the same income and CBFS contributions are maximal. In the simulation, two trends appear. Families with low base incomes tend to choose Wage Option 1, whereas families with high base incomes tend to choose Wage Option 2. However, in the early years, when the income target is low, most families choose Option 2. In later years, when the target is higher, most choose Wage Option 1. By the end of the simulation, essentially all members choose Wage Option 1. The income target rises to a final value of about 107,000 T&D, which means that family post-CBFS income rises to a similar value (104,000 T&D). Note that all families receive this income, regardless of whether zero, one, or both persons are employed.

In a real LEDDA, there would likely be circumstances under which the simple Wage Option system used in the simulation would not be adequate. For example, the simple Wage Option system does not address the issue of single adult, one-person families. Thus, a real LEDDA would use a more sophisticated Wage Option system to incentivize all or nearly all members to eventually choose Wage Option 1.[5]

While Figure 6.1 implies that four major CBFS earmarks exist, in practice these would be split into a larger number for more fine-grained control. Seven earmarks are used in the simulation, and a real LEDDA might use even more. The seven in the study are earmarks for standard business loans, Principled Business loans, nonprofit loans, standard business subsidies, Principled Business subsidies, nurture engagements, and nonprofit donations. (As noted previously, there is also a small governance earmark, but it was not used in the simulation.)

---

[5] For example, the income target might be increased for single adults to compensate for the benefits of shared living costs within a family. On the other hand, any such increase should not be so large as to discourage family formation. Many other approaches are possible.

Loan Certificate Trading System

When a member loans tokens or dollars to a member organization via the CBFS, the online software system records the transaction. As part of this, the lending member receives a loan certificate that indicates the balance due. The certificate is updated every time the debtor makes a scheduled payment. Most of this work is done behind the scenes, making the system user-friendly and efficient. For example, an individual member does not need to sign loan contracts or arrange payment schedules. She simply has to check a box next to an applicant's name on an online form and fill in the loan amount offered. Once a loan is made, payments appear as deposits in her account according to a standard repayment schedule. The collection of loan certificates that a member holds is called a *loan portfolio*.

At certain times, members might wish to retrieve tokens or dollars from their loan portfolios faster than repayment schedules allow. For example, a member might need extra currency to purchase an expensive item. This is achieved through a loan certificate trading system. The trading system resembles a simple version of the stock market, except that loan certificates are bought and sold, rather than equity, and profits are limited to the remaining face value of a loan certificate.

Suppose a member wants to retrieve tokens from a 400-token loan that is half paid off. The remaining face value of the loan certificate is 200 tokens. The owner could offer this certificate on the trading system, and another member might be willing to pay, say, 190 tokens for it. In the exchange, both members gain. The original owner collects most of the tokens that he loaned to an organization, and the buying member gains a certificate worth 10 tokens more than she paid.

If an organization begins to show potential for default, its loan certificates would likely be viewed as less valuable. Thus, they would trade on the exchange at a higher discount. This could provide opportunities for savvy traders; some businesses once viewed as high-risk will later turn themselves around, making their certificates valuable once again.

The purpose of the trading system is to allow members to help one another—someone needs tokens or dollars today and others are willing to assist in providing them. Indeed, nearly every member would use the trading system at some point. A cordial and cooperative atmosphere could be encouraged by various means, not the least of which are cultural norms. Further, because profits are limited to the face value of loan certificates, the rewards for greedy behavior are limited. And if necessary, a LEDDA could place restrictions on the total amount that could be earned annually through the trading system.

6.3 Legal Aspects of Local Currencies

Local currency systems operate legally in the United States, and this chapter ends by examining the legal issues in more detail. The Constitution prohibits states from coining money. It does not, however, prohibit private parties from issuing coins, and it does not address the issuance of private paper money or electronic money.[149]

Congress prohibited the private issuance of metal-based coins in 1864. Issuance of paper currency by a private person or corporation was not prohibited, as long as that currency was not fractional (with value less than $1) and as long as it did not resemble paper money issued through the government.[6]

State laws can be more restrictive than federal laws. The legality of local currencies in a few states might rest on the question of competition with national currency, and might depend on the type of entity issuing the currency. For example, some laws might not apply to currency issued by nonprofits.

Federal and state securities regulations might also apply to local currencies, particularly if there is a profit-sharing agreement, if the currency is issued by a for-profit organization, and/or if the currency is transported over state borders.

---

[6] In 1865, Congress imposed a 10 percent tax on banks that issued notes for general circulation in order to discourage the practice. The tax was extended to include notes issued by persons in 1866, and cities and municipalities in 1867. The Supreme Court later clarified that the tax only applied to promissory notes that were intended to compete with the national currency. The tax was repealed in 1976 as obsolete. Arguably, modern local currencies would not have been subject to the tax; they are not promissory notes, and because they are not in widespread circulation, they do not compete with the national currency.

Legal concerns are built into the LEDDA framework. One advantage of designing the token as a local currency is that the potential for legal conflicts is reduced. Tokens are not transported over state borders. As a local currency, the token does not compete nationally with the dollar. And legal conflicts are reduced by the profit-neutral characteristic of the CBFS. Members do not buy investment shares with their CBFS contributions, or earn interest on token or dollar loans.

Legal conflicts might be reduced further by organizing a LEDDA as a nonprofit. Another option that could conceivably affect rulings in some states would be to organize a LEDDA as one of the new socially responsible corporate forms, such as a B-Corporation (Chapter 7).

A few words on crowdfunding are in order, given that the CBFS is a type of crowdfunding operation. Crowdfunding refers to raising funds for a business, artistic, or other project via small contributions from a large number of people. For example, KickStarter is a popular crowdfunding website that generates pledges for artistic ventures. In 2011, more than 27,000 projects were started, almost 12,000 of which were successfully funded in full. Total pledges exceeded $99 million.[150] KickStarter members do not earn profits on pledges.

As another example, the Kiva website helps people make micro-loans. As of 2012, it had helped to arrange over $291 million in loans from more than 697,000 individuals around the globe. Kiva lenders do not earn interest on loans; they only receive repayment of the principal.

Crowdfunding operations were given a boost in 2012, when President Obama signed the JOBS (Jumpstart Our Business Startups) Act. As mentioned in Chapter 4, it contains several provisions that encourage crowdfunding as a means to raise equity capital.[75] This law applies to investment opportunities in which securities are offered. As such, it does not apply to funding offered through the CBFS.

On a different legal issue, members could not use a LEDDA to avoid taxes. The IRS has experience with local currencies and barter systems, and has developed guidelines and procedures for collecting taxes that are due. The transparency of the LEDDA framework, as well as its purpose, would, in all likelihood, be looked upon favorably by the IRS and other state and federal agencies.

Chapter 7

Principled Business Model

> *"Work without love is slavery."*
> —Mother Teresa (1910–1997)

As mentioned in previous chapters, one purpose of the Crowd-Based Financial System is to fund new and existing for-profit member businesses. Many, perhaps even a majority of funded businesses would be Principled Businesses. A Principled Business is a cross between a nonprofit and for-profit business model. The model is designed to appeal to groups and entrepreneurs who might otherwise desire to start a nonprofit, but who also want to own their business and compete in the marketplace for self-sustaining revenues. The model is consistent with a general trend in recent years toward an increasingly blurred distinction between for-profit and nonprofit sectors.[151]

A true partnership exists between LEDDA members and Principled Businesses. Individual members support Principled Businesses via token-and-dollar purchases, loans, and/or subsidies. In turn, a Principled Business operates transparently to fulfill its stated social mission and to help implement LEDDA policies. The Principled Business model is a critical element of the LEDDA framework; it is a business structure designed to thrive in the token–dollar economy, and to embody concepts of consumer–business cooperation.

A Principled Business is certified as such by a LEDDA if it meets a set of criteria. But it legally organizes under one of several forms. A Principled Business could organize as a sole proprietorship, partnership, Limited Liability Company (LLC), or cooperative.[152, 153] Or it could organize as one of the newly emerging socially responsible corporate forms, which include Benefit Corporations (B-Corporations), Low-Profit Limited-Liability Companies (L3Cs), and Flexible Purpose Corporations.

Depending on the legal form chosen and desires of the business, it could make decisions via a variety of governance structures and share ownership via a variety of styles. A Principled Business could hold ownership tightly within a small group and employ a traditional top-down form of governance. It might operate as a Worker Self-Directed Enterprise (WSDE), where decision-making power and ownership are widely shared.[154] Or it could choose other approaches or combinations of approaches.

This chapter focuses on Principled Businesses that organize through the new socially responsible corporate forms. Slightly modified versions of the Principled Business model could be available for sole proprietorships, partnerships, LLCs, and cooperatives that organize through other forms. C- and S-Corporations would have to convert to one of the socially responsible forms before they could be certified as Principled Businesses.

7.1 Public Corporations

The importance and role of the corporation in the United States has changed dramatically through the years. Political leaders in colonial America and the new republic held a remarkable distrust of corporations, stemming in part from the injustices they suffered under the hands of the British East India Company, the mega-corporation of its day. It was East India Company tea that was thrown overboard during the Boston Tea Party of 1773.

Accordingly, in the late 1700s and early 1800s, states severely restricted the behavior of corporations. Corporations were not allowed to purchase other corporations, their ability to raise funds was limited, their charters lasted only for a limited period (e.g., 20 years), and they could not spend money to affect elections or public policy. Nor were they viewed as "persons" under the law.

Today corporations can purchase other corporations, raise unlimited funds, write charters that last in perpetuity, and affect both elections and legislation. They now enjoy some of the same rights and responsibilities as natural persons (see box).

Corporate Personhood Under the Law

Up through the mid-1800s, corporate law in the United States tended to focus on protection of the public interest over shareholder interests. Due to legal restrictions, many private firms, including Standard Oil, avoided the corporate form altogether, and were set up as trusts or partnerships. As the century progressed, the promise of greater corporate tax revenues and registration fees led some states, notably Delaware, to enact more permissive, "corporation-friendly" laws.

In 1819 the U.S. Supreme Court, in its hearing of *Dartmouth College v. Woodward*, granted corporations numerous new rights. Corporate charters were no longer subject to arbitrary amendment or abolition by state governments, for example.

By the late 1800s, railroads were the nation's most politically powerful corporations. In the now-famous 1886 Supreme Court case *Santa Clara County v. Southern Pacific Railroad*, the summary notes of a court clerk, who was also a former railroad executive, indicated that corporations enjoyed the same rights under the Fourteenth Amendment as did natural persons. This issue was not decided directly by the Supreme Court. Regardless, the effect was that from this point forward, corporations were viewed as "persons" under the law and were granted due rights.

Over the years, the Supreme Court expanded and clarified the rights of corporations, most notably in 2010, with *Citizens United v. Federal Election Commission*. The Court held that corporate funding of independent political broadcasts during elections was a matter of free speech and could not be limited. Thus, corporations are now free to spend unlimited amounts to influence elections.

Directors and officers of public corporations have a fiduciary duty to maximize shareholder wealth. If they fail to do so, they can face shareholder lawsuits, lose their positions, and damage their reputations. On the other hand, many who succeed in maximizing shareholder wealth are handsomely rewarded. Maximization of shareholder wealth generally goes hand in hand with maximization of corporate profits. For convenience, both are referred to here as *profit maximization*. The pressure to maximize profits has intensified since the 1970s, with increased competition and deregulation of the transportation, communications, energy, and finance industries.[155]

This is not to say that CEOs of public corporations care only about profits. Many, if not most, are concerned with a wide range of issues, including worker safety, and social and environmental impacts. Further, many, if not most, are concerned with producing quality products. But because of their fiduciary duty, they must act to promote shareholder interests as a top concern. And many executives are given strong incentives to act ruthlessly in doing so.

In general, a corporation will improve profits by reducing operating costs (e.g., by reducing staff size and worker pay) and by increasing revenues (e.g., by charging higher prices). Operating costs can also be reduced by externalizing them. Externalizing a business cost means transferring it to someone else, usually the public. For example, companies that reduce health-care benefits to workers transfer these costs to the workers themselves, or to the public if the workers cannot afford to pay them. As another example, companies that pollute the environment rather than disposing of waste responsibly externalize their waste disposal costs; the public pays through increased health-care costs and in other ways. Corporations externalize their costs in myriad ways, but almost by definition, these are not included in accounting reports. According to Nobel laureate Joseph Stiglitz, externalities destabilize markets:

> *Market failures arise whenever there are externalities, consequences of an individual's or a firm's actions for which they do not pay the cost or receive the benefit. Markets, by themselves, lead to too little of some things, like research, and too much of others, like pollution.*[156]

Of course, corporate leaders can also make decisions that help their employees, society, and the environment. Indeed, corporations produce many useful, even amazing products. And U.S. corporations are responsible for about $14 billion in annual charitable giving.[157] But the good that corporations do, or want to do, is tempered by the pressure to maximize profits. Arguably, even better and more amazing products could be produced, science could progress faster, and corporations could benefit society to a greater degree if they were more transparent and their focus was on maximizing well-being, rather than profits. This is what the Principled Business model is designed to accomplish.

Who are the shareholders that public corporations serve? In 2010, the top 1 percent wealth class owned 35 percent of all stock equity. The lower 80 percent wealth class, the vast majority of Americans, owned only 8.4 percent.[158] While many in the lower 80 percent wealth class own stocks, their average portfolio size is tiny compared to that of the top 1 percent. Thus, the investment system acts as a type of positive feedback loop to hyper-concentrate wealth—the more one has, the more one can invest, and the more one gains. As such, benefits of the investment system disproportionately accrue to the wealthy.[159]

In light of the fact that a small population of investors owns a large share of all stocks, it should come as no surprise that a small group of corporations owns a large share of all others. In 2011, researchers at the Swiss Federal Institute of Technology analyzed a database containing 43,000 transnational corporations and their owner relationships. In constructing an ownership map, they discovered that global corporate control has a dominant core of just 147 interlocking super-firms. Most of these are financial institutions, including Barclays Bank, JPMorgan Chase, and Goldman Sachs.[160] Almost identical to the stock market, less than 1 percent of the companies control 40 percent of the total network wealth.

The relentless drive for profits, abuses of power, undue influence over elections and legislation, and the hyper-concentration of wealth in a tiny minority of corporations, executives, and investors have eroded the public's trust in large corporations. An outpouring of anger has been focused at banks in the wake of the 2008 global financial crisis. The 2013 "Confidence in Institutions" Gallup poll indicates that only 22 percent of adults have either a "great deal" or "quite a lot" of confidence in big business.[15] A 2011 Rasmussen poll suggests that 68 percent of likely voters believe big business and Congress are on the same team, working against the interests of common citizens.[161]

7.2 Socially Responsible Corporate Forms

If a central problem of corporations is that they are driven by profit maximization, then a reasonable solution is to develop new corporate forms that place less emphasis on profit and more on social responsibility. Much work has already been accomplished in this area. Dozens of states offer or are considering offering alternative corporate forms.[1] These include L3Cs, B-Corporations, and Flexible Purpose Corporations.[162, 163]

In general, the new corporate forms promote greater transparency and expand the purpose of the corporation to include a social mission. Corporations using the new forms are expected to make a profit, but they must balance their desire for profit with a social purpose. They can be funded through traditional means and, in some cases, by philanthropic foundations. In fact, one reason for creating the L3C model was to allow foundations to support corporations that are working toward social aims.

Although there are differences between L3Cs, B-Corporations, and Flexible Purpose Corporations, the basic ideas are the same. All are recognized by states as having a broad legal mandate that stretches beyond profit maximization. For example, directors can prioritize environmental concerns along with profit when making decisions. Directors are protected from shareholders who might otherwise force them to focus narrowly on profits. On the other hand, shareholders have additional rights to hold directors accountable for failure to act in accordance with the corporation's social mission.

In addition to these three socially responsible corporate forms, an important informal model has also been proposed: the Social Business.[164] The Social Business differs from the other corporate models in that it has funders, rather than investors. Social Businesses do not pay dividends. The business itself can make a profit, but profits stay within the business to allow expansion and improvement.

---

[1] It is not necessary that each state approve new corporate forms. Once a single state approves a form, it is available for use in all states. A corporation can organize in one state but operate in another.

Figure 7.1: The corporate motivation spectrum.

Nonprofits and profit-maximizing corporations define the two extremes of the profit-motive spectrum. L3Cs, B-Corporations, Flexible Purpose Corporations, and Social Businesses fall somewhere in between, as indicated in Figure 7.1. The four socially responsible alternatives enjoy the best of both worlds. They can harness profit as a motivational force and a means to self-sufficiency. And they can fully leverage the entrepreneurial experience that is present in the business community. Yet they are not forced to narrowly focus on profit and can consider social and environmental impacts as well.

Social Business

Because the Principled Business model shares some similarity with the Social Business, it is worthwhile to mention a few characteristics of the latter. The Social Business is the brainchild of Muhammad Yunus, founder of Grameen Bank and recipient of the 2006 Nobel Peace Prize for developing the concept of microcredit. No U.S. state recognizes the Social Business as a legal form. Rather, a business gains the title of Social Business by meeting a set of (broadly defined) criteria. Most Social Businesses that exist have been created outside the United States, under the guidance of the Grameen Creative Lab or its affiliates.[165]

One important aspect of a Social Business is that funders do not receive dividends. Funding is done only to produce social gains. Essentially, funding occurs via interest-free loans. In his books, Yunus argues that the definition of a Social Business must include the criterion that it does not pay dividends to investors.[164, 166] According to Yunus, this restriction acts to keep the social purpose crystal clear, and avoids the confusion that can arise when investors expect both a profit and a social benefit. He fears that if motives are mixed, over time the social mission will lag behind the drive for profit.

While the Social Business concept has substantial merit, it is not well-suited for a LEDDA. The criteria are broadly worded and do not address several important issues, such as political activities and transfer of assets during dissolution. The Principled Business model builds on ideas from the Social Business and nonprofit models to offer an approach attuned to the needs of a LEDDA.

Nonprofits in the United States

Before examining the Principled Business model in detail, a point of reference is gained by examining the nonprofit. The structure and behavior of nonprofits is tightly regulated. Nonprofits are formed as corporations, but they cannot be bought or owned by individuals or groups. The concept of ownership does not apply to nonprofits, except to say that they are owned by the public. A nonprofit is managed by a board of directors, and exists to serve a public purpose. That purpose might be educational, charitable, religious, or scientific, for example. A nonprofit is prohibited from transferring profits to any individual, other than through reasonable salaries. Upon liquidation, any revenues gained must be donated to charity. A nonprofit must act in the public's behalf, not for private gain. If a nonprofit acts like a for-profit corporation, it faces fines, taxes, and loss of its nonprofit status. Finally, nonprofits are required to make certain financial data public so that their income and expenses can be scrutinized.

Restrictions on ownership, assets, secrecy, and use of profits help to instill public confidence that the organization serves its mission and that donations are used efficiently. Despite these restrictions, however, the nonprofit sector is growing faster than both the government and business sectors.[167]

The number of nonprofits increased by 25 percent (to 1.6 million) between 2001 and 2011. According to the Congressional Research Service, charities recognized under section 501(c)3 of the IRS code employ more than 7 percent of the entire U.S. workforce.[168] If other nonprofits, such as political organizations, are included, the sector is estimated to employ 10 percent of the nation's workforce. Nonprofits (largely charities) that serve households represented more than 5 percent of GDP in 2010. In 2009, charities reported approximately $1.4 trillion in revenues and nearly $2.6 trillion in assets.

The fact that the nonprofit sector is large and growing suggests that there is need for its services and a desire by at least some organizers to serve public, rather than private interests.

7.3 Principled Business

The Principled Business model borrows heavily from the Social Business and nonprofit models. It is designed to address issues of transparency and accountability, and to place a higher priority on the maximization of well-being than the maximization of profit. Yet it also offers a clear path by which companies can gain self-supporting revenues. It encourages cooperation among businesses, promotes a close partnership with members, and allows organizers to harness the experience and skills present within the entrepreneurial community.

A Principled Business formed as an L3C, B-Corporation, or other socially responsible form has legal duties and protections granted by these corporate forms. In particular, executives have a legal duty to balance the drive for profit with a social mission. Principled Business must also meet criteria specified by a LEDDA. The criteria reflect the purpose of a LEDDA. Specifically, they help to prevent three situations from occurring: use of revenues to enrich individuals, other than through wages consistent with the income target; use of funds to act or create a business branch or product line inconsistent with the firm's stated social mission; and growth of a Principled Business to such an extent that it becomes an unwanted monopoly and/or too big to fail.

The proposed criteria are listed below. Some refer to a company's business plan, which is submitted to the membership as part of the application for Principled Business status. The term "Principled Business" is not intended to imply that other forms of business are unprincipled. Rather, it refers to a business that meets the following criteria:

1. A Principled Business acts and spends revenue in accordance with its submitted business plan, and consistent with its social mission.

2. A Principled Business does not pay dividends to investors or shareholders.

3. A Principled Business adheres to basic environmental stewardship practices, as demonstrated through certification with an approved third party.

4. A Principled Business operates in a transparent fashion. Financial data that 501(c)3 nonprofits and publicly traded corporations must disclose are made public. In addition, funding sources and statistics on the distribution of compensation are disclosed, as is any other information that the membership deems reasonably necessary for making informed purchasing and funding decisions. Measurements of externalized costs and social and environmental impacts are disclosed, where these can be practically and economically obtained.

5. Upon dissolution and after payment of creditors, a Principled Business must transfer any remaining assets to nonprofit charities or to other Principled Businesses in which no board member has a financial interest. Determinations made by a bankruptcy court take precedence. Ownership of a Principled Businesses cannot be transferred to an entity that is not a Principled Business or nonprofit.

6. A Principled Business cannot substantially fund other for-profit businesses that are not Principled Businesses. It can wholly purchase other businesses, as long as the combined entity continues to act as a Principled Business.

7. A Principled Business adheres to a conflict-of-interest policy. Board members having financial or familial conflicts of interest must recuse themselves from decision-making when conflicts occur.

8. A Principled Business cannot spend money to influence elections or legislation, except as detailed and justified in the business plan. Any such expenditures are fully transparent.

The first three criteria loosely follow that of a Social Business. The remaining five criteria loosely follow that of a nonprofit. Although these criteria are more restrictive than the law demands with respect to for-profit corporations, they still should be enforceable. Courts are inclined to uphold business contracts that are freely negotiated in good faith.

Taken together, the criteria describe a business that is privately owned, privately steered on the community's behalf, and who's assets revert to the community (via nonprofits or Principled Businesses) at dissolution or transfer. In effect, the membership lets entrepreneurs use its money to achieve worthwhile aims. In this sense, a Principled Business is not unlike a nonprofit. Both compete for zero-cost CBFS funding. The primary difference is that voting through purchasing decisions (Chapter 3) tends to play a larger role for Principled Businesses. Member nonprofits obtain most of their ongoing funding through the CBFS, while Principled Businesses obtain most of theirs through the marketplace. Either way, the membership makes the decisions. Of course, both Principled Businesses and nonprofits can obtain funding and revenue from outside the membership too.

7.4 Certifying a Principled Business

A group seeking to form a new Principled Business submits an application to the membership via the CBFS. If the group is also seeking funding, it would extend its application to include funding. A key component of the application is a business plan, which describes intended social, economic, and environmental impacts. The plan states the social mission; describes products or services; specifies how products and wastes are recycled, reused, reduced, or upgraded; describes product lifetime resource use; estimates revenue and profits; summarizes expected wage distributions, and explains how they align with income targets; estimates volume and type of purchases from local supply chains; specifies dissolution procedures; identifies expansion plans; describes accounting methods for externalized costs; and indicates the desired maximum size. The plan also specifies how any windfall revenues are used.

Applicants would be encouraged to include numerous scenarios in order to address different contingencies, such as slow or rapid revenue growth. Since business conditions are uncertain and can change with time, the plans are flexible and can be updated.

Obviously, an applicant's business plan would become public knowledge. This might pose a problem for some entrepreneurs, but many others would be willing to share business plans. For example, a clinic or neighborhood bakery might not be very concerned about making a business plan public. And the rewards for doing so can be substantial. Not only can a group gain funding and goodwill by becoming a Principled Business, it can also gain valuable community input and access to a pool of intellectual property (discussed later in this chapter).

There is a growing movement toward greater openness within many sectors of society.[169] This is evidenced by open-source software, open-access publishing, open education, open government, open hardware, and open design. The Ecuadorian government has recently commissioned a study to help that country transition to an "open, commons-based knowledge society."[170] In each case mentioned, the word *open* refers to some information or process or dialogue being made freely available to the public. The transparency of the Principled Business model is in keeping with the spirit of other open initiatives.

Once an application for Principled Business certification has been submitted, the review process could be extensive. Members, councils, and other groups might offer analysis, summaries, and recommendations based on business plan quality and community need. Analysis might be based in part on results from computer simulations that estimate impacts on token and dollar flows, and (eventually) on member well-being.

After the review process is completed, members decide whether to approve or deny the application. If denied, the applicant could still operate as a standard business and seek loans and subsidies as such through the CBFS. If approved, members would also decide on funding, if that is part of the application.

Once a Principled Business is approved (or an existing business is approved for new funds), the business signs a contract with the LEDDA acknowledging that it will act in accordance with information contained in its application. If the business acts in substantial disregard of its application, warnings might be issued. In severe cases, penalties in tokens and/or dollars could be levied, and/or Principled Business status (and even membership of owners) could be revoked. If multiple LEDDAs existed, they would share such disciplinary information.

As an aside, applications for loans or subsidies for standard businesses would be similar, but abbreviated. Only some criteria of a Principled Business would need to be met, and an applicant could choose to omit some types of information from its application. But the more information an applicant provides, and the more it mimics a Principled Business, the better its chance of receiving funds. Competition for CBFS funds, and for member support in the marketplace, could help to steer businesses over time toward the Principled Business or Principled-Business-like models.

True to the crowd-funding approach, support from a large number of members would usually be necessary in order to obtain the full amount of CBFS funds requested. It might happen, however, that one or a few members choose to contribute all or most of the requested amount. While this is allowed, a fail-safe mechanism prevents the CBFS from funding highly unpopular businesses. If a supermajority of the membership votes to deny an application for funding, no CBFS support can be offered. Of course, the applicant can still seek funding through traditional avenues, such as banks and investors.

7.5 Diversity of Principled Businesses

A wide variety of businesses could apply for Principled Business status. This includes farmers markets, community newspapers, mills, parts factories, construction companies, medical clinics, auto repair shops, advertising companies, coffeehouses, and radio stations. Such inclusiveness does not dilute the meaning of a Principled Business; all must meet the defining criteria. Each would serve a LEDDA and global public in its own unique way.

As a general rule, members may wish to create a diverse set of small- and medium-sized Principled Businesses. A local economy, and token circulation, are made stronger through diversity. And diversity helps reduce risk in lending portfolios. By offering small loans to many businesses, member can protect themselves from damage that a single default could make.

Inevitably, some Principled Businesses (and standard businesses) will default on their loans, but if the system is well designed, the default rate should be low. For example, the microloan program at Kiva.org has a repayment rate of nearly 99 percent.[171] Other studies suggest that the default rate for microfinance ranges from 2 percent to 5 percent.[172] Lessons learned at Kiva and other microloan programs could be applied to CBFS funding. The public vetting process should also help reduce the number of defaults; loan applications are scrutinized by a large number of members, and the reputation system provides information on the history of applicants.

Successful businesses obviously produce the greatest benefits to a LEDDA, but members would want to take some risks in choosing which businesses are funded. Higher-risk businesses might pursue more creative and innovative projects than do less-risky ones. A diverse lending portfolio would include some higher-risk businesses. Subsidies could also be offered to higher-risk businesses. In fact, this is one purpose of the subsidy arm of the CBFS.

7.6 Intellectual Property

LEDDA members would likely want to fund Principled Businesses that develop new inventions and make scientific discoveries. Inventions and discoveries play critical roles in improving well-being, and can help member organizations produce goods and services with high efficiency and at the least environmental cost. As well, discoveries might help members find new ways to repair environmental damage or generate energy. Some inventions and discoveries might lead to better consumer products and services, including better health care and disease prevention. Further, innovation and discovery are an expression of creativity. Humans are compelled to explore their universe and discover new and deeper scientific truths. A LEDDA would want to encourage creative exploration. Thus, almost certainly, some Principled Businesses would generate intellectual property (IP).

The U.S. government also encourages innovation and development of new technologies, artistic expressions, and inventions. It does so partly by offering copyright and patent protections. As a classic hypothetical, suppose that a pharmaceutical company is considering a plan to spend millions of dollars on research in order to develop a new drug. It knows, however, that without patent protections, a competing firm could jump in at the end and unfairly manufacture the drug. The competitor could sell the drug at a lower cost, or at a higher margin, because it didn't have large research costs to defray.

Thus, the argument goes, if the inventing company could not obtain patent protection, it would not invest in research. As a result, the new drug would not be produced. IP laws are intended to remove unfair competition and stimulate innovation by granting sole licensing rights (a monopoly) to the inventor for an extended period.

The actual situation is more complicated. The history of IP protection suggests that the monopolies it helps create often substantially harm, rather than benefit, society. In their book *Against Intellectual Monopoly*, Boldrin and Levine argue that IP laws are unnecessary, and creators' property rights can be sufficiently protected in the absence of such laws.[173] Using numerous historical examples as evidence, they claim that IP laws tend to hinder, rather than encourage, innovation. Indeed, rapid innovation has occurred in many industries without IP protection. A great deal of the innovation in software and computer science occurred prior to 1980, before IP protection was available for the products of that industry.

Debate on the utility of IP protection is widespread.[174] The open-source software movement is itself a reaction to the negative aspects of IP restrictions. Members of the open-source community create products that are licensed royalty-free to any interested party. Proponents of open-source, open-copyright, open-design, and related movements claim that without IP restrictions, ideas will spread faster, find greater application, and be improved upon more rapidly.[169]

Another concern about IP law involves the size of royalties. To the degree that royalties constitute economic rent, they can produce negative social and economic consequences and raise ethical issues. Economic rent is *extra* payment for a resource (capital, land, labor, information), in excess of opportunity costs. That is, payment in excess of what could be obtained by using the resource in other ways.[2]

---

[2] By choosing a certain use for a resource, one gives up the market opportunities that could be obtained by using it differently.

Economic rent is due to an advantage, such as high demand or a monopoly, rather than productive effort. It stems from conditions of imperfect competition. For example, a pharmaceutical company might charge a premium price for a drug if the company holds a patent that keeps competitors out of the market. That price might be in excess of what the company would be willing to accept, and still make profit on, in a more competitive market.

One problem with economic rent is that it leads to higher prices. Especially when a monopoly is created (via IP restrictions or otherwise), economic rent can also serve to hyper-concentrate wealth. Concentration is furthered when wealthy rent-seekers try to increase their advantages by influencing legislation and policy. As Bivins and Mishel explain:

> *[T]he increase in the incomes and wages of the top 1 percent over the last three decades should be interpreted as driven largely by the creation and/or redistribution of economic rents, and not simply as the outcome of well-functioning competitive markets rewarding skills or productivity based on marginal differences. This rise in rents accruing to the top 1 percent could be the result of increased opportunities for rent-shifting, increased incentives for rent-shifting, or a combination of both.*[175]

In light of these concerns, and due to the importance of scientific development, the LEDDA framework incorporates an alternative approach to IP. One possible direction would be to develop a licensing system based on the Creative Commons model. Usage rights to this book, for example, are offered to the public via a Creative Commons license (see front pages). Creative Commons licenses pertain, however, only to materials that fall under copyright rules (like books). For these, the creator is automatically assigned rights. Patents, in contrast, are a more complicated issue. Rights to an invention are not automatically assigned to the creator, who must apply to the government for them. Management and litigation costs are also typically higher for patents than copyrights.

One approach to making patents friendly to open innovation communities (OICs) is the Defensive Patent License (DPL), developed by Schultz and Urban.[176, 177] In brief, defensive patenting is the practice of seeking patents in order to discourage offensive lawsuits, as opposed to more traditional aims of seeking licensing revenue or excluding competitors.[3] The DPL is in keeping with the values of Creative Commons license; a DPL allows an inventor to seek patent rights with some assurance that those rights will not later be used offensively. Thus, the DPL is:

> ... a standardized open patent license designed to encourage the creation of a broad, decentralized network of OICs that both patent their innovations with a commitment to defensive purposes and license them on a royalty-free basis to any others who will do the same.[176]

Anyone can use the licensed IP as long as he commits to a defense-only stance. The goal is to create a large repository of patents that has the same deterrent power (against offensive patents) as the large patent portfolios held by major players, but that has costs and benefits distributed across DPL users.

While the DPL provides a starting point, LEDDAs may require a modified approach that meets additional needs. One option is to require that all Principled Businesses join a patent pool, administered by a LEDDA or, preferably, by the association of LEDDAs. IP pools have become common in recent years as industries seek to obtain resources and improve their efficiencies.[178] An interesting example aimed at public benefit is the Eco-Patent Commons, an IP pool administered by the World Business Council for Sustainable Development (WBCSD).[179] The pool makes patents available, without royalty, in order to address a wide range of sustainability issues, including pollution, climate change, and energy use.

As a rough sketch, access to IP in a LEDDA pool would be licensed royalty-free to all Principled Businesses, but restrictions would help inventors recoup opportunity costs. Suppose a Principled Business manufactures headphones and spends $1 million to develop a novel electronic technology. The firm assigns rights to the technology to the pool, and the pool applies to the U.S. Patent and Trademark Office for

---

[3] A defensive patent strategy is aimed at filing patents on innovations primarily to ensure that no other party blocks the inventor's practical use. An offensive patent strategy is aimed at blocking competitors from using an innovation. Defensive patents are a deterrent to offensive patents.

patent protection. All Principled Businesses can use the technology royalty-free, except those that produce a headphone product that competes in the same market. That is, except for direct competitors. But the competitor can use the technology once the inventor recoups its opportunity costs. Alternatively, if agreeable to the inventor and competitor, the latter can license the IP at a fee that effectively shares costs. Academics and other individual members are free to use the technology for any non-commercial purpose.

If the IP was in use by one or more Principled Businesses, the pool would not license it to other parties, unless the users requested it. If no Principled Business was interested in the technology, a license could be offered for fee to member standard businesses (or for no fee, as with the DPL). If none of these were interested, a license could be offered for fee (or no fee) to outside parties. In developing a royalty structure, the pool would seek primarily to recoup opportunity costs incurred by the inventor, as well as costs incurred by managing the pool. Like the DPL, the pool would also act as a deterrent to offensive patents.

An IP pool, and/or use of the DPL, could stimulate creativity, in-novation, and the rate of scientific discovery. Indeed, with a coop-erative approach to intellectual property and ample CBFS funding, LEDDAs could become hotbeds of creativity. Income inequality due to economic rent could also be minimized. Moreover, access to free IP could encourage new Principled Businesses to form, leading to ever-larger IP pools in a virtuous cycle of economic development.

Chapter 8

National Monetary and Financial Systems

> *"I have never yet had anyone who could, through the use of logic and reason, justify the Federal Government borrowing the use of its own money. ... I believe the time will come in this country when [the public] will actually blame you and me and everyone else connected with the Congress for sitting idly by and permitting such an idiotic system to continue."*
>
> —U.S. Rep. Wright Patman (1893–1976)
> Chair, House Committee on Banking and Currency

The previous chapters introduced LEDDA economic direct democracy and identified the role of the token in achieving it. In this chapter, emphasis shifts to the national monetary and financial systems. The national monetary system defines how the dollar supply is managed, including how new dollars are created, added to, and removed from circulation. The national financial system, which includes banks, securities markets, and pension and mutual funds, defines how dollars are used to fund business and promote economic growth.

The token is not a national currency; a LEDDA is a local organization. Yet it is useful to examine the national monetary and financial systems in order to contrast them with the Token Monetary System and Crowd-Based Financial System. Further, the knowledge gained acts as an incentive for developing the LEDDA framework. On inspection, the long-term stability of the national systems will be shown to be uncertain, giving some urgency to the search for new approaches that might help stabilize local economies in times of stress.

This chapter describes the national monetary and financial systems in the broadest strokes. The purpose is to capture the big picture and, in so doing, to highlight alternative approaches offered in the LEDDA framework.

8.1   Eight Differences

In both subtle and obvious ways, the national monetary and financial systems influence nearly every aspect of our lives. The volume of money influences the inflation rate and cost of credit. The very design of the financial system, particularly the profit motive that drives it, influences which businesses receive funding, what they make, and how their workers and the environment are treated. To the degree that the financial system produces extreme wealth for some, it also affects politics; political and financial power are deeply intertwined. Very few aspects of modern life remain untouched by the monetary and financial systems.

Eight differences between the TMS/CBFS and national monetary and financial systems are summarized below:

1. **Debt-free money creation.** New dollars enter the economy primarily via interest-bearing debt. That is, commercial banks loan money into existence. In contrast, tokens are created by a debt-free process.

2. **Focus on economic development.** Public corporations and many standard businesses are driven by profit maximization. Further, the default yardstick for national economic progress is the GDP, which only measures economic output. Together, profit maximization and reliance on the GDP focus attention on economic growth, rather than economic development. A LEDDA focuses on the latter, measuring its progress with well-being indexes.

3. **Inflation-free money.** Inflation serves several purposes in the dollar economy, and the Federal Reserve strives to maintain a steady annual inflation rate of about 2 percent. Inflation does not serve a purpose in the token–dollar economy, and the token is intended to be inflation-free.

4. **Income equality.** Extreme inequalities of income and wealth exist in the dollar economy. These are partly due to the for-profit nature of the financial system; wealthy investors can use their money to gain even greater wealth. A LEDDA funds business and nonprofits through a profit-neutral mechanism, the CBFS. In the process, it achieves income equality.

5. **Environmental stewardship.** A LEDDA promotes the view that the economy and well-being depend on a clean, healthy environment, which includes a stable climate and vibrant ecosystems. Whereas environmental protection is often portrayed as a job killer in the dollar economy, a LEDDA should be capable of aggressive environmental protection while maintaining full employment.

6. **High transparency.** The national financial system is not particularly transparent, and problems and abuses can be difficult to identify and rectify. In contrast, all elements of the LEDDA framework are transparent. Members can monitor token and dollar flows, and thus can spot problems and abuses if and when they occur.

7. **Alternative conceptual models.** Standard economic models are limited in several important ways. Economists using them were unable to see the 2008 global financial crisis coming. Conceptual models of the LEDDA framework incorporate additional approaches. Further, transparency within the LEDDA framework provides sufficient data to support useful models.

8. **Community funding decisions.** In the dollar economy, wealthy investors and big banks have tremendous influence over which firms and projects receive funding. In contrast, LEDDA members share decision-making power, as exercised though CBFS funding decisions.

Each of these topics, with the exception of community funding decisions, is discussed in more detail here, under its own section. Community funding decisions were discussed at length in Chapter 3.

8.2 Debt-Free Money Creation

Prior to roughly the mid-1900s, the money supply of most countries was backed by some physical commodity, such as gold. If a nation found a new deposit of gold, or if it looted gold from other countries, its money volume would increase.[1] Modern economies do not back their currencies with gold or other commodities. Rather, money is created by fiat (by regulation and law). That modern money is created by fiat—one could say, through an accounting procedure—might strike some as a design flaw. But rather than a flaw, it is a feature. It provides flexibility. Under a gold-backed currency, the money supply of a country could only expand if additional gold were obtained. With fiat money, an economy can grow at its intrinsic, natural rate.

One can think of money as a carrier of information. Money carries information much like a vote carries information. People use money to communicate needs, desires, hopes, and fears; money helps people organize human capital and natural resources. This vote-like property of money, combined with transparency and income equality, is intrinsic to LEDDA economic direct democracy. Viewed as an information carrier, it is completely natural to create or destroy money via accounting procedures. Consider what occurs leading up to a presidential election. If the population has changed size, potential votes are created or destroyed through a simple accounting rule: all adult citizens who register receive the opportunity to cast one ballot.

Taking the voting analogy one step further, if election regulators gave each registered citizen the opportunity to cast 10 ballots instead of one, the voting power of the population would stay the same. But each vote would be worth one-tenth its previous value. This would be vote inflation. In the same way, creating too much money can cause economic inflation, and creating too little can cause deflation.

---

[1] The value of gold itself has never been constant; it has fluctuated with supply and demand throughout history.

The Federal Reserve (the "Fed," the U.S. central bank) is tasked with the job of establishing monetary policy that produces maximum employment, stable prices, and moderate, long-term interest rates, which means controlling inflation. The goals of low unemployment and low inflation are usually at odds in the dollar economy, and balancing them is no small challenge. Too many dollars or too fast a circulation tends to increase employment but cause inflation, and too few dollars or too slow of circulation tends to decrease employment and cause deflation. The dollar economy is dynamic and can be upset in numerous ways, yet the volume of money, as well as its circulation rate, must be kept within a limited, favorable zone. The dollar circulation rate tends to be somewhat stable, so we shall focus hereafter on the volume of money in circulation, especially on the process used to create money.

The Fed, Banks, and Dollar Creation

The Fed has only a few traditional tools with which to influence the money volume. It can buy/sell Treasury securities and raise/lower the discount rate (the short-term interest rate that the Fed charges to banks when it makes loans). To set the stage for a more complete description, assume that the government has, at numerous times in the past, paid for deficit spending by creating and selling interest-bearing Treasury securities to the U.S. public, banks, and international buyers. The following explanation gives the "realistic" version of money creation; the "textbook" version taught in some undergraduate classes is arguably less accurate, if not misleading.[146]

There are two types of money. The first, *central bank money* is created by the Fed. The vast majority of money, however, is of the second type, *commercial bank money*, which is created by commercial banks when they make loans. The process of creating commercial bank money is called fractional reserve banking. Its roots reach back to at least 1694, with the Charter of the Bank of England. Part of the justification for allowing banks to create most of the money supply is that the process is considered by some to be more stable and immune from politics, compared to money creation by government. The Federal Reserve system, established by act of Congress in 1913, was a compromise between competing views.

Not only do commercial banks create most of the money supply, they—and not the Fed—drive the process. The Fed has limited tools with which to control the volume of bank lending. Banks make lending decisions based on (prudent, one hopes) business principles. If their lending practices are too strict, they risk a loss of potential interest income. If their practices are too lenient, the banks risk high default rates.

To help ensure stability of the financial system, the Fed requires banks to keep a certain percentage of deposits on reserve (typically, 10 percent). The rest can be used for other purposes, including lending. Reserves allow banks to fulfill typical depositor withdrawal requests. On any given day, only a small percentage of depositors request withdrawals, so keeping a small amount of reserve on hand is usually sufficient for the task.

Reserve requirements do not have a large influence on lending volume. If banks need more reserve funds, they can borrow them from other banks (interbank lending) or from the Fed (the lender of last resort). Also, when needed, the Fed can create money that can be used for bank reserves. It creates new dollars electronically and uses them to purchase Treasury securities held by banks. Banks bid on the price they are willing to accept, and the Fed buys securities from the lowest bidder. The Fed gains securities and banks gain new dollars. When it wishes, the Fed can also reduce the volume of money in circulation by selling its Treasury securities back to banks. The Fed gains dollars and banks gain securities.

When a bank customer takes out a loan, the bank creates all or most of the money for it. As the loan is repaid over time, the debt is retired. Thus, lending creates money, and repayment of principal destroys money.

As long as most banks continue to expand their lending practices, the money volume continues to expand. But if they loan too little, the money volume might expand too slowly, risking an economic slowdown. An extremely sluggish rate of lending can lead to an economic depression. On the other hand, if banks make too many loans, then inflation could rise past the target set by the Fed. And if banks make too many loans due to poor lending decisions, the default rate can rise too far. Extreme default rates can stress banks, causing them to reduce interbank lending, and thus also commercial lending. Bank stress caused by toxic assets and subsequent reduction in interbank lending were primary factors in the 2008 global financial crisis.

The Fed can control the lending activity of banks to a degree by setting the discount rate, which in turn affects the interest rates that banks charge for loans.[2] A high discount rate leads to higher borrowing costs and fewer loans. But in circumstances where the discount rate is already low, such has been the case since the 2008 global financial crisis, the Fed's ability to influence bank lending is limited (see box "Quantitative Easing").

The LEDDA Approach to Token Creation

The LEDDA framework uses a different approach to create money. A LEDDA creates tokens by fiat, and in this sense is similar to a bank, but it does so without the creation of debt. In effect, a LEDDA creates money and gives it away for free, not for fee. And it does so in a transparent process that is governed by the membership.

Similar to the Fed, a LEDDA strives to achieve low unemployment and maintain a stable value for the token and token–dollar. But arguably, it has better tools to achieve these aims, and in the LEDDA framework these aims are more mutually compatible. Rather than adjusting interest rates, as does the Fed, a LEDDA adjusts the "control dials" of a TES, which include the rate of token creation/destruction and earmark and demurrage rates. The interest rate for the token and token–dollar is constant, at zero; all CBFS loans are interest-free.

By adjusting these dials, a LEDDA controls the volume of tokens, the rate of circulation, and the rate of CBFS funding (and thus the rate of job creation). In addition, members also control the rate and quality of token and token–dollar circulation through their CBFS funding decisions. If members make wise lending, subsidy, and donation decisions, circulation will benefit. For example, members might fund a certain business or business sector in part because of its role in the local supply chain and, subsequently, its capacity to improve

---

[2] The rate that banks charge one another for interbank loans is called the *federal funds rate*. The federal funds rate tends to parallel and be slightly higher than the discount rate. The *prime rate*, the interest rate banks charge to favored customers, is almost always higher than the federal funds rate.

token–dollar circulation. Likewise, members might fund a certain business because it provides a desired consumer product or service, which can also improve token–dollar circulation, and well-being.

Quantitative Easing

The 2008 global financial crisis ushered in a prolonged period of high unemployment and anemic lending. Soon after the crisis began, bailouts were given to banks and the Fed lowered the discount rate below 1 percent to control damage. But unemployment remained stubbornly high and lending slow. In late 2008, with traditional tools exhausted, the Fed resorted to an unconventional measure called quantitative easing.

Some described it as a "Hail Mary pass," a long-shot effort to right a sinking economy. In quantitative easing, the Fed creates new money and uses it to purchase long-term Treasury and mortgage-backed securities from banks and other financial institutions. Since 2008, several rounds of quantitative easing have occurred, and currently it occurs as an ongoing process rather than in rounds. Since 2008 the Fed has injected roughly $3 trillion into the banking sector.

Quantitative easing can have several impacts. First, it can instill confidence in the business and investment community; it shows that the Fed is taking bold steps to improve conditions. Second, it can remove toxic assets from bank balance sheets, and thereby encourage interbank lending and more commercial lending. Third, quantitative easing can lower long-term interest rates, stimulating lending. Fourth, banks can use some of the money received for commercial lending.

But quantitative easing has not led to a marked increase in lending activity, a policy dilemma that some call "pushing on a string." The Fed can give banks access to dollars but can't make them lend. Some worry that the Fed will not be able to adequately remove the money it created if inflation begins to rise too high. Others worry that the flood of money encourages reckless financial behavior by banks, or that stock price increases secondary to quantitative easing benefit mostly the wealthy.

Dollar Debt

Given that banks create dollars as debt, and that the federal government finances deficit spending by issuing debt (Treasury securities), it follows that the total debt load increases hand-in-hand with economic expansion. The associations between various types of debt and the GDP are illustrated in Figure 8.1. The solid black line on the top in each panel is Total Credit Market Debt Outstanding (TCMDO), a measure of total debt in the economy.[3] As can be seen, public and private debt have grown rapidly since the 1950s. In fact, except for a few bumps, debt has grown exponentially.

Note that total debt is growing faster than the GDP. Multiple factors play a role. One is that consumers and businesses are spending a larger share of their budgets on debt services. This includes services for a growing volume of student loans, now over $1 trillion.[181] Debt has increased due to decades of stagnant wages for the middle class—U.S. consumers borrow to maintain a comfortable lifestyle. In addition, military spending has expanded the federal debt. And after the 2008 financial crisis, the federal debt has grown due to bailouts, stimulus packages, and higher social spending for those in need. Last, but not least, total debt has increased due to interest charges on unpaid debt.

An obvious question to ask is, how much debt is too much? Or to be more specific, what are the optimal and sustainable amounts of consumer, business, federal, and total debt, and how high can they rise before they cause harm? These questions can be asked of absolute debt levels (Figure 8.1), but debt/GDP or related ratios might be even more important (Figure 8.2).

There is now considerable debate on these questions among economists and in the public. It stands to reason that some thresholds exist above which debt would substantially hinder growth (and economic development) and increase the risk of financial crisis. But no one knows for sure what these thresholds actually are. Can the federal debt/GDP ratio rise much further than its historic maximum of about 1.2, set in 1944? At that time, the nation was in debt due to World War II. But the population was young relative to today, natural

---

[3] TCMDO includes debt from financial and nonfinancial sectors, including public sectors. "Nonfinancial business + household debt," shown in the figure, includes corporate and non-farm non-corporate business debt. "Gross federal debt" is the sum of the "debt held by the public" and "intragovernmental" debt. USD = U.S. dollars.

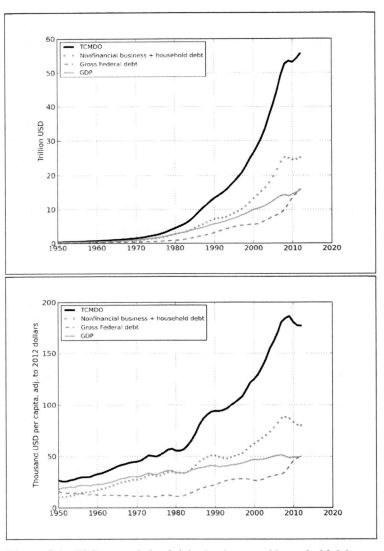

Figure 8.1: GDP, gross federal debt, business and household debt, and TCMDO. Nominal (upper panel) and per capita adjusted to 2012 dollars (lower).[180]

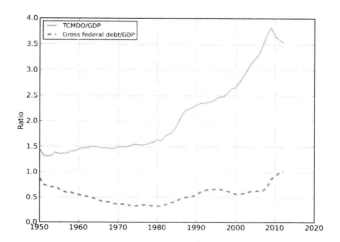

Figure 8.2: Debt to GDP ratios.[180]

resources were still plentiful, and the prospects for rapid growth were good.

When considering the limits of debt, several potential consequences can be weighed:

- Government debt might "crowd out" private investment, thus restricting economic growth. When the government captures a large share of available investment resources. interest rates tend to rise. making it more expensive for business to obtain credit.

- As debt increases, so does the money supply. An excessive expansion of the money supply can result in inflation (see box "Modern Monetary Theory").

- High debt increases rollover risk. The federal government and many private borrowers roll over a portion of debt each year, borrowing again to make payments on old debt. If interest rates were to suddenly spike. private and public debt service costs could become intolerable.

- Debt transfers wealth to banks. Since 1950 a growing share of consumer spending has gone toward interest payments (and payment of other financial services and insurance). Likewise, a growing share of total corporate output (as gross value added) can be attributed to the financial sector itself. Trends are shown in Figure 8.3.

- As wealth is transferred to banks, some have grown "too big to fail." Attorney General Eric Holder famously stated in 2013 that some are now too big to prosecute, a perspective from which he has since retreated.[182] Still, executives of financial institutions seem to be off-limits to prosecution. Although the risky behavior of banks was partly responsible for the 2008 financial crisis, exceedingly few criminal charges have been filed. This is in contrast to successful prosecution of more than 800 bank officials following the savings and loan crisis of the 1980s.[183]

- The pain of debt accumulation is felt mostly by low- and middle-income groups. In 2010, over 26 percent of families below the 20th income percentile had a high debt burden compared to only 3 percent for those above the 90th income percentile.[84]

In summary, debt can have serious downsides if it grows too large. The Congressional Budget Office has warned that if the economy does not grow, and if the rate of public debt accumulation is not reduced, the nation could face markedly increased financial risks within a decade or two.[184] Given that dollars are created via debt, that debt expands with economic growth, and that private debt can be transferred to public debt (through deficit financing of social welfare programs, for example), debt-related problems are not easily solved. The LEDDA framework avoids most of them by creating tokens in a debt-free process and lending at zero interest.

Modern Monetary Theory

Modern Monetary Theory (MMT)—developed by Randall Wray, Bill Mitchell, Warren Mosler, and others—seeks to describe how the national and global monetary systems actually work in practice. MMT sees public debt as a mechanism to expand the economy. As such, it views efforts to greatly reduce or pay off public debt as misplaced. Further, because the dollar is created by fiat, it sees little danger that the United States will become insolvent. Rather, the real risk of large budget deficits, according to MMT, is inflation.

A clear difference between the LEDDA approach and MMT is domain: while a LEDDA pertains to a local, token–dollar economy, MMT pertains to dollar macroeconomics. The instruments also differ. MMT discusses the role of deficit spending and taxes, while a LEDDA is concerned with the rates of (debt-free) token creation and Crowd-Based Financial System (CBFS) contributions. But there are conceptual similarities between MMT and the LEDDA approach. For example, overproduction of dollars or tokens is viewed as an inflation risk. Further, both CBFS contributions and taxes are seen to play similar roles, from an MMT perspective. Both complete a full circuit of money flow, stabilizing money value.

Mitchell explains public debt from the MMT perspective: "The only issues a progressive person might have with public debt would be the equity considerations of who owns the debt and whether there an equitable provision of private wealth coming from the deficits. There is a debate to be had about that, but there is no reason to obsess over the level of outstanding public debt. The government can always honor its debt; it can never go bankrupt."[185] According to Mitchell, "From a macroeconomic point of view, the spending and tax decisions of government should be such that total spending in the economy is sufficient to produce the level of real output at which firms will employ the available labor force."

Finally, "None of this is to say that budget deficits don't matter at all. The fundamental point ... is that the risk of budget deficits is not insolvency but inflation. ... We believe that budget deficits can be excessive and can be deficient as well. ... [The] aim of government is to make sure that they're just right to employ all available productive capacity."

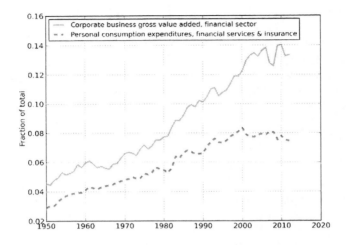

Figure 8.3: Growth of the financial industry.[180]

8.3 Focus on Economic Development

"The profit motive, when it is the sole basis of an economic system, encourages a cutthroat competition and selfish ambition that inspires men to be more concerned about making a living than making a life."

——The Reverend Martin Luther King Jr. (1929–1968)

The fee that we pay to banks for creating money is called *interest*. Of course, interest is charged elsewhere in the economy, too, such as for person-to-person and business-to-business loans. Interest plays a number of beneficial roles in the financial system. For example, interest payments to savers encourage people to store money in bank accounts, where it can be used for lending. Also, the Fed uses interest rates to influence economic activity, as we have seen. But any benefit that interest provides to the dollar economy is achieved by some other means in the token–dollar economy. Interest and debt due to interest play no useful roles.

Looking back in history, not every financial system has relied on interest. In particular, interest-bearing loans were prohibited by the

Catholic Church during the Middle Ages (see box), and have always been prohibited in Islamic culture.

A Brief History of Interest in Europe

Records of interest-based finance date back to the time of King Hummarabi in ancient Babylon (circa 1770 BCE). The Code of Hummarabi stipulates various rules for loans, including a maximum allowable interest rate and the conditions under which debts must be forgiven.

The practice of charging interest continued into ancient Greece, although both Plato and later Aristotle condemned it.[186, 187] By the time of Aristotle (384–322 BCE), debt accumulation had already precipitated social and economic unrest in Greece, as it had in Babylon long before.

Interest-based lending continued into the Roman era. With the decline and eventual fall of the Western Roman Empire (circa 476 CE) and the onset of the Middle Ages, a shift occurred. Based in part on the arguments of Aristotle, in part on the human suffering caused by loans under the Romans, and in part on prohibitions to usury in the Old Testament, interest-based lending was prohibited by the Catholic Church. The Church regarded usury as morally decrepit and sinful.

Although Catholics were prohibited from lending with interest to other Catholics, Jewish law did not prohibit lending to non-Jews. As Catholic peasants and merchants continued to need loans, Jews, who were excluded from many other forms of commerce, became brokers who filled the need.[188, 189]

By the 1400s, alternative sources for loans became available. At the urging of Franciscans, public funds for the poor (*montes pietatis*) were established. Because they charged low interest, just enough to cover expenses, they were generally accepted by the Church. Also in that century, the Medici banking family rose to power in Florence. Along with several other banking innovations, their system of bills of exchange generated a profit without charging interest, and so was welcomed by the Church.

It is easy enough to see that interest increases the debt owed. Indeed, total interest payments on some long-term bank loans can exceed the principal. Further, some portion of private and public debt is rollover debt. It is also easy enough to see that interest and rollover debt favor growth of the financial sector (Figure 8.3), and that this occurs, to some extent, at the expense of other sectors. Finance costs are a burden on business. But it might not be readily apparent that interest-induced debt requires economic growth (which is not necessarily the same as economic development).

Suppose that a business takes out a ten-year, $100,000 loan. Further, suppose that over the course of the loan, the business will pay $30,000 in interest fees. The money to pay interest charges can come from a variety of sources, but it can't come from the loan itself, at least not in total. Repayment of a loan with loan proceeds would only pay back the principal. Money to pay the interest might come from savings or the sale of assets, and some can come indirectly, through inflation. But the preferred, and perhaps least painful source, is economic growth. If the business uses the loan to increase its revenues, then interest can be repaid without resorting to other sources. Indeed, a central purpose of lending is to fund economic growth. One can say that lending with interest drives economic growth, or alternatively, that the expectation of growth makes lending with interest feasible.

Interest is a form of profit on money. In this respect, interest and equity investment are similar. An investor buys partial ownership of a business in the hope of recouping the original investment amount (akin to principal) plus some extra profit (akin to interest). Thus, one can say that investing for profit also drives economic growth, or alternatively, that the expectation of growth makes investing for profit feasible. The situation is a little different when investing via the stock market, as shares of ownership are traded somewhat detached from actual business revenues and profit. But the same principle holds.

The interest/investment system works well enough, as long as economic growth actually occurs. Sometimes things go wrong, however. Suppose growth in the national economy is low—say, below 3 percent in real GDP—perhaps due to the burst of an asset bubble.[4] Under these conditions, average business revenues and profits are stagnant or might fall, more debt is rolled over, unemployment tends to rise, and consumer spending tends to decrease. Due to economic

---

[4] Real GDP is inflation-adjusted GDP. In contrast, nominal GDP is unadjusted for inflation.

uncertainties, corporations can begin to limit capital expenditures that would otherwise fuel future growth.[5] With profits weak and debt accumulating, banks and investors have less incentive to risk money in funding new business. So instead they stockpile money or invest in safer, but less profitable and less productive assets, like government bonds. The process can feed upon itself, driving growth lower still. If growth falls too far, it might reach a critical, even negative level. Deflation leading to depression can ensue and/or a banking crisis unfold.

Two problems are evident. First, the national financial system lacks robustness. If a downturn is severe enough, the economy can have difficulty righting itself. Typically, the government steps in with some sort of stimulus package, perhaps funded by deficit spending. The more debt in the economy, however, the more difficult it is to obtain political agreement on stimulus details. The Fed might step in, too. For example, it might flood banks with new money in hopes of stimulating lending. As noted in the box "Quantitative Easing," this also has its risks.

The second problem is that the focus is on growth in output (or lack thereof), as evidenced by changes in the GDP. But as discussed in Chapter 2, the GDP is a poor measure of economic development (i.e., well-being). The interest/investment system is driven by the expectation of growth, but growth in output can be achieved by wasteful consumerism, war, planned obsolescence, and other processes that can reduce, rather than increase, well-being. Also GDP growth does not say anything about how new wealth is distributed. Thus, the growth that is achieved is not necessarily *smart*. Economic growth is not necessarily economic development.

The LEDDA framework, in contrast, is designed for stability, even under conditions of zero and negative growth. Funding occurs through the CBFS in a profit-neutral mechanism. It is not driven by interest/investment concerns, and thus is not dependent on the expectation of economic growth. Rather, funding is driven by concerns of economic development. Moreover, a token–dollar economy should be relatively immune to boom-bubble-bust cycles, which have plagued

---

[5] Non-financial corporations had a higher share of cash on their balance sheets in 2010 than at any time in nearly half a century.[190]

the U.S. economy since the nation's birth (see box "Boom-Bubble-Bust Cycles").[6]

8.4 Inflation-Free Money

As already noted, the Fed is charged with pursuing policies that encourage maximum employment and a stable value for the dollar, two aims that often conflict in the dollar economy. In seeking a balance between a stable dollar and unemployment, the Fed favors a small amount of inflation (about 2 percent). A small, positive inflation rate acts as a buffer against deflation, which we have seen is difficult to correct. But at times, inflation rises too high. It rose to double digits in the 1970s, for example.

A small rate of inflation has other benefits. For example, it can encourage people to spend money on goods and services; money buys more today than it will tomorrow. But inflation can also have negative consequences. For instance, it harms savers and families who live on fixed incomes, and it can increase the costs of doing business.

Inflation does not serve a useful purpose in a TES, and the token is intended to be inflation-free. Any positive impact that inflation provides in the dollar economy is obtained by other means in the token–dollar economy. As noted, for example, an adequate circulation of tokens and token–dollars is achieved in part through adjustments of earmarks and the demurrage rate. Further, a guiding principle of TES operation is that if token inflation occurs, then token volume must be reduced or other mitigating steps taken to regain stability. Not only would this correct inflation, if it occurs, it would also reduce the expectation of inflation, which is itself inflationary.[191]

---

[6] The causes of business cycles are still uncertain and receive spirited debate. According to Keynesian economics, they are viewed as fluctuations in aggregate demand that cause the economy to temporarily fixate at an equilibrium different from the full employment rate. Proponents of the real business cycle theory see business cycles not as a failure of markets, but rather as the most efficient operation, given shocks such as innovations, bad weather, and stricter environmental regulations. The Austrian school views the cause as excessive growth in bank credit, exacerbated by expansive central bank policies that keep interest rates low for extended periods. Excessive credit, in this theory, leads to speculative bubbles and lowered savings.

Boom-Bubble-Bust Cycles

In boom years, demand is high in one or more sectors of the economy, production grows, the price of stocks or other investment rises, and those who have invested early make sizable profits. Attracted by the profits, more investors jump in, sending prices higher. Many of these investments are bought *on margin*, which means that they are bought with borrowed money. Low interest rates make margin purchases attractive.

At some point, the investment volume exceeds the real business opportunities. Yet momentum continues to propel investments, and prices rise higher. This is the bubble—the elevated, unsustainable rise in price. Eventually prices rise well past their supported limits, the bubble turns into a bust, and prices plummet. Investors and lending institutions can suffer substantial losses.

In severe cases of boom-bubble-bust, the entire economy can be affected. The bust creates a panic. Banks hold excessive amounts of devalued assets on their books. Fearing further decline, they stop making loans. Normal business activity, which relies on access to credit, slows. Before 1933, when the Federal Deposit Insurance Corporation (FDIC) was created to insure deposits, such situations often led to bank runs. Because banks keep only a fraction of depositor money on reserve, cash is quickly exhausted during a run.

Periods of over-speculation, busts, panic, recession/depression, and bank runs have been common in U.S. history. Prior to World War II, major incidents occurred in 1819, 1837, 1857, 1873, 1893, 1907, and 1929, or on average once every 18 years. Some experts cite as many as 15 panics prior to the 1929 crash.[192] The Federal Reserve was established in 1913 in part to prevent new panics. But it was unable to prevent the stock market crash of 1929 and the ensuing depression.

Financial crises have continued to occur throughout recent decades. These include the 1973 oil-price shock, the 1987 Black Monday crash, the 1989 savings and loan crisis, the 2001 dot-com bust, and the 2008 global financial crisis. Altogether, there have been 12 recessions since 1940.[180] Like panics throughout the 1800s and early 1900s, some of these were associated with risky bank practices and speculation.

The orthodox view on the causes of inflation has already been discussed; inflation is "always and everywhere a monetary phenomenon," to quote Milton Friedman. That is, inflation is believed to be caused by a money supply that is too large relative to the amount of output, or goods and services purchased.

Heterodox theories of inflation include or focus on other factors, including wage-increase pressures. For example, a worker group might successfully bargain for higher wages. This results in increased manufacturing costs, which are passed on to consumers. As a result, other worker groups bargain for still higher wages to cover increased costs of living and to provide a cushion for future price hikes. Viewed this way, inflation can be affected by the distribution of worker income, and by the distribution of income among workers, employers, and investors.

If dollar inflation is a complex issue, token–dollar inflation is even more so. For instance, the relationship between the token and dollar is dynamic, and local. The token share of income can change over time, and restrictions might be placed on the bulk sale of tokens for dollars, and vice versa. Much work remains to develop means to identify, quantify, and prevent token and token–dollar inflation. But there are reasons to expect that zero token inflation is achievable, given the conditions of high transparency, education, group cooperation, and income equality that would be present in a LEDDA. Further, a LEDDA could, if needed, create tokens via the "substitution," rather than "addition," pathway (Chapter 6). By doing so, it could increase token volume without necessarily increasing local inflationary pressures.

How high can incomes rise?

Given the relationship between money volume and inflation, and the high degree of income equality within a LEDDA, there is also a relationship between member mean income and inflation. An increase in member mean income implies an increase in the local (token-plus-dollar) money supply. So how high can mean member income rise without causing local inflation?

This is, of course, a difficult question to answer. In the LEDDA Microsimulation Model, post-CBFS family income rises to a maximum of about 104,000 T&D annually. Of this, families receive about 35 percent in tokens (about 37,500 tokens), and the rest in dollars (about

$69,500). The pre-CBFS income target (per family) is about double this. The target was chosen for three reasons. First, it results in a post-CBFS family income that is just above the initial 90th percentile of family income. It is assumed in the simulation that this is high enough to attract 90 percent of families—the target population—into membership. Second, it is high enough so that every family in the target population eventually has incentive to choose Wage Option 1 (Chapter 6). Third, it results in a dollar income that is roughly on par with the national average. Recall from Chapter 5 that due to income inequality, national mean family income is far higher than median family income. Thus, in the simulation, LEDDA members gain a dollar income on par with the national average and, in addition, gain a substantial token income that is dependent on the token share of income (TSI).

The maximum TSI is limited by several factors, all of which are ultimately related to inflation. Consider for a moment an income made up of fixed dollars but flexible token amount (which would depend on how many tokens are created through the "addition" pathway). If tokens are created in excess of member needs, or likewise, in excess of outlets available for token spending, then the value of the token might fall. Members would have more tokens than they could effectively use. Thus, the capacity to increase token income without causing inflation is intimately tied to the number of businesses that accept tokens, the rate at which they accept them, and their ability to use tokens in producing goods and services.

Conceptually, all would increase together over time. The token share of income starts small when few organizations accept tokens and the token share of sales is small. Over time the token share of income rises as new organizations accept tokens, as they accept a larger percentage of sales in tokens, and as businesses find new outlets for their tokens. In the simulation, the final token share of income, 35 percent, is chosen as a compromise. It is high enough to raise T&D incomes to the desired level, but not so high that outlets for token spending and token share of sales cannot keep pace.

What are the upper limits for token outlets and the token share of sales? Again, this is a difficult question to answer. Roughly half of U.S. retail-sector sales revenue is generated by independently owned (mostly small- to medium-sized and locally owned) businesses.[193,

194] Many might be interested in LEDDA membership. Further, independent businesses in the restaurant and retail sectors recirculate, on average, about 46 percent of revenue locally, compared to 18 percent for national chains. That is, national chains tend to export a greater share of local revenue to distant regions. These observations suggest that the token share of income and token share of sales can rise substantially, especially if most of the new businesses that a LEDDA funds are independently owned, and if members weigh the impacts on token circulation when making purchasing and CBFS funding decisions.

The capacity to increase the token share of income without causing inflation is also dependent on education, transparency, and data collection programs. Without transparency and data collection, the circulation rate of tokens, the rate of inflation, and the potential impacts of purchasing and funding decisions on these, would be difficult to assess. Education can help members understand that if incomes are to rise but inflation kept at zero, they must play a role. For example, members can avoid supporting businesses that engage in predatory price hikes or that fail to pay employee wages in keeping with the income target. And they can spend wisely on a diverse assortment of goods and services, rather than paying premium prices for a select smaller set.

8.5 Income Inequality

"If a free society cannot help the many who are poor, it cannot save the few who are rich."

—John F. Kennedy (1917–1963)

Income inequality was discussed in Chapter 5, but there is more to the story. The profit-based, interest/investment-driven national financial system funds businesses, as it is supposed to do. But as already suggested in this chapter, the LEDDA framework uses alternative means that might do the job better.

Indeed, financial markets (e.g., stock markets)—a central feature of the national financial system—might not be the efficient resource allocators they are often assumed to be. Robert Shiller jointly shared the 2013 Nobel Prize in Economics for suggesting that observed volatility of asset prices is incompatible with the efficient market hypothesis (in which market prices fully reveal all relevant information and investors act rationally using this information).[195] Irrational or sentiment-driven investors can have a permanent impact on financial markets.[196]

Other economists, including John Maynard Keynes and Hyman Minsky, went even further, arguing that financial markets are not self-correcting, and if unregulated (or lightly regulated) are inherently unstable and capable of causing crises.[197]

To the list of arguments, we can add one more, the focus of this section: by allowing wealth to create wealth—that is, by allowing lending and investments to create wealth—the majority of benefits accrue back to the wealthy.

As noted in Chapter 5, income inequality is greater in the United States than in almost every other developed nation.[88, 7] It has been steadily rising since the 1970s and is now at an extreme that was last seen in 1928, on the eve of the Great Depression.[198] The top curve in Figure 8.4 shows that the per capita inflation-adjusted GDP increased steadily from about 1950 to 2008. The bottom curve, however, shows that real wages for the middle class (production and non-supervisory workers) stopped rising with the GDP around 1970 and have been stagnant ever since.

If the middle class did not benefit from the past 40 years of GDP growth, then who did? Families in the 80th–100th income percentiles prospered nicely during the past 40 years, as shown in Figure 8.5. But the biggest gains went to families above the 95th percentile. Though not shown in the graph, income gains for the top 5 percent were overshadowed by even larger gains for the top 1 percent. Their massive gains are passed on to new family generations through inheritance.

Gains from rising GDP have largely gone to corporations and wealthy investors. Record-breaking corporate profits in recent years have been buoyed by 1970s-level employee wages and a higher percentage of part-time hirings.[200] Gains in per capita corporate profit relative to GDP are shown in Figure 8.6, where an exponential curve has been fit to after-tax corporate profits to mark the trend.

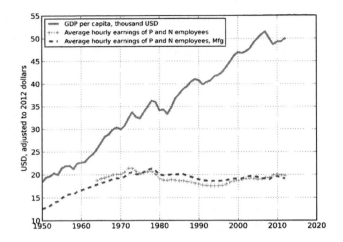

Figure 8.4: Real GDP per capita and real wages for production and non-supervisory (P and N) employees in manufacturing (Mfg) and all sectors combined.[180]

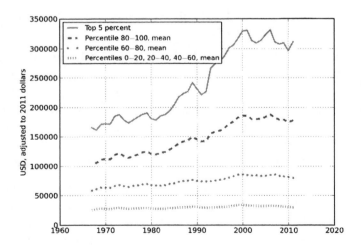

Figure 8.5: Growth in real family income by percentile.[199]

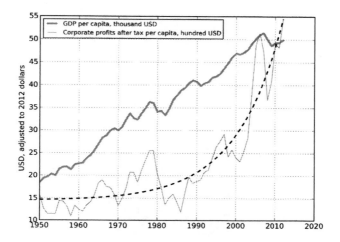

Figure 8.6: Rise of real corporate profits versus GDP, per capita basis (dotted line: exponential fit).[180]

Figure 8.7 shows the nation's wealth distribution in 2007. Households in the top 1 percent financial wealth class enjoyed 43 percent of the total wealth pie. In contrast, households in the bottom 80 percent financial wealth class, that is, the vast majority of Americans, were left with only a 7 percent slice. Most of the income received by the ultra-wealthy stems from investments. In 2008, income from wages and salaries made up only 19 percent of total income reported by households making over $10 million.[158]

Wealth accumulates, as Thomas Piketty points out, because return on investment tends to exceed the rate of economic growth.[159] Piketty, the celebrated French economist and author of *Capital in the Twenty-First Century*, bluntly states, "I have proved that under the present circumstances capitalism simply cannot work."[201] It leads to "patrimonial capitalism," he says, an aristocracy of money passed from parents to children.

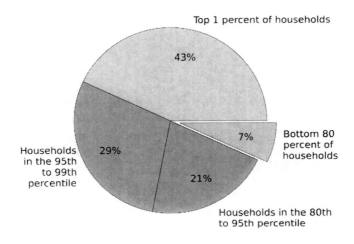

Figure 8.7: 2007 U.S. financial wealth.[158]

8.6 Environmental Stewardship

"Anyone who believes exponential growth can go on forever in a finite world is either a madman or an economist."

—Kenneth Boulding (1910–1993)
Co-founder of General Systems Theory

In a finite world, exponential growth cannot continue forever. A striking quality of exponential growth is that when it is graphed, change seems minor for a very long time, then mild, and suddenly, explosive. The U.S. economy has grown exponentially since the nation was founded. By the time the 2008 crisis hit, change had entered the explosive range.

Figure 8.8 shows growth in real GDP (adjusted to 2012 dollars) from 1800 onward, given on a total and per capita basis. The dotted lines indicate the close fit to exponential curves. They are extrapolated

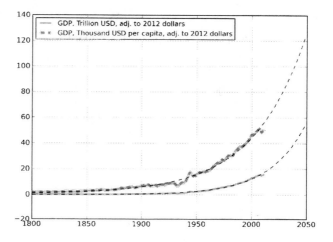

Figure 8.8: Exponential growth of real GDP since 1800.[202]

to 2050 for effect. Real GDP has been increasing at a rate of about 3.1 percent per year, a value that can be considered the *thermostat setting* to which the U.S. monetary and financial systems are permanently tuned. If growth is lower in any year, unemployment tends to increase.[7]

Due in large part to abundant natural resources and stable climate and ecosystems, we have been able to consistently achieve 3.1 percent growth thus far. But it will become increasingly difficult—perhaps exponentially so—to continue this level of growth into the future. The trajectory shown in Figure 8.8 requires that the real GDP double between 2012 and 2035. Said another way, the same amount of growth that took 212 years to achieve must happen again in the next 23 years. And once it is achieved, the total must double again in the following 23 years, and so on, forever. But this degree of economic output is incompatible with ecological stability. In short, the environment, society, and the economy are on a collision course.

---

[7] A linear regression model of annual unemployment change versus annual change in real GDP for the years 1950–2012 suggests that on average, real GDP growth of 3.3 percent produces zero change in unemployment. Unemployment tends to rise at lower growth and fall at higher growth. At real GDP growth below about 2 percent, unemployment has always risen.[180]

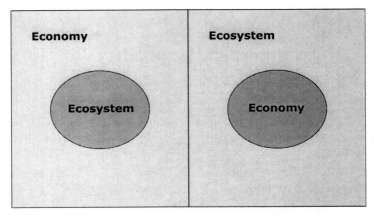

Figure 8.9: Two views of the ecosystem/economy.[205]

The solution, of course, is to build an economy that is geared toward well-being—toward economic development—rather than economic growth. This is the purpose of the LEDDA framework. Time is running short, however. Some of the damage we are doing to the environment is essentially permanent (relative to the human lifespan). Topsoil loss, for example, can take hundreds of years to repair. Impacts from climate change are expected to continue for thousands of years.[203] And extinctions are irreversible, at least using today's technology.

Economy within the ecosystem

The basic laws of physics tell us that economic activity produces some degree of waste, no matter how efficient. This suggests that there are ecological limits to economic output. Some scientists believe that we exceeded those limits in the 1970s, when the population was about half of what it is today.[204] But for many economists, the idea of ecological limits doesn't hold much weight. They see the environment as a subset of the economy, instead of the reverse. The two views are contrasted in Figure 8.9.

The differences between the two views are profound. If one believes the view shown on the left, then there is no natural limit to economic activity. The economy contains the ecosystem (and nearly everything else). Since the economy is not constrained by the ecosystem, it can grow without end. Even if an environmental crisis were to occur, it would occur within the economy as a whole. For any given crisis, economic pressures would lead to technical or other types of solutions. If too many greenhouse gases were in the atmosphere, new industries would arise to profit from removing those gases. The crisis itself could help the economy to grow. If one nonrenewable resource runs out, technology will discover a way to replace it.

The right-hand panel shows an entirely different situation. Here the economy is seen as a subset of the ecosystem. As such, there is a natural limit to its size. Moreover, the economy is seen to *depend* on the ecosystem. If the economic output grows too large and begins to harm the environment, it will be forced to shrink to a more sustainable size. If in the process of expansion it causes excessive environmental damage, entire ecological systems might collapse, which could force the economy to collapse.

The economy depends on the ecosystem in a number of ways. It relies on nonrenewable resources (such as oil) and renewable resources (such as timber, soil, and food). It needs clean air and water, bees to pollinate certain crops, and beneficial bugs to eat the ones we call pests. The ecosystem is complex and we depend on it in many ways, some of which we barely understand.

Some things we have learned can seem surprising. For example, most of the oxygen we breathe is produced by the uncountable numbers of tiny marine algae (phytoplankton) floating in the world's oceans. If we ruin the oceans, we destroy our oxygen supply. Ominously, a 2010 report suggests that phytoplankton levels have dropped 40 percent since 1950.[206] A 2011 report warned that the world's oceans are moving into a phase of extinction due to overfishing, pollution, and climate change.[207] And a 2012 report warned that the rate of ocean acidification due to a rise in atmospheric greenhouse gases is at its highest rate in the last 300 million years.[208]

Climate change is among our biggest social, ecological, and economic threats. Every region in the U.S. and around the world is expected to experience substantial negative impacts if emissions of greenhouse gases are not rapidly and dramatically reduced.[209] In addition to changes in ocean chemistry and ecology, sea level has already risen eight inches and could rise another one to four feet by 2100. New evidence suggests that irreversible collapse of the West

Antarctic ice sheet has already begun, which alone could increase sea level by 10 to 13 feet.[210] With a 10-foot rise, the United States would lose roughly 28,800 square miles of land, an area about the size of West Virginia and Delaware combined, and home today to 12.3 million people. Trillions of dollars in property damage could occur.[211]

Coastal flooding and the expected increase in severe weather patterns (heat, droughts, floods, hurricanes) are expected to increase heat-related deaths; favor the spread of tropical diseases; disrupt food, water, industrial, energy, and other socioeconomic networks; and cause migrations of environmental refugees.

Climate change can affect a region through multiple indirect means. Floods can spread pollution, for example. Global agricultural topsoil is being lost to erosion so fast that one rough estimate suggests all agricultural topsoil will be gone in 60 years. Already, 40 percent is classified as either degraded or seriously degraded, and productivity is dropping.[212] Iowa has lost about half of its topsoil to erosion.[213] Extreme and more frequent rainfall events caused by climate change make topsoil erosion even more rapid.

There is ample scientific evidence to suggest that the right-hand panel of Figure 8.9 is the more realistic one. However, viewing the economy as a subset of the ecosystem does not mean that humans are destined to live a life of material hardship and need. Rather, it means we must learn to live intelligently and show greater care for the planet, its systems, and all its inhabitants. The economy must become smart, even ultra-smart.

To achieve progress, industrial and commercial sectors must become highly efficient in their use of energy and resources. The production of waste and pollution must be minimized. Nearly every product must be redesigned for cradle-to-cradle, rather than cradle-to-grave, management. Reduce, reuse, and recycle must become the norm. And products must be designed for updates wherever practical. Planned obsolescence must itself become obsolete. Massive investment is needed in new technologies and education. Factories must be retooled, buildings insulated and retrofitted, and infrastructure repaired.

Monumental funding is needed to switch to a smart economy. Unfortunately, the profit-driven national financial system is poorly suited for the task. Combating climate change and addressing other social and environmental challenges could actually reduce GDP, even while increasing well-being. For example, GDP would drop if energy were conserved, all else being equal. Nor is deficit funding of government programs well suited for the task; Congress is in gridlock and the debt burden (and shift of wealth to the financial sector) is already high.

While government and the financial system have important roles to play, the LEDDA framework provides an additional means to help raise the funds necessary to achieve the bold social, environmental, and economic goals that demand our attention.

8.7 High Transparency

The U.S. financial system and the dollar economy in general are far from transparent. According to the International Monetary Fund, "Weak financial institutions, inadequate regulation and supervision, and lack of transparency were at the heart of the financial crises of the late 1990s as well as the recent global financial crisis."[214] The "shadow banking system"—the network of relatively unregulated credit intermediaries outside the regular banking system—played a major role in the 2008 crisis. To this day, no one knows it true size, but one estimate places its 2012 value at $100 trillion.[215]

Even regulated banks are known to engage in illegal behavior. Total fines for U.S. and European banks were a record $43 billion in 2013.[216] And banks have been fined millions of dollars in recent years for money-laundering activities that aid drug cartels.[217] A 2008 U.S. Senate report estimates that each year the Treasury loses approximately $100 billion in tax revenue to secret offshore tax accounts.

Offshore tax havens and billion-dollar bank fines make front-page news, but transparency problems go deeper. Insufficient data collection, limited access to data, and suboptimal analytic methods make even seemingly straightforward economic variables, like the GDP, difficult to pin down. Lequiller and Blades, in a report for the Organisation for Economic Co-operation and Development (OECD), paint the picture:

> *National accounts data are therefore approximations. It is not even possible to give a summary figure of the accuracy of the GDP. Indeed, national accounts, and in particular GDP, are not the result of a single big survey for which one might compile a confidence interval. They are the result of combining a complex mix of data from many sources, many of which require adjustment to put them into a national accounts database and which are further adjusted to improve coherence, often using non-scientific methods.*[218]

In a staff report for the Federal Reserve Bank of New York, Dennis Kuo et al. provide a similar view, this time focused on short-term interbank lending, which played a major role in the 2008 global financial crisis:

> *Despite the importance of U.S. dollar term interbank markets, little hard data is available to researchers to measure and analyze term dollar interbank transaction interest rates, volumes, and maturities.*[219]

As more examples, Federal Reserve and U.S. Census surveys cannot provide robust statistics of top—and therefore average—family income and wealth because privacy regulations do not allow them to publish data that could be used to identify specific individuals. Income and wealth of the top 1 percent are so extreme, and by definition the number of families so small, that publication of accurate data would make identification of specific individuals relatively simple.

The same holds true for surveys on business characteristics. Accurate information on large, privately held corporations is particularly difficult to obtain, as these businesses are not subject to securities regulations. And accurate state and local economic data are, in general, more difficult to obtain than national data. Not only are individuals easier to identify when the population in question is small, but survey costs increase dramatically when local-area resolution is required.

To provide just two examples with particular relevance to LEDDAs, very little public information is collected on county-level supply chains or county trade balances. Such data must be inferred from a collection of other sources. Further, a shortage of local and national data exists in other domains that have economic components, such as health care, education, politics, and the environment.

Thus, in spite of the large and growing volume of information that is available from the Federal Reserve, U.S. Census, and other public agencies, there is still a serious shortage of data for those who are attempting to model the economy. Enormous benefits could be gained by increasing transparency and making data more open. By one estimate, if governments made available data more open, $3 trillion in additional value would be added to the global economy annually.[220] Collection of new and more refined data could likewise produce massive economic impacts.

The purpose of transparency in the LEDDA framework is to give members all the information that they need to understand how their token–dollar economy is functioning, and how their state of well-being is changing. Among other uses, such data are indispensable for creating helpful simulation models of token–dollar flow and of changes in well-being. And data are needed to spot abuses and to monitor the effectiveness of implemented solutions. Members are responsible for guiding their token–dollar economy, and without timely, accurate, and accessible data, their choices will be suboptimal, if not destructive. Thus, members must have access to all information needed to make informed decisions, but not more. That is, a trade-off exists between openness and privacy.

Compared to current norms that favor low transparency, the openness–privacy balance in a LEDDA would fall on the side of openness. Only by becoming more open can a society understand itself. Openness breeds honesty and trust, and discourages selfish behavior. It also facilitates science in its quest to understand the world. And openness allows for greater participation; if data are made available, anyone can get involved in examining problems and finding solutions. For all these reasons, one could say that the *fuel* of a LEDDA is open data. Of course, abuse of data and the potential for abuse, both by members and non-members, are also concerns that must be addressed.

It is premature to identify all the social, economic, and environmental information that a LEDDA would collect and make public. The framework remains under development, and transparency and data collection needs will change over time. The membership of individual LEDDAs and the association of LEDDAs will make ongoing decisions regarding these issues. But some likely transparency requirements have already been discussed. For example, the transparency requirements of the Principled Business model were discussed in Chapter 7.

The TES was also described in Chapter 6 as a transparent system. Quite likely, periodic (for example, daily) summary statistics of each member's token account would be made public. So too would summary statistics for the token accounts of nonprofit organizations and for-profit businesses (especially Principled Businesses).[8] Armed with this information, members would have reasonable knowledge of how tokens are flowing, to whom, and when.

Further, since dollars are part of the token–dollar economy, similar disclosures would be necessary for dollar accounts. This refers primarily to the dollar account tied to a member's token account. Recall from Chapter 6 that a LEDDA would partner with a willing credit union, local bank, or public bank to develop and manage dollar accounts. Certainly, the token is much easier to track than the dollar due to its electronic nature and local distribution, but means to make dollar accounts adequately transparent can be devised.

In considering the openness–privacy trade-off, it might help to remember that no person or organization is forced to join a LEDDA. Membership is optional. Thus, openness within the LEDDA framework is not an infringement of constitutional rights. Courts are inclined to uphold contracts that are freely negotiated in good faith. Also, as member incomes rise and become more equal, the perceived need for privacy might diminish to some degree.

8.8 Alternative Conceptual Models

The essence of science is to discover what is true—to observe phenomena honestly and impartially in order to understand them. By offering rich and deep perspectives in sociology, psychology, biology, ecology, medicine, economics, and other fields, scientific

---

[8] A record of individual purchases made by persons or organizations would not necessarily be made public, however.

inquiry reveals ever-deeper truths about nature, human society, and the meaning of well-being. Through science we gain understanding, for example, about what motivates human behavior, what promotes social cohesion, and what improves human health. The purpose of a LEDDA is to maximize well-being, and it uses science to understand how this can be achieved. Said another way, the *method* of a LEDDA is science.

The workings of our natural and social worlds are highly complex, often too complex to be understood by casual observation. Today more than ever, humanity needs science to help it act rationally, maturely, and wisely for the benefit of all. The growing severity of ecological threats stands as but one example to show how foolish humans can be when science is ignored. As human civilization progresses, and as human-constructed systems—political, financial, economic, or otherwise—become more complex, science must play an ever more central role. Dirk Helbing, writing in the journal *Nature*, captures this notion:

> *It is time to recognize that crowd disasters, conflicts, revolutions, wars, and financial crises are the undesired result of operating socio-economic systems in the wrong parameter range, where systems are "unstable." In the past, these social problems seemed to be puzzling, unrelated, and almost "God-given" phenomena one had to live with. Nowadays, thanks to new complexity science models and large-scale data sets, one can analyze and understand the underlying mechanisms, which let complex systems get out of control.*[221]

In the quote, Helbing is speaking primarily of averting disaster, but a LEDDA is intended to thrive, not merely survive. In the same way that data collection and complex models can help avert disaster, they can also help achieve greater well-being.

Models should reflect actual conditions with as much fidelity and richness as can be achieved within the limits of practicality. On this note, it is worthwhile to point out some of the shortcomings of current microeconomic and microeconomic models.[9]

---

[9] Microeconomic models are concerned with the behavior and decisions of individual (but generic) persons and businesses. Macroeconomic models are concerned with the economy as a whole, and so focus on such issues as unemployment, the trade balance, and the GDP.

Since the 1950s, the primary conceptual basis underlying dominant microeconomic models has been *rational choice theory*. It models behavior *as if* individuals are the primary economic actors; are motivated solely by rational self-interest; have access to full and perfect information; and have the cognitive ability and time to fully weigh every choice. In recent years, the trend has been to increasingly base macroeconomic models on microeconomic principles, and thus rational choice theory.

Of course, every model is an abstraction of reality, and as such, every model is wrong; what matters is a model's usefulness. But an increasing number of social scientists have questioned both the core assumptions of rational choice theory and the usefulness of models built on it. Sen, for one, calls rational choice theory "remarkably alienating."[38] Geoffrey Hodgson has pointed out its unfalsifiable nature (the theory can't be proved wrong, and is therefore not testable—it is true by its own definition).[222]

Surely, humans do not act as if motivated only by private gain. Even if the concept of private gain is expanded to include group cooperation for mutual benefit, observation tells us that humans often act in ways that are unrelated to self-interest. For example, in response to the 2010 Haiti earthquake, governments, nonprofits, and individuals raised and spent nearly $2 billion in emergency aid.[223] Haiti is a small, poor island nation. Not all of this outpouring of assistance can be construed as self-interested behavior.

Numerous studies in neuroeconomics, behavioral economics, and other fields suggest that rational choice theory offers an inadequate description of human nature.[224] Physiology experiments indicate, for example, that "reward" pathways in the brain show similar patterns of activation when people either receive money or donate to charity.[225] Further, people who spend money on others, rather than themselves, report higher levels of happiness.[226]

By viewing the economy as a conglomeration of self-interested players, rational choice theory risks becoming a self-fulfilling prophecy.[227] If economic theory tells us that people are driven by self-interest, then we develop policies that not only assume self-interested behavior but also reward it as a means to achieve desired outcomes. As a result, the economy grows increasingly steeped in self-interested behavior over time.

Further, by focusing on self-interest as a motivation, we fail to develop policies that reflect a more complete and accurate view of human nature. As discussed in Chapters 1 and 5, humans are complex creatures driven by a wide range of motivations. Moreover, humans are social, and do not always act as individuals; the entire concept of a LEDDA is based on the notion that people can act as a group to make *purposeful* economic decisions—to help one another through cooperation.

Conventional macroeconomic models have two other weakness: they do not typically include the financial system as a component; and they increasingly rely on microeconomic principals, expressed through dynamic stochastic general equilibrium (DSGE) models.[10] The trouble with the first is that the financial system obviously does affect the greater economy; the 2008 global financial crisis is proof. The trouble with the second is that equilibrium models, while useful, are limited. They are not well suited for studying dynamic systems that swing out of equilibrium, as we know economies can. Further, equilibrium models are not well suited to studying the distribution of income and wealth. *The Economist* put it this way, referring to the 2008 crisis:

> *The crisis showed that the standard macroeconomic models used by central bankers and other policymakers ... neither represent the financial system accurately nor allow for the booms and busts observed in the real world.*[228]

Models matter. They inform public policy and shape cultural worldview. In the aftermath of the 2008 global financial crisis, economists

---

[10] DSGE models attempt to bridge microeconomic decisions (e.g., regarding personal savings, consumption) with macroeconomic outcomes (e.g., economic growth, business cycles) using a set of equations and an equal-sized set of unknown variables. The models are dynamic in that they depict how an economy evolves over time. They are stochastic in that they take into account random shocks to the economy. Typically, they predict macroeconomic events using a small set of (exogenous) parameters. The equations are solved using numerical solutions based on log-linearization at an equilibrium point, which means that DSGE models are ill-suited for studying systems that are not in equilibrium, prone to non-equilibrium events, or are driven by irrational behavior (like asset bubbles). Because they do not model interactions between individual persons or businesses (as do agent-based models), they cannot provide distribution information on income or other variables. The usefulness of DSGE models has been increasing in recent years, however, as they have become larger and more complex.

were asked why they did not see it coming. The typical answer was that the crisis stemmed from such a rare combination of occurrences and accumulated errors that it was, for all practical purposes, impossible to predict. But in fact, a small set of economists did see the crisis coming.[229, 230] As a group, they shared several characteristics: most explicitly modeled the financial system as a component, and most examined the economy from an accounting, stock and flow, approach, rather than through a general equilibrium model. As a result, they could see the buildup of debt, and they could see the impending instability. (It is now widely understood that banks and bank credit played key roles in precipitating and extending the crisis.)

In light of the failure of conventional economic models to provide adequate warnings to the 2008 crisis, many within the profession have made efforts to broaden their approach. While improvements to DSGE models, such as "bounded rationality," look promising, some scientists have called for bold new approaches and modeling projects. Farmer and Foley, for instance, have suggested that the United States develop a large-scale agent-based economic simulation model.[231]

Unlike DSGE models, agent-based models simulate interactions between multiple players, which can include large numbers of individuals and businesses. As such, agent-based models can assess stability in non-equilibrium conditions, and can provide income and wealth distributions as output. Progress with large-scale, agent-based models has already been made in Europe, with initiation of the EURACE project.[232]

The LEDDA Microsimulation model is also an example of a stock–flow consistent agent-based model, only at the county level. It is but the first model developed for the LEDDA framework; others are to follow. While early models will focus on dollar–token flow, later ones will increasingly examine more comprehensive indicators of community well-being, human capital, and states and flows of energy, wastes, and other resources. In time, a variety of models will be developed, based on a diversity of methods and perspectives, and meeting a range of needs. The computer models funded by LEDDAs will be available to the public via open-source licenses, thereby allowing any member to engage in assessment, if he or she desires.

As a concluding note, the relevance of the tractor–race car analogy used in Chapter 1 might now seem more apparent. Major structural differences exist between the Token Monetary System and Crowd-Based Financial System, on the one hand, and the national monetary and financial systems, on the other. Structural differences also exist between the Principled Business model, described in Chapter 6, and publicly held corporations. Because of these and other structural differences, radically different operating characteristics and outcomes can be expected for a token–dollar economy. Debt levels, environmental damage, resiliency, income and wealth distributions, and knowledge transfer are all affected. The LEDDA framework is not a reformed tractor, it is a race car designed from the ground up to serve its intended purpose.

Chapter 9

Collaborative Governance System

"I know no safe depositary of the ultimate powers of the society but the people themselves; and if we think them not enlightened enough to exercise their control with a wholesome discretion, the remedy is not to take it from them, but to inform their discretion by education."

—Thomas Jefferson (1743–1826)

This chapter is, in a sense, Part B to Chapter 3. That chapter introduced LEDDA economic direct democracy and focused on the mechanics of purchasing and CBFS funding decisions. This chapter focuses on the mechanics of formal deliberation and voting in the Collaborative Governance System.[1] The CGS provides opportunity for all members of a LEDDA to participate in the creative, collaborative, problem-solving process of developing and amending rules and setting policy. In this way, the CGS provides members with meta-influence over their token–dollar economy.

---

[1] The term *collaborative governance* is commonly used to denote types of online direct democracy. Related terms include open-source governance, open democracy, and e-governance.

The Collaborative Governance System is based on a hybrid form of direct democracy. Members hold ultimate decision-making power, as opposed to representatives elected through a voting scheme. But the CGS is more flexible than traditional direct democracy systems. Members are encouraged to participate via direct democracy mechanisms, but they can also delegate their power to do so to proxies. Any such delegation is reversible on demand and can be given for specific issues or with limitations. Further, the CGS includes mechanisms for members to seek recommendations from others, including CGS committees, nonprofits funded to provide recommendations, and persons or groups who elect to offer recommendations. Thus, the CGS (and token–dollar voting) reflects a synthesis of ideas from direct democracy, participatory democracy, and delegative democracy (liquid democracy).[45, 46, 47, 48] For convenience, the remainder of this chapter assumes that members choose to make decisions themselves. But in a real LEDDA the proxy process would be available and likely used widely.

There are at least two reasons why a LEDDA would want to engage its full membership in decision-making. First, doing so distributes control equally among all members. Given that power over one's economic destiny is a component of well-being, distributing power helps a LEDDA to fulfill its purpose. Second, a LEDDA can tap the experience, skills, and creativity of all its members when it tries to solve a problem. The modern term for this is *crowdsolving*. Netflix famously used crowdsolving in 2009 to improve the algorithm by which it predicts the movies a customer might enjoy. Rather than hire engineers and statisticians, the company set up a website, posted a huge data set of movie and subscriber information, and offered a $1 million prize to anyone who could improve its algorithm by 10 percent.[233] For Netflix, the price of the prize was small compared to the value of the product it received.

Of course, a group majority can also be shortsighted, irrational, and even tyrannical. But that is not a valid reason to avoid direct democracy. Political representatives can also act in these ways. The CGS is designed to be transparent, efficient, and fair. It is also supported by beneficial cultural norms and educational programs. Under these conditions, one can expect members to be at their best.

9.1 Three Branches of Collaborative Governance

Not unlike the federal government, the CGS is divided into three branches: administrative, legislative, and judicial. But in practice, it resembles a city government more than it does the federal government. In particular, it has some resemblance to the council–manager form of local government, as well as the government of ancient Athens, the world's first well-documented direct democracy (see box).[234] As an aside, our word *idiot* comes from ancient Greece. It referred to someone who did not participate in politics and other public affairs.

Considering similarities to the council–manager and Athenian forms of democracy, the design of the administrative and judicial branches of the CGS is not particularly novel. It borrows from and builds upon ideas that have worked in the past, tailoring them to an online format that meets the needs of a LEDDA. The legislative branch of the CGS, however, has a novel design.

If the Collaborative Governance System is to succeed, each of its three branches must satisfy the same set of design requirements:

1. It must be efficient. It must use financial and human resources efficiently. If members feel that their time is wasted or their input ineffective, or if involvement is too demanding, they will choose not to participate.

2. It must be transparent, secure, and fair. Members will not fully participate if they feel that the system is unfair or biased, or that power is unevenly distributed. Transparency is essential to demonstrate fairness and to address problems that arise.

3. It must be effective. The system must lead to useful and well-supported decisions. This requires that members of a LEDDA be informed, and that the system lend itself to functional, rather than dysfunctional discussions.

The design of each branch, discussed below, helps to ensure that these requirements are met.

Direct Democracy in Ancient Athens (507–338 BCE)

The institutions of Athenian direct democracy consisted of two main bodies: the Assembly, which was open to adult male citizens, and the courts. Groups other than adult male citizens of Athens could not participate. The Assembly passed all laws and made all major decisions. It met about 40 times per year, often with 6,000 or more in attendance (about 20 percent of those qualified to attend). At each meeting, a series of speakers would offer their points of view on an issue, and the public would vote by raise of hands.

Courts were composed of a large number of jurors, with no professional judges or lawyers. Athenians were notorious for litigation, and courts met roughly 150 days per year. After hearing a case, jurors would vote by ballot. Typically, several hundred people would sit on a jury, but in important trials (often political trials), as many as 2,500 jurors might participate.

Subservient to the Assembly was the Boule, a council, composed of hundreds of administrative officials. The purpose of the Boule was to handle the day-to-day operations of the government. Between attending the Assembly, serving on the Boule, and participating in juries, a large portion of citizens were involved regularly in the self-governance process. To ease the strain of spending so much time on community affairs, at times jurors and others were paid stipends.

Athenians struggled with some of the same governance problems that nations face today. They realized how easily elections could be manipulated by the wealthy. Therefore, instead of electing officials in the Boule, most were chosen by lot from a group of qualified applicants. And they chose juries by lot on the day of the trial to reduce bribery and corruption. Magistrates, selected yearly by lot, administered the courts. The oligarchs saw democracy as a form of tyranny over the rich and were constantly plotting to replace democracy with their own rule.

9.2   Administrative Branch

The purpose of the administrative branch is to manage the day-to-day operations in accordance with LEDDA bylaws, the wishes of the membership, and local, state, and federal laws.

As envisioned, the administrative branch comprises standing councils, overseen by a central council. Council members are chosen mostly by lot from a list of applicants.[2] The goal is to have a large percentage of the membership serve on a variety of councils over time. In this way, knowledge and skills are distributed in the population, and then passed on to new generations.

Selection by lot (sortition) avoids many of the problems associated with either election by vote or selection by appointment. The citizens of Athens used selection by lot to prevent wealthy and well-connected candidates from dominating the electoral process. Selection by lot also avoids the cronyism that can occur with selection by appointment. And selection by lot is efficient and inexpensive. It also lessens voter fatigue.

Recent research suggests that even within a representative democracy, choosing some portion of legislators by lot could improve performance.[235] Indeed, a 2012 poll of likely American voters indicated that 43 percent believed people who are randomly selected from a telephone book would do a better job than current legislators.[236] Only 38 percent disagreed.

As in Athens, a small number of administrative positions could be chosen by election. This could include, for example, the chief executive officer of a LEDDA. To reduce the influence of wealth, such elections would be financed by a LEDDA. Furthermore, a rated voting system or similar alternative could be used to maximally convey voter preference.

For reasons of efficiency, LEDDA councils play a role in legislation. The issues that a LEDDA faces would span a wide range of topics, from simple to technical, and from uncontroversial to controversial. Councils would be asked to obtain expert recommendations, when needed. Further, they would be asked to triage issues based on the anticipated degree of controversy among members. Issues viewed as minor and uncontroversial would be handled by the councils themselves in a transparent process. Certain types of uncontroversial issues might be subject to a public comment period before decisions

---

[2] Qualifications for applicants and the evaluation process could be handled in several ways. For example, a search committee could develop a list of qualifications for each committee position. Members would apply for the positions that interest them.

are made. Issues viewed as somewhat controversial would be elevated to the next level; councils would prepare motions, which would then be presented to the full membership for discussion and vote. Issues viewed as more controversial would be elevated to the full collaborative legislative process, as discussed below. The membership could elevate any issue themselves via online petition.

9.3   Legislative Branch

The legislative branch implements the formal collaborative process of developing and amending rules and policies, referred to here as legislation. To allow a massive group of members to efficiently participate at low cost, interactions would occur largely via the online system. Face-to-face meetings of small or even mid-size groups, perhaps guided by trained facilitators, could supplement the online activities.

Perhaps the world's first example of an online collaboration system used to make governmental decisions is the LiquidFeedback implementation operated by Friesland, a small district in Germany.[237] LiquidFeedback, an open-source software project, has also been used by the German Pirate Party and other groups.[48, 238]

Similar to LiquidFeedback, the CGS allows for reversible delegation of proxy power, uses a form of preferential voting, and strives to ensure that minority voices are heard.[3] Also like LiquidFeedback, voting in the CGS is not secret. Secure, secret voting via an online platform would be extremely difficult, if not impossible to achieve. Non-secret voting is in line with the general trend of transparency and openness found throughout the LEDDA framework. Policies would be needed, however, to help ensure that voting transparency is not abused.

Another example of online collaboration in action is Wikipedia, the popular encyclopedia. Anyone can contribute to a Wikipedia article. The article is built up, contribution by contribution, edit by edit, often through the efforts of a large number of individuals. While Wikipedia

---

[3] Preferential voting includes ranked and range voting systems. In the latter, voters score candidates or proposals using a point system.

can act as an inspiration for collaboration, it does not offer a solution for collaborative democracy. Legislative issues can be highly contentious. While the Wikipedia model does have some controls to keep discussions productive and prevent abuse, they are not sufficient for the purpose of writing legislation. Nor does Wikipedia contain a mechanism for reaching formal decisions.

Yet one more example of online collaboration is open-source software development. It too requires a communications system to facilitate dialogue and decision-making. Karl Fogel speaks to this point in his guide to building successful open-source projects:

> *Because the Internet is not really a room, we don't have to worry about replicating those parts of parliamentary procedure that keep some people quiet while others are speaking. But when it comes to information management techniques, well-run open-source projects are parliamentary procedure on steroids. Since almost all communication in open-source projects happens in writing, elaborate systems have evolved for routing and labeling data appropriately; for minimizing repetitions so as to avoid spurious divergences; for storing and retrieving data; for correcting bad or obsolete information; and for associating disparate bits of information with each other as new connections are observed.*
>
> *Active participants in open-source projects internalize many of these techniques, and will often perform complex manual tasks to ensure that information is routed correctly. But the whole endeavor ultimately depends on sophisticated software support. As much as possible, the communications media themselves should do the routing, labeling, and recording, and should make the information available to humans in the most convenient way possible.*[239]

Like open-source projects, the success of the CGS ultimately depends on the development of a sophisticated communications system. The basic idea is that the system would help members interact in a manner that efficiently steers them toward widely supported decisions. The question is, how can this best be accomplished?

Evolutionary Computation

Taking a bird's-eye view, the legislative process can be seen as a form of evolution in which a draft bill is refined by the actions of members over time. In this respect, it has certain similarities to evolutionary computation, a mathematical technique widely used in science to find suitable answers to difficult problems. A prime example of evolutionary computation is the genetic algorithm, which mimics the biologic evolution of DNA in response to environmental pressures.

Briefly, a genetic algorithm finds solutions to a problem over a series of rounds, called generations. In the first generation, initial solutions, called chromosomes, are randomly created and scored. The equation used to score the solutions reflects their fitness to the given problem. In subsequent rounds, chromosomes are mutated in some way. Some mutations are due to simple random changes, while others are due to merging two highly fit chromosomes.

Round by round, the genetic algorithm implements a survival-of-the-fittest approach. As a result, each generation tends to produce one or more chromosomes that are better than the best ones seen previously. Typically, early rounds produce dramatic improvements in fitness. As rounds continue, improvements become smaller, until eventually little, if any, further gain is made. At that point, the system has reached a solution. Depending on the problem, it might not be a "global" optimum (the best out of all possible solutions), but it is usually a "good" solution, the best of all that were tried.

As envisioned, the legislative process within the CGS mimics evolutionary computation. In the first round, an initial set of solutions is created and scored. These are not random solutions, however. Councils create an initial set to start the process. And solutions are not scored by a fitness equation. Rather, they are scored by members according to the degree that solutions meet a member's approval. For example, a member might score a solution as 6 on a scale of 1 to 10, where 1 is strongly disliked and 10 is strongly liked.

In subsequent rounds (generations), the solutions are modified. This occurs not by random mutation, but by the editing activity of members. Members can edit the solutions of their choosing and devise entirely new solutions, if they desire. After the editing for a round has been completed, members score the solutions that interest them.

All the edits and scores are recorded by the system, and then computationally processed in order to summarize meanings. For example, similarity scores between solutions are computed and used to identify clusters of highly similar solutions. Depending upon the issue at hand, many clusters might form, each representing a distinct approach to a solution. And some solutions might be unique, not falling into any identified cluster. The summaries produced can help members to understand how their views compare to those of others; what affinity groups are forming and dissolving; what range of solutions is being considered; what unique views are being offered; what components could be borrowed to improve favorite solutions; and what adjustments could be made to favorite solutions in order to elicit higher scores from others.

As rounds continue, the evolutionary process tends to produce one or a few solutions that are particularly fit—that is, particularly popular. At some point the process comes to an end. Ideally, it ends because sufficient agreement has been reached to select a winning solution. The criteria for winning might be, for example, a score of 7 or more by 70 percent of the membership. A LEDDA would set this criteria in its rules, along with other aspects of the legislative process.

For some issues the evolutionary process might not converge to a well-liked solution within a reasonable number of rounds. A similar situation can occur in other types of communities that strive to reach consensus or near consensus in their decision-making processes. Karl Fogel provides an example from the open-source community:

> *The more experienced people are with open-source projects, the less eager I find them to settle questions by vote. Instead they will try to explore previously unconsidered solutions, or compromise more severely than they'd originally planned. Various techniques are available to prevent a premature vote. The most obvious is simply to say "I don't think we're ready for a vote yet," and explain why not. Another is to ask for an informal (non-binding) show of hands. If the response clearly tends toward one side or another, this will make some people suddenly more willing to compromise, obviating the need for a formal vote. But the most effective way is simply to offer a new solution, or a new viewpoint on an old suggestion, so that people re-engage with the issues instead of merely repeating the same arguments.*

In certain rare cases, everyone may agree that all the com-
promise solutions are worse than any of the non-compromise
ones. When that happens, voting is less objectionable, both
because it is more likely to lead to a superior solution and
because people will not be overly unhappy no matter how
it turns out. Even then, the vote should not be rushed. The
discussion leading up to a vote is what educates the electorate,
so stopping that discussion early can lower the quality of the
result.[239]

When no solution meets the criteria for success after a reasonable number of rounds, two avenues of action remain open to members. First, they can vote to continue the deliberation process for additional rounds, hopefully resulting in a solution that does meet the criteria. Second, they can vote to lessen the criteria and continue deliberation. For example, they might choose to lower the stopping criteria to a score of 7 or more from 60 percent of the membership (rather than 70 percent), and continue for an additional number of rounds.

If at the end of these rounds, a winning solution still has not been found, the same two avenues of action remain open. For highly intractable issues, that have gone through many additional rounds, the criteria might be lowered to a majority vote.

There may be times when lowering the criteria is the best available option. But this choice would not be made lightly, as there are potential costs. If the criteria are lowered, the winning solution is less likely to be of high quality and to receive strong and wide support. Over time, this could lead to frustration and resentment that might undermine a LEDDA.

Cultural norms could spur members to work toward widely supported decisions. The cultural norms nurtured by a LEDDA should encourage cooperation, respect, productive problem-solving, active participation, and other beneficial behaviors. Karl Fogel had this to say about the role of cultural norms in the open-source world:

A recognizable culture has slowly emerged, and while it is
certainly not monolithic—it is at least as prone to internal dis-
sent and factionalism as any geographically bound culture—it
does have a basically consistent core. Most successful open-
source projects exhibit some or all of the characteristics of

this core. They reward certain types of behaviors, and punish others; they create an atmosphere that encourages unplanned participation, sometimes at the expense of central coordination; they have concepts of rudeness and politeness that can differ substantially from those prevalent elsewhere. Most importantly, longtime participants have generally internalized these standards, so that they share a rough consensus about expected conduct.

Unsuccessful projects usually deviate in significant ways from this core, albeit unintentionally, and often do not have a consensus about what constitutes reasonable default behavior. This means that when problems arise, the situation can quickly deteriorate, as the participants lack an already established stock of cultural reflexes to fall back on for resolving differences.[239]

Besides cultural norms, additional motivators could be developed. For example, the rules of a LEDDA might indicate that decisions made using a lowered stopping criteria would need to be revisited after a set period of time for reaffirmation, modification, or repeal. Such a rule would dissuade members from using lowered criteria.

The goals of the decision-making process are to make quality decisions, to minimize the size of the dissenting minority, and to make members feel that their voices were heard and that the process was fair and complete. In this way, many in the minority would still likely be willing to lend their support to the winning solution. The ideal is to obtain 100 percent support, regardless of the voting outcome.

Details of the Legislative Process

The previous discussion provides a rough outline for the legislative process. To summarize, a range of solutions is considered, and these evolve in a series of editing rounds. The criteria for winning is set such that widely supported decisions are encouraged. This basic approach could be implemented in a number of ways. For example, each solution might be presented in simple text, similar to that of traditional legislative bills. Text might work well for some issues, particularly if they are not complex and the proposed solutions are simple and short.

Several refinements to simple text could be made. For example, a controlled natural language system could be employed, at least to some degree. This consists of a dictionary containing an expressive subset of words. These words, and sentences made using them, are understood by a computer so that computer-facilitated logical reasoning can occur. As a simple example a member could type the statement "Miguel works in a school." Then he could ask the system, "Does this rule affect Miguel?" The system should be able to answer correctly. This technology has already been proposed for online e-government discussion forums.[240]

Many other options are available to help gather, store, and process information. For example, members could create searchable, issue-specific personal home pages, where they could post links and explain their views. Home pages could also display responses to comprehensive questionnaires designed to help others understand the concerns, questions, and alliances of members on an issue. Questionnaire responses could also be computationally analyzed, resulting in summaries of membership stances. Further, responses would likely change as rounds progress, and trends could be tracked and summarized. Apart from personal home pages, other communication elements could also be employed (see box).

Still other possibilities exist. There may be some issues whose solutions are best expressed as flowcharts, called *blueprints* here. A blueprint is a graphical depiction of a solution, showing the relationship between its different elements. The basic idea mimics what often occurs when people sit down to solve a problem: they draw a sketch and then make changes to it until it embodies an acceptable solution.

Imagine two architects trying to design the plumbing layout for a house. They create a draft blueprint, which shows where the water comes into the house, how it flows toward each bathroom, and how it returns to the main sewer line. To create this blueprint, they typically use special drawing software, which allows edits to be easily made. The two architects edit and re-edit the blueprint until they are satisfied. Collaborative democracy in a LEDDA could work the same way. Members could use online software to edit and re-edit sets of drawings. Rather than being blueprints for a house, these would be blueprints that depict solutions to a legislative issue.

Alternative Communication Elements

Alternative or complementary communication elements that could be used singularly or in combination include:

- **Questions/answers:** These are polls or queries that would allow a member to request responses from a selected sub-group or the entire membership. To make responses manageable, the system could summarize results.

- **Fact statements:** These are very short statements of fact, perhaps just a few sentences in length. Fact statements submitted by members would be reviewed by an impartial panel for accuracy. If accepted as fact, the statements could be referenced by others and used as a common basis for logical arguments, similar to the process of judicial notice.

- **Policy papers:** These are written statements, perhaps several pages in length, that explain aspects of an issue in some detail. Members could submit policy papers in order to influence and guide the overall decision-making process. For example, a policy paper might explain the legal ramifications of several popular solutions, or might argue why a particular solution is the best one. A maximum length could be set on policy papers to encourage concise writing and help ensure that no one voice dominates the discussion.

- **Informational briefs:** These briefs would be shorter than policy papers, perhaps just a paragraph or two in length. They would allow a member to submit information pertinent to a specific component of a solution. For example, an informational brief might explain why a particular budget item in a particular solution includes the cost of an engineering consultant. As members edit a solution, they could click on links to informational briefs associated with that solution.

- **Recommender system:** To help members home in on the most useful information, a recommender system could be used. A simple version is the "Like" button found on many websites. A more complicated version is the one Netflix uses to suggest interesting videos to its members.

There are three advantages of editing a blueprint rather than editing text. The first is that for some issues, particularly complicated ones, a blueprint might be more easily understood than text. In fact, that's why we use blueprints rather than words when describing the construction of a house. As the saying goes, a picture is worth a thousand words.

The second advantage is that a computer can understand a blueprint (essentially a graph) much better than it can understand text. This would facilitate the computational assessment of results during each editing round. To further support computation, blueprints could be annotated using a controlled natural language, rather than normal text.

The third advantage is that a blueprint would already be in a standard (graph/flowchart) form that facilitates automatic rule checking and development of intelligent systems. Blueprints could be designed to meet selected Unified Modeling Language (UML) specifications. UML is commonly used to visualize software development, and as well has been used to visualize legislation.[241]

Further, UML-compliant blueprints could be analyzed by computational tools in order to produce animated "live" graphs, and/or to identify legislative anomalies, such as dead-end rules, unreachable elements, inconsistencies, and missing rules.[242] Such anomalies are common in legislation but can be difficult to detect without computational assessment.

Ultimately, a LEDDA could develop an "intelligent" electronic body of legislation that could be queried by members to obtain answers on specific issues. Artificial intelligence applied to law is already a formal field of study, complete with professional journals and international conferences.[243, 244]

By starting from scratch, unburdened by incompatible structures, LEDDAs are in a unique position to make rapid progress toward development of an intelligent legislative system.

9.4 Judicial Branch

"Never forget that justice is what love looks like in public"
—Cornel West (1953–)
U.S. philosopher, academic, activist, and author

The third branch of the Collaborative Governance System is judicial. It has two primary purposes, the first of which is to help members settle disputes with one another and/or with the LEDDA itself. The second is to balance the powers of the administrative and legislative branches. The judicial branch does not replace existing legal systems. If a member breaks local, state, or federal laws, this would necessarily be handled by outside authorities.

In a large LEDDA, disputes will inevitably occur. It is important for a LEDDA to handle these internally to the degree practical. Doing so would be time- and cost-efficient for members, compared to formal court. And it would provide additional avenues to encourage cooperation, honesty, justice, mutual respect, and other qualities that a LEDDA values.

To minimize the cost and complexity of the judicial branch, internal disputes could be handled through a mediation and arbitration system. Briefly, mediation is an alternative to formal court. A trained mediator assists two (or more) disputing parties to negotiate a settlement. In some cases, the mediator might offer suggestions for a reasonable settlement. Neither party has a legal obligation to settle the dispute through mediation.

In contrast, arbitration is more formal. Binding arbitration is a substitute for formal court, and the parties are obligated to abide by the arbitrator's decision. Typically, one or three arbitrators are involved in deciding a case, in a process that resembles a mini-trial. It usually proceeds faster than a case in court, and at lower cost. In general, mediation is attempted first. If that fails, arbitration is used. Where possible and practical, a LEDDA could develop an internal mediation and arbitration system, rather than relying on outside contractors. An appeals procedure could also be developed.

The second purpose of the judicial branch is to balance administrative and legislative powers. Councils within the judicial branch could offer or obtain expert opinions on the legality of proposed or executed administrative and legislative actions, relative to a LEDDA's rules and local, state, and federal laws.

The judicial branch also plays a role in other aspects of a LEDDA. For example, it interacts with the reputation system. As mentioned in previous chapters, reputation is a form of currency within a LEDDA. One's reputation can be harmed by breaking the rules, and the judicial branch determines if rules were broken.

The judicial branch could also participate in creation of an intelligent electronic legal system. Such a system could help arbitrators to make consistent judgments, and help LEDDA members to monitor those judgments. It could also help members to understand when and how rules apply, and the consequences of breaking them. An intelligent legal system would help ensure that the judicial process is efficient, fair, and transparent. It would complement an intelligent legislative system, as described previously in this chapter.

As a final remark, the Collaborative Governance System is not the first proposal for an online form of democracy. For example, the website metagovernment.org lists numerous projects in various stages of development, each with a different approach. The work on delegative democracy by Brian Ford has been an inspiration for several efforts.[46] Considering the diversity and creativity of approaches that are under investigation and development, a rich source of inspiration exists for continued development of the Collaborative Governance System. Indeed, some ideas, such as proxy voting, are already incorporated. As the system develops, more opportunities for cross-pollination will be possible.

Chapter 10

Starting and Operating a LEDDA

"The difference between what we do and what we are capable of doing would suffice to solve most of the world's problems."
—Mahatma Gandhi (1869–1948)

The LEDDA framework has now been described in some detail, and this final chapter addresses practical issues related to starting and operating a LEDDA. These include initial planning and organizing, and the fun part: deciding how to use CBFS funds to achieve social, economic, and environmental goals.

Ideas are offered from the viewpoint of a popular, successful LEDDA. Recall from Chapter 4 that the average-sized county described in the simulation reached full employment by Year 15. By Year 18 it was generating about 2 billion tokens plus dollars annually in CBFS funds. The funding ideas explored in this chapter consider possibilities if funding were available on that scale.

10.1 LEDDA Startup

How do the first LEDDAs get started? The process would necessarily be different for the first LEDDA, which would be involved in a scientific pilot trial. The process would also be different for LEDDAs started far down the road, after the framework has begun to spread and an association of LEDDAs has formed. Rich collective knowledge and a great many resources would likely be available by that time to help new LEDDAs get off the ground. In this section we focus instead on LEDDAs that would start in the first few years after the pilot trial has ended.

The first step in starting a LEDDA is social organizing and sharing of information. The Principled Societies website could help in these efforts by offering a sign-up list or newsletter targeted to individual U.S. counties and county-equivalents in other nations.[1] It might also provide educational materials for use in attracting members. And it could offer training programs for local organizers.

Once enough individuals and organizations within a community have shown interest, a new LEDDA might legally form.[2] In the United States, a LEDDA would likely organize as a nonprofit corporation or as an L3C, B-Corporation, Flexible Purpose Corporation, or other socially responsible corporate form (Chapter 7). The operating documents (bylaws, articles of association) could be based on templates developed by the Principled Societies Project. Operating documents act as a type of constitution, and any person who has interest in becoming a member of a particular LEDDA could review that organization's documents.

After a LEDDA has legally formed, it would likely seek funding to cover startup costs. The Principled Societies Project can help by suggesting fundraising activities and introducing organizers of incipient LEDDAs to corporate donors, philanthropists, and foundations. It is premature to provide firm estimates of startup costs, but expenses should not be so large as to be prohibitive.

The primary funding needs in the first few years are for planning studies, computational and communications resources, and office

---

[1] At the time of this writing, the Principled Societies Project is taking the lead in developing the LEDDA framework. The Project's role could evolve over time.

[2] In the simulation model, a LEDDA formed with 5 percent of a county's population.

expenses and wages for a small professional staff. After the first several years of operation, a LEDDA should become self-supporting in operating expenses via the CBFS governance earmark.

A large number of activities would occur prior to issuing the first tokens. Planning studies would assess community resources, capacity, interest, and needs. Public meetings would provide opportunities to introduce ideas, answer questions, and discuss results from planning studies. A publicity campaign would occur. And data would be collected and computer simulation models adapted to local conditions.

Like Toyota, IBM, and many other large for-profit corporations, the viability and vitality of a LEDDA would depend on the qualities and quantities of the flows within its system. The success of a LEDDA rests in part on its capacity to develop a robust token–dollar circulation among individual and organization members. But other items must flow properly as well. These include raw materials, manufactured supplies, waste products, energy, information, and so on. Companies like Toyota have devoted substantial time and effort toward optimizing their network flows, and over time a LEDDA would have to do the same.

Planning for flows would begin in the startup period, with initial focus on token–dollar flow. To assist, a simulation model could be made available online or off-line so that the public could watch the virtual circulation expand and gain strength as increasing numbers of individuals and organizations indicate interest in membership. In this way, the incipient LEDDA would have a useful, working estimate of token–dollar flow before any person or business makes a formal commitment. No LEDDA should start operations before it has reason to believe that its token–dollar circulation would be successful.

Over time, organizers of the incipient LEDDA would gather more data from prospective members for use in modeling. In parallel, organizers could play an increasingly active role in growing the circulation network. In particular, they could invite existing businesses to join that might improve token–dollar flow. They could also develop a set of Requests for Proposals (RFPs) to encourage the formation of certain kinds of Principled Businesses or standard businesses. The idea of invitations and RFPs is to create the right mix of businesses, and enough individual members, so that token–dollar circulation can serve community needs and be free of dead-end paths and bottle-necks.

An incipient LEDDA might use an RFP, for example, to signal its desire to fund a Principled Business that produces ethanol from locally available organic waste materials. This business might supply member farmers with fuel for their tractors, providing the latter with a new outlet for the tokens they receive from customers.

Similarly, an incipient LEDDA might develop an RFP for a gasket company or other parts manufacturer, if the parts it produces could be used by other member businesses. In this way, supply chains within the membership could expand. Pollution and energy use might also be reduced due to local production and reduced transportation distances.

As yet another example, an incipient LEDDA might develop an RFP for a recycling company that accepts certain waste products from existing member businesses, processes the materials as needed to make them more valuable, and then sells the finished product to other member businesses. In this way, value is retained in the LEDDA, pollution is reduced, and token circulation is improved.

Once enough non-binding commitments for membership are received, initial analysis completed, and public meetings held, plans could be finalized and memberships formalized.[3] The new members would select interim councils and committee members of the Collaborative Governance System. Software would be mounted on the LEDDA's server, dry-run tests conducted, trainings offered, and finally, the software system would go live. After a period of testing, during which time members could grow accustomed to the software, the software would be ready for real interactions and the first tokens would be created and distributed to member accounts.

10.2   Businesses Diversity and Distributive Enterprises

With proper planning, a Token Exchange System should be ready to spring into operation on Day One. Soon after token–dollar flow

---

[3] Individuals and organizations who join a LEDDA can cancel their membership at will. If necessary to ensure TES integrity, however, mild restrictions might be placed on the transfer of their tokens to other members.

begins, members would start making (automated) contributions to the CBFS. Shortly after that, members would start making funding decisions. In the early years, CBFS funds would likely be small; many families would choose Wage Option 2 (Chapter 6), and thus make contributions on a percentage of token incentive bonus rather than total income. But over time, the income target would rise, more families would choose Wage Option 1, and CBFS contributions would increase. As they do, CBFS applications would likely increase in volume, and members would have growing power to support the organizations of their choosing.

Initially, a LEDDA might focus its funding efforts on building program capacity. This could include building the capacity of Collaborative Governance System staff, offering education programs to help new entrepreneurs develop quality business plans and CBFS applications, and offering skills-training programs to members in order to prepare individuals for work in LEDDA-funded organizations.

Because CBFS funds would be limited in the first years, the organizations that initially form due to CBFS funding would likely be small. As funds grow in later years, the capacity to fund new, larger organizations would increase. But a focus on funding new, small organizations in the early years is not wasted effort. Small firms tend to be more beneficial to a community than are large corporate chains. Typically, they purchase a higher percentage of products from local suppliers, pay higher wages, have fewer layoffs, and are less likely to relocate. In a nationwide study of county income, employment, and poverty for the period 2000–2009, Anil Rupasingha concluded that "local entrepreneurship matters for local economic performance and smaller local businesses are more important than larger [ones]."[245] A similar study for the period 2000–2007 found that the county-level density of small, locally owned businesses was positively associated with per capita income growth, whereas a negative association was seen between income growth and the density of large, non-local businesses.[246]

Moreover, effects of small businesses might extend past economic indicators. A 2012 study found that counties with a greater concentration of small, locally owned businesses tend to have healthier populations than do counties that rely more heavily on large businesses. Rates of mortality, obesity, and diabetes were lower in the former group.[247]

A wide assortment of the products and services used by individuals and businesses within a community would become candidates for local production. Initial funding might focus on production of relatively simple products like soap, toothpaste, paper towels, food, beverages, and clothes, as well as on common services like cleaning, graphic arts, accounting, and repair. But over time, the CBFS could fund increasingly large and complex organizations that offer more sophisticated products and services. For example, a mature LEDDA could fund cable services, film production, trade schools, hospitals, and manufactures of computers, engines, and solar panels.

As the membership increases, the size of the IP pool (Chapter 7) would grow, fueling even faster business growth. And as the LEDDA framework spreads, efforts to produce sophisticated products and services could be aided by manufacturing and trade agreements between cooperating LEDDAs. Knowledge, skills, financial risk, and resources could be shared. As just one possibility, small groups of LEDDAs could manufacture their own smartphones using design, IP, practices, and tools openly shared among all LEDDAs.

Smartphones are used as an example only because they are a common product; the same scenario could hold true for many types of products. But this does not mean that a LEDDA or a cooperating group of LEDDAs would want to produce every product and service that they use. CBFS funding decisions should be based on consideration of a wide range of factors.

As mentioned in Chapter 5, members use the CBFS to allocate funds, but in actuality, they allocate themselves; members democratically decide how they will contribute their time and energy to the local economy. They fund their own jobs and their own care. As such, members should fund the jobs that are most useful and meaningful to their community. Decisions should take into account member well-being, as well as effects on the global public. Consideration can be given to a host of social, economic, and environmental factors. It might be, for example, that airplane engines are best made by Boeing in Seattle, cars best manufactured by Ford in Detroit, and pineapples best grown by Del Monte in Thailand. Or it might be otherwise.

After considering efficient use of local human and natural capital and other factors, a LEDDA might decide to focus funding on a fixed set of products and services. But there should be no shortage of these to choose from. As mentioned in Chapter 5, a LEDDA would likely have many economic, scientific, social, artistic, public health, manufacturing, and environmental goals that it would like to achieve. Therefore, the real task put before the members is to decide what the needs of the LEDDA and greater community actually are, and to fund accordingly.

The ideal set of products and services targeted for local production is certain to change as technology changes. In particular, it should become increasingly practical to produce an astonishing variety of products via local, small-scale production. In the near future, distributed, low-cost manufacturing operations will be facilitated by technologies, such as three-dimensional (3D) printing, new discoveries in materials science, and innovations in technology access, such as fabrication labs (fab labs).

By itself, 3D printing could revolutionize manufacturing by allowing a person or small group to "print" products of nearly any complexity using plastic, metal, rubber, ceramics, or other stock material.[248] Scientists are even using 3D printing to manufacture live tissues for body part replacements, a process called bioprinting.[249] Fab labs tend to contain all the equipment necessary, including 3D printers, to produce just about any type of part that an entrepreneur might need.[250]

New research in 3D printing technology is leading to production of large, architectural-scale objects. And already one small company, RedEye On Demand, has plans to produce a fuel-efficient car made from printed parts. The three-wheeled, two-passenger vehicle has a plastic body as strong as steel and runs on a hybrid electric/diesel engine.[251]

Using open-design, open-source software, and machines found in an average fab lab, it took another group, WikiSpeed, just three months to build an award-winning prototype car that achieves 100 mile per gallon.[252, 253] Not a clunker, it accelerates from zero to 60 mph in less than 5 seconds and tops out at 149 mph.

WikiSpeed is an example of a *distributive enterprise*, a transparent company that seeks its own open replication.[254] Such open business models are highly compatible with the LEDDA framework and could play an important role in hastening its spread. Further, transparency and open replication are compatible with a common component strategy, in which products are manufactured using lower-cost generic parts.[255] With their emphasis on knowledge sharing, open business models can increase the speed of discovery and hasten the implementation of new technologies.

10.3   Targeting Economic Sectors

To start an examination of funding possibilities for a mature LEDDA, it is useful to consider the distribution of consumer spending in the U.S. economy. The token–dollar economy is unique, and members in a mature LEDDA probably will not have the same spending habits and needs as is seen in the current dollar economy. Improved urban design, for example, including better mass transit and greater pedestrian and bicycle traffic, could reduce transportation costs. Nevertheless, current consumer spending patterns provide a framework for discussions.

As illustrated in Figure 10.1, the Bureau of Labor Statistics breaks consumer spending into eight major categories. Six (all but the "apparel" and "other goods and services" sectors, the smallest in the group) are discussed separately under their own headings. Possibilities exist in these two small sectors also, of course.

Food and Beverage

Of all economic sectors, food/beverage is perhaps the easiest to target, so it is discussed first. Even without new developments in technology, a substantial portion of food production, distribution, and retail sales can occur through small, locally owned businesses. LEDDAs can target this sector by funding new and existing local farms, grocery stores, food distribution and manufacturing companies, and restaurants. The potential is large; former U.S. Deputy Secretary of Agriculture Kathleen Merrigan has called the local food movement "the biggest retail food trend in my adult lifetime."[257]

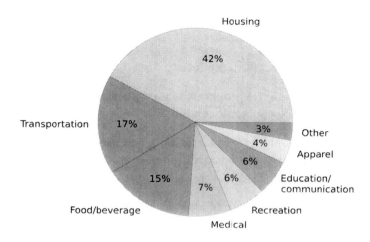

Figure 10.1: Typical consumer expenditures in 2011.[256]

This sector is also important from environmental and health perspectives. By funding organic and well-managed farms, a LEDDA could reduce environmental impacts due to fertilizer and pesticide use, as well as due to transportation of food from distant locations. Further, it could promote soil health and reduce erosion. And it could promote human health by increasing the availability of fresh fruits and vegetables. But just as with other products discussed earlier, not every food item is ideal for local production.

Taking small farms as an example category within the food/beverage sector, a LEDDA could:

- advertise and promote farmers markets via its online system, thereby expanding the customer base

- encourage member grocery stores and restaurants to carry or use locally grown produce

- advertise and promote community-supported agriculture (CSA) projects, which directly connect farmers with consumers

- fund salaries for additional county workers, allowing them to certify farms and conduct other regulatory activities in a timely fashion

- offer existing farmers subsidies and interest-free loans

- fund the startup of new farms and of businesses that use or distribute local farm products

- fund educational programs that emphasize the benefits of locally grown, organic produce

- fund research on organic farming and permaculture methods, especially in consideration of heat, drought, and other climate change stresses[4]

- fund research on use of agricultural lands to absorb greenhouse gasses

- fund research aimed at developing new products, including oils and fuel, from agricultural wastes.

A LEDDA could also target the supply chains that farms use. One example already mentioned is a LEDDA-funded Principled Business that produces locally made fuel for farmers. As well, a LEDDA could fund a seed company that develops varieties suited to local climate and soil conditions. About 75 percent of the genetic diversity in food crops has been lost over the past century as farmers worldwide have abandoned diverse local varieties in favor of genetically uniform, high-yielding varieties.[259] Especially in this era of climate change, maintaining diversity could be important for survival.

While these examples focus on small farms, a similar action list could be developed for other types of businesses within the food/beverage sector, including grocery stores, food packaging and manufacturing businesses, and restaurants. And apart from commercial farms, a LEDDA could encourage urban food production. A great deal of production capacity goes unused within a typical metro area. Homeowners and renters have access to yards, porches, and rooftops in which they could grow small amounts of produce for sale. Such small operations could provide new sources of revenue to members, as well as improve the health of their community.

---

[4] Permaculture—permanent [agri]culture—is a design system that promotes sustainable food production and culture. It seeks to work with ecosystems, rather than against them, focusing on perennial, rather than annual, food plants.[258]

City plots may also be available for growing food for personal or community use. A study conducted for the city of Oakland, California, for example, suggests that 5 percent to 10 percent of the city's vegetable needs could be met through gardens located on available undeveloped and public lands.[260] The City of Seattle recently initiated what will become a seven-acre community food forest, where any resident is welcome to harvest fruits and vegetables.[261, 262] Designs of the food forest are based on permaculture principles.

Housing

Housing is the largest sector of consumer spending. If members could use tokens in partial payment of rents and mortgages, token circulation would benefit. But rent and mortgage payments often go to distantly owned and operated financial institutions. Even rent paid by a tenant to a local homeowner might be applied to a mortgage held by a faraway corporation. Thus, deep expansion into the housing sector would require that a LEDDA develop its own mortgage institutions or that it fund organizations to purchase land and property.

An intriguing idea is to purchase land and property to be held in a "land commons." Environmental groups such as Nature Conservancy already do this to protect biologically important parcels.[263] In a LEDDA land commons, long-term leases could be offered to member businesses or families. But the membership could retain the option to lease to different members or use the land for new purposes (parkland, for example), once lease terms are complete. The concept has similarity to the house leasing system available to professors on some university campuses.

The housing sector, along with the commercial building sector, is also important from an environmental perspective. Residential and commercial buildings accounted for nearly 40 percent of total U.S. energy consumption in 2012.[264] One way to reduce climate change risk is to make all new construction energy-efficient and as carbon-neutral as practical. Existing buildings could be retrofitted with insulation, daylighting, and other technologies that reduce energy demand. And when appropriate, existing buildings could be demolished, recycled, and replaced by ones that are more energy-efficient.[265] The European Commission's Low Carbon Roadmap proposes that emissions from the built environment could be reduced by around 90 percent by 2050.[266]

In the United States, a LEDDA's efforts to retrofit and replace buildings could be accompanied with advocacy programs to encourage city planners to improve existing zoning laws. Updated zoning could facilitate energy-efficient construction and transportation, including increased pedestrian and bicycle traffic. With appropriate zoning, cities could become more "livable."[267] As one effect, zoning changes could provide new opportunities for employees to live closer to their jobs.

Transportation

Transportation accounts for 17 percent of consumer spending, the second-largest sector. Several examples have already been given by which LEDDAs could target this sector. To expand, LEDDAs could fund businesses that produce cars, bicycles, and other types of vehicles, as well as their fuel. A LEDDA could also fund trucking businesses, auto repair shops, car rental agencies, taxi companies, and organizations that facilitate automobile co-ownership. CBFS funds could be used to support city and county governments in their efforts to build bicycle paths, expand mass transit, update zoning laws, and enhance transportation in other ways.

A substantial percentage of the nation's bridges, rails, roads, and other transportation structures, as well as its dams, energy facilities, schools, parks, wastewater plants, and other infrastructure are overdue for repair or replacement. As mentioned in Chapter 4, the American Society for Civil Engineers gives U.S. infrastructure a failing grade of D+, and estimates that $3.6 trillion will be needed over the next six years (by 2020) to make needed changes.[81] As part of the rebuilding effort, a LEDDA could help fund local infrastructures that are designed to reduce climate change risks and withstand damages.[268]

Energy

Although not detailed in Figure 10.1, energy costs are part of the housing and transportation sectors. A LEDDA could help usher in a new energy landscape, the signs of which are already appearing.

On the supply side, decentralized electricity production via "utility-in-a-box" solar cells plus battery storage is soon to be less expensive than electricity generation at large centralized facilities and transportation over grids. According to a 2014 Rocky Mountain Institute report, cost parity will arrive as soon as 2020 for tens of millions of commercial and residential customers.[269] With demand-side improvement, cost parity can be achieved even sooner. In less than a decade, many communities will be able to cut the cord entirely to distant utilities.

The Rocky Mountain Institute projections are based on existing technology, but new technology is also being developed. If new technologies reach a degree of maturity soon, cost parity could come faster, or the solar–battery approach could be replaced with less costly or more efficient approaches. For example, new catalytic materials could lead to lower-cost storage devices and less environmental damage.[270] Artificial photosynthesis—nanoparticle structures that mimic tree leaves or forests—could facilitate solar water-splitting to make hydrogen fuel.[271] Hydrogen fuel bypasses the need for battery storage altogether.

Low-carbon sources accounted for 17 percent of the world's total energy supplies in 2010. To successfully address climate change, some experts estimate that their share would have to triple or quadruple by 2050.[272] Demand-side improvements could greatly assist. Using available technologies, the increased efficiency in the transportation, housing, and commercial building sectors could reduce global energy use by more than 70 percent.[273]

LEDDAs could help communities make progress on both the supply and demand sides. Members could help fund utility-in-a-box installations, research in materials science, insulation of existing homes and businesses, and construction of new energy-efficient buildings. Further, the IP pools of Principled Businesses could help ensure that roadblocks to the access and use of new energy-related technologies are removed.

Medical Care and Recreation

The medical care and recreation sectors combined account for about 13 percent of consumer spending. They are considered together here because some types of recreation improve fitness and other types improve psychological well-being. Either way, recreation and medicine are linked—both facilitate wellness, the absence of physical and psychological disease.

There is abundant room for activity in this sector. The U.S. health-care system is the most expensive of all developed nations and yet performs poorly on several basic measures.[274, 275] Bloomberg recently ranked it 46th in the world for efficiency, just behind Iran.[276] The number of general practitioners per capita is low, as is the quality of primary care.[277] As well, both access and quality of care are suboptimal for minority and low-income groups.[278] Costs are rising faster than economic growth, and are on track to contribute to crisis levels of federal debt within the next few decades.[184] Total annual health-care costs for a family of four are now more expensive than groceries.[279]

Further, while the health-care system excels at treating some conditions, its record on promoting wellness and keeping people out of the medical system is rather dismal. The obesity rate is soaring, and with it, rates of diabetes, heart disease, hypertension, stroke, and other chronic diseases.[280, 281] Direct and indirect medical costs attributable to obesity were $147 billion in 2008 alone. If trends continue, half of all Americans will be obese by 2030. Unfortunately, it looks as if trends will continue. Despite a recent report to the contrary, which looked at a small dataset, obesity in children, especially severe obesity, is on the rise.[282]

The four leading causes of death in the United States—heart disease, cancer, respiratory disease, and stroke—are all chronic, non-communicable, and largely preventable diseases. Heart disease alone accounts for one in three deaths, at a cost of more than $300 billion per year in direct medical care and lost productivity.[283] If the major risk factors for chronic diseases were eliminated—if people were supported in making healthier dietary, fitness, smoking, and other lifestyle choices—about 40 percent of cancers and 75 percent of heart disease, stroke, and type 2 diabetes could be prevented.[284] The Centers for Disease Control and Prevention estimates that if national rates of these diseases were brought down simply to the lowest now observed among U.S. states, about 21 percent of premature deaths due to cancer, 34 percent of premature deaths due to heart disease, and 39 percent of premature deaths due to lower respiratory disease could be prevented.[285] By reducing risk factors, Americans could save hundreds of billions of dollars per year in treatment costs and lost productivity, and enjoy healthier, happier, and longer lives.

By way of example, the best-selling drug of all time is Lipitor, a cholesterol-lowering medication. In its peak sales year, 2006, Pfizer sold $13 billion of the product. Yet it appears that preventing heart disease, the end goal of Lipitor, might be done as or more effectively, and certainly more safely and less expensively, through diet and lifestyle changes. A recent large clinical trial suggested that 30 percent of heart attacks, strokes, and deaths from heart disease could be prevented in high-risk people simply by switching to a Mediterranean-style diet.[5][286] A similar reduction in heart disease risk has been claimed for Lipitor, yet some medical professionals believe its effectiveness has been overestimated.[287]

A recent metastudy of results from over 300 randomized controlled trials suggests that physical activity alone rivaled some heart drugs and outperformed stroke medicines.[288] Modeling suggests that simply eating an apple a day could be as effective as statin medications (like Lipitor) for preventing strokes and heart attacks, and would have fewer side effects.[289]

Less than 10 percent of all cancer cases can be attributed to genetic defects; all others have their roots in the environment and lifestyle.[290] In other words, cancer is largely a preventable disease. In one study, men who exercised the most were 68 percent less likely to develop lung cancer and 38 percent less likely to develop colorectal cancers, compared to the least active men. Moreover, for those diagnosed with either cancer, exercise reduced the risk of death.[291] Evidence suggests that healthy diets can also reduce the risk of cancer spread and death after diagnosis, while diets high in saturated and trans fats— found in meat and processed foods—have the opposite effect.[292]

By encouraging members to stop smoking, eat healthy, and exercise, a LEDDA could reduce treatment and drug costs, disease rates, and deaths, and could improve health and well-being. In a study on over 6,000 people, those who made four lifestyle changes— exercising, eating a Mediterranean-style diet, maintaining a normal

---

[5] A Mediterranean diet is characterized by olive oil, fruits, nuts, vegetables, legumes, fish and seafood, and red wine, but low consumption of dairy products and meat.

weight, and quitting cigarettes—reduced their all-causes death rate by 80 percent.[293] Similarly, in a study involving more than 1,000 individuals aged 70 to 90, switching to a Mediterranean diet and healthy lifestyle reduced the all-causes death rate by more than 50 percent.[294] In a study of over 65,000 people, eating seven or more portions of fruit and vegetables daily reduced the risk of death by 42 percent, compared to eating less than one portion.[295]

Just as a LEDDA can promote health by encouraging members to eat more fruits and vegetables, it can reduce disease by discouraging members from eating too many animal products. A study on 6,000 adults suggests that those who eat a diet rich in meat, milk, and cheese during middle age experience a 400 percent increase in cancer death risk and a 175 percent increase in overall death risk, compared to those who eat a low-protein diet.[296]

About 5 percent of the U.S. population eat a vegetarian diet, and about 2 percent eat a vegan diet.[6][297] In a study on more than 70,000 people, the risk for all-cause mortality was 12 percent lower for those who ate any type of vegetarian diet versus non-vegetarian diet.[298] Mortality risk was 19 percent lower for those who ate a vegan versus non-vegetarian diet. Vegetarian/vegan diets have also been shown to reduce risks of hypertension, diabetes, and high blood cholesterol, as well as improve depression, anxiety, work productivity, and quality of life, compared to non-vegetarian diets.[299, 300]

Education and support programs that encourage healthy lifestyle choices are but two of the many ways that LEDDAs could help improve wellness. Members could use the CBFS to fund organic farms and farmers markets, as well as bicycle paths and pedestrian urban designs, as mentioned. That is, they could fund products and environments that support healthy living. Members could also fund parks and fitness centers, as well as clinics, mental health programs, elderly care, and research centers that emphasize preventive medicine.

Further, they could fund programs that reduce hazardous emissions, increase the density of urban forests, or that otherwise reduce urban air pollution. Globally, 2 million deaths per year can be traced to air pollution.[301] Urban forests are protective; a study based on

---

[6] Vegetarian diets typically contain no meat products; vegan diets typically contain no fish or animal products of any kind, including dairy.

data from 15 states concluded that tree loss increases death rates due to cardiovascular and lower respiratory tract illness.[302] Moreover, U.S. urban forests absorb carbon from the atmosphere, and are already producing an estimated $1.5 billion annually in economic benefit.[303]

Members could also fund university research, and use nurture engagements to support students in the health and medical fields. Students in biology, chemistry, psychology, sociology, and other fields that support medicine could also be supported. By using CBFS funds in this way, members could increasingly develop a comprehensive understanding of personal and community wellness.

Members of a LEDDA or group of LEDDAs could also use CBFS funds to provide their own comprehensive health-care plan, ideally one focused on preventive medicine. Already, a single-payer plan has been suggested for New York City; it would function somewhat like Medicare and reportedly save the city $1 billion over three years.[304] Economist Gerald Friedman has recently calculated that a national single-payer "Medicare-for-all"-type program could save the nation more than half a trillion dollars in the first year of operation alone, enough to offer every American improved care at lower cost.[305] A substantial portion of the gains would come from reduced paperwork and negotiated drug prices. A LEDDA or group of LEDDAs could develop a small-scale version of such a program for use at the local level.

Education and Communication

> *"Education is the most powerful weapon which you can use to change the world."*
>
> —Nelson Mandela (1918–2013)

In this and previous chapters, frequent mention has been given to using the CBFS to support students and improve schools and colleges. This could include expansion of academic and research programs in response to LEDDA activities. The LEDDA framework brings to life a novel synthesis of ideas, and entirely new courses in business, finance, political science, and other disciplines would be necessary. The role of education in facilitating the functional aspects of the framework has also been stressed. Education can help members make wiser purchasing and funding choices, as well as disseminate information about how the Token Exchange System and LEDDA economic democracy operate. Further, continued academic research is needed to improve the framework, and discover better solutions to social, economic, and environmental problems.

A LEDDA could also fund new approaches to delivering education. As in nearly all arenas of modern life, new technologies raise new possibilities. In this section, we briefly discuss a complementary means by which a LEDDA might make education more affordable and accessible.

Online distance learning, including Massive Open Online Courses (MOOCs), is one of the most promising new technologies in education access. To provide a few examples, University of the People is a nonprofit online school that offers tuition-free online classes and degrees to underserved students around the globe.[306] The university received accreditation from the Distance Education and Training Council in 2014, and by 2016 expects to enroll 5,000 students.[307] Most courses are taught by volunteer instructors and professors.

Developed by the Massachusetts Institute of Technology and Harvard University, edX offers free university-level courses in a wide variety of disciplines to students around the globe.[308] edX provides certificates of successful completion, but itself does not offer course credit. Schools that partner with edX can offer credit at their discretion. The learning platform, called Open edX, is developed as open-source software with help from Stanford University, Harvard, MIT, Google, and others.[309] Open education is also being advanced by groups such as The OpenCourseWare Consortium, which provides free and open digital publication of high-quality educational materials for use in college courses worldwide.[310]

For-profit groups, such as Coursera and Udacity, are also developing online courses.[311, 312] Although courses are free, fees may be charged for certificates of completion or other services.

A LEDDA or group of LEDDAs could fund traditional education programs, as well as programs that build on the ideas of edX, University of the People, OpenCourseWare Consortium, and others. Alternatively, or in combination, a LEDDA or group of LEDDAs could partner with these organizations to offer new approaches to learning. Moreover, a group of LEDDAs could, if desired, develop its own "open" university, offering courses tailored to the needs of members and the greater community.

10.4   Climate Change and the Environment

"Today, more than ever before, life must be characterized by a sense of Universal responsibility, not only nation to nation and human to human, but also human to other forms of life."
—The 14th Dalai Lama (1935–)

Climate change and environmental problems have been mentioned numerous times in this book. To emphasize the dangers at our doorstep and the need for bold action, this section provides further information.

It is now clear that humans are depleting natural resources at an unsustainable rate.[313] Global fish stocks have all but collapsed; about 85 percent are over-exploited, depleted, or are protected for recovery.[314] Global reserves of numerous strategic minerals, including gold, tin, lead, zinc, silver, and copper, could run out within 20 to 40 years.[315] Even groundwater is running out. A case in point is the once enormous Ogallala aquifer. The Ogallala lies below the Great Plains and is the main source of drinking and irrigation water for large parts of Oklahoma and seven other states. It is being pumped so fast that some geologists fear it could run dry within 25 to 30 years.[316]

Human disturbances of ecological systems increase the risk of ecosystem collapse.[317] To provide a few examples, agricultural runoff in the Mississippi river basin has caused a dead zone the size of New Jersey to form in the Gulf of Mexico.[318] More than 50 percent of U.S. wetlands have been destroyed in the past 200 years.[319] Nearly all ocean fish and shellfish, including tuna, contain traces of mercury.[320, 321] Habitat destruction and pollution, together with climate change, have already caused the extinction rate to spike. Today, for the first time since the dinosaurs disappeared, the species extinction rate is faster than the rate at which new species evolve.[322] Some scientists warn that the next great species die-off could be on the horizon.[323]

Of all environmental challenges, climate change is perhaps the most dangerous. And its effects might not come slowly. A 2013 report by the National Academy of Sciences warns of crossing potential "tipping points" that could induce massive damage within years rather than decades.[324] While the global temperature rise has slowed down in recent years, investigators see this as temporary; long-term predictions remain grim.[325] Researchers speak of an "economic time-bomb" if Arctic warming and loss of sea ice result in a significant release of methane; global costs could run in excess of 60 trillion dollars.[326]

The impacts of climate change are likely to include more frequent and intense droughts, hurricanes, floods, heat waves, and forest fires. Tropical diseases are expect to spread into new areas, and famine is expected to increase. Looking at just one of these, heat, extreme events such as seen in Australia in 2009 are projected to cover quadruple the amount of global land by 2040.[327] Even more extreme events will go from being essentially nonexistent today to covering around 3 percent of the global land surface by 2040. Under a high-emissions scenario, they could cover 60 percent of the global land surface by 2100.

Cities will need to build new levies, improve infrastructure, and provide other types of engineering protections. New York City is planning to spend $20 billion over the coming decades to reduce the impacts of severe weather.[328] Flood management costs alone for 136 U.S. coastal cities are expected to increase by about $50 billion per year.[329] Because flood defenses have been designed for past conditions, even a moderate rise in sea level could lead to soaring losses. And cities and counties will need to rebuild after damage has occurred. The global average temperature has so far risen only a fraction of a degree, yet the frequency of billion-dollar extreme weather events in the U.S. is increasing rapidly. In the 1980s, there was an average of about 1.5 events per year. Today there are close to 10.[330]

Costs are rising exponentially along with the damage, and if this trend continues—as is expected—there may come a point at which debt-burdened national governments are unable to offer cities necessary assistance and relief. Lacking a coherent national policy and fearing for the future, U.S. cities and counties are starting to take the initiative.[331, 332, 333] Michael Bloomberg, while mayor of New York, summarized the situation:

> *National governments have largely failed to act, while cities embody the spirit of innovation we need. When it comes to climate change, cities are where the most exciting progress is being made.*[334]

The viewpoint is widely shared. In its 2014 report, the Intergovernmental Panel on Climate Change (IPCC) stressed the vital role that urban areas can play in cutting greenhouse gas emissions. More than 52 percent of the global population live in urban areas, and urban areas account for as much as 76 percent of energy use and energy-related CO_2 emissions.[335]

LEDDAs can help cities and counties to move forward faster. Highlighting some previous discussions, members could use CBFS funds to support recycling programs, mass transit, pedestrian urban design, the expansion of urban forests, the redesign of products for cradle-to-cradle life cycle and easy upgrade and repair, the insulation of existing buildings and the construction of new energy-inefficient ones, and the installment of distributed electricity-generation systems. Biologists, engineers, and construction workers could be funded to conduct environmental reclamation efforts. Forests could be replanted, agricultural soils rebuilt, and streams and watersheds protected. Infrastructure, including bridges, dams, and levees, could be upgraded. Importantly, the LEDDA framework provides a means by which all of this might be done while strengthening economies, increasing incomes, and achieving full employment.

10.5 Interrelated Problems

It should be clear by now that the major economic, social, and environmental problems facing society are interrelated—diet, health, habitat loss, pollution, aquifer depletion, and climate change provide but one example.

It is generally much more efficient in terms of land, water, fuel, and fertilizer to raise plants for direct human consumption than to raise plants for animal feed, and then to consume the animals.[336]

Moreover, large livestock operations are a major source of ground- and surface-water pollution. In some instances, spills have killed millions of fish.[337] Further, the life cycle and supply chain of raising livestock currently accounts for about 18 percent to 51 percent of total greenhouse gas emissions.[338]

The late environmental scientist Robert Goodland, whose estimate falls at the high end of the range, calculated that replacing just 25 percent of today's livestock products with vegan alternatives could almost completely meet international climate change treaty objectives.[339] Fredrik Hedenus et al. state bluntly that "reduced ruminant meat and dairy consumption will be indispensable for reaching the 2-degree Celsius target with a high probability."[340] Rajendra Pachauri, chair of the Intergovernmental Panel on Climate Change, has recommended vegetarianism as a viable strategy to help mitigate climate change and protect habitat.[341]

Some relationships between diet and health—specifically, low-meat, low-dairy diets and health—have already been discussed. But more connections exist. Two million people in the United States are infected with superbugs each year, and 23,000 die as a result.[342] Superbugs—bacteria resistant to some or all antibiotics—evolve from normal bacterial strains due to the overuse and misuse of antibiotics.

According to the World Health Organization, the problem is so serious that it threatens the achievements of modern medicine.[343] Already, drug-resistant infections are estimated to cost Americans up to $26 billion per year.[344] It may not be long before human suffering and health-care costs rise even more dramatically; diseases once easily treated with antibiotics could soon be lethal.

Dietary choices play a role. About 80 percent of the antibiotics used in the United States are incorporated into feed for cows, pigs, chickens, and other farm animals to help them grow larger.[344] Bacterial resistance can develop both within feedlots and, due to runoff water and waste spills, within the larger environment. By reducing the intake of animal products, and implementing better farming practices and regulation, the use of antibiotics could be expected to fall. Human exposure to contaminated animal products could be expected to fall as well.

In tallying health and environmental expenses, as well as government subsidies, Dave Simon has calculated that the hidden cost of animal food production borne by the U.S. public is more than $400 billion per year.[345] According to Simon, a typical $5 hamburger actually costs American consumers and taxpayers a total of about $13.

Interrelated problems require comprehensive solutions. We can develop an economy that is smart, as suggested in Chapter 8. But this means that we too must become smart, see the big picture, and make wise lifestyle choices. By doing so, we can enjoy better health, greater happiness, stronger economies, and a more vibrant environment.

10.6 Next Steps

This book has outlined the basic ideas of the LEDDA framework, but much work remains. To name a few tasks pending before a live pilot trial can be initiated, it is necessary to conduct academic studies, improve designs, expand models, and develop software. These tasks might be completed within several years, but only with a Herculean effort—and that requires assistance and secure funding. Support from readers and well-wishers is needed, as well as from foundations, corporations, and philanthropists.

On this note, allies might be found within all sectors of society. The following quote is revealing:

> *Business-as-usual cannot get us to sustainability or secure economic and social prosperity; these can be achieved only through radical change, starting now.*

The quote sounds as though it could be a passage from an earlier paragraph of this book, but it is taken from a report titled *Vision 2050: The New Agenda for Business*, authored by the World Business Council for Sustainable Development, a CEO-led organization established to galvanize the global business community to create a sustainable future.[346] Its executive committee contains representatives from Dow Chemical, Shell, ConocoPhillips, and other large corporations. The report itself was co-chaired by current or former executive officers from Alcoa, PricewaterhouseCoopers, Storebrand, and Syngenta.

Among the many other quotable statements in the report, the authors write, "Business leaders will need to manage companies through unprecedented transformational change, in parallel with governments getting the right policies and incentives in place." They talk of incorporating the cost of externalities into accounting systems, starting with carbon and ecosystem services, and of addressing the development needs of the poor, of halting deforestation, and of dramatically reducing the use of all natural resources. Once these calls might have sounded radical, but when executives of multinational corporations make them, they simply sound like good business sense.

The assessments and suggestions in the report are complementary to the proposals contained in this book. In fact, the basis of this book is developing new policies and incentives—the chief difference is that the focus is on implementing them at the local level, rather than federal level, with the direct goal of democratizing the economy and improving well-being.

Allies might also be found in the nonprofit sector, which accounts for roughly 10 percent of the U.S. workforce. In this book it can include schools and colleges, research institutes, charities serving households, public service agencies, churches, and government agencies. But many nonprofit organizations struggle due to lack of funding. In recent years, schools and colleges have suffered from budget cuts and revenue shortfalls, for example. The LEDDA framework can help. Recall that the nonprofit sector doubles in size in the LEDDA Microsimulation Model (Chapter 4). This occurs partly because all new hires in the sector receive ongoing CBFS support at 100 percent of wages. In addition, dollar donations more than double, apart from CBFS funding. The framework has potential to breathe new life into this important sector of the economy.

Philanthropists, too, will likely be moved by the message contained in this book. With a relatively small amount of funding, the framework could produce a radical change in course—a turn from a path that leads over a cliff to one that leads over a bridge. A legacy is waiting to be made.

With your help, development of the LEDDA framework could be smooth and rapid. Please visit the Principled Societies Project at http://www.PrincipledSocietiesProject.org and sign up for our newsletter. The website also provides opportunities, small and large, to get involved. Donations are welcomed.

I end with a quote from American engineer, designer, author, inventor, and visionary R. Buckminster Fuller (1895–1983) that captures the spirit behind the LEDDA framework:

> *You never change things by fighting the existing reality. To change something, build a new model that makes the existing model obsolete.*

About the Author

John Boik is founder of the Principled Societies Project, the organization developing the Local Economic Direct Democracy Association (LEDDA) framework. Boik received a B.S. in civil engineering from the University of Colorado, Boulder; a master's degree in acupuncture and Oriental medicine from Oregon College of Oriental Medicine, Portland, Oregon; and a Ph.D. in biomedical sciences from the University of Texas, Health Sciences Center, Houston. He completed postdoctoral work at Stanford University, in the Department of Statistics.

References

[1]   U. S. Geological Survey. Forecasting California's Earthquakes—What Can
        We Expect in the Next 30 Years?. 2008. URL:
        http://pubs.usgs.gov/fs/2008/3027/.

[2]   C. Solberg, T. Rossetto, H. Joffe. The Social Psychology of Seismic Hazard
        Adjustment: Re-evaluating the International Literature. Natural Hazards and
        Earth System Sciences. 2010;10:1663–1677. URL:
        http://www.nat-hazards-earth-syst-sci.net/10/1663/2010/
        nhess-10-1663-2010.html.

[3]   World Bank. Turn Down the Heat: Why a 4 Degree Celsius Warmer World
        Must be Avoided. 2012. URL:
        http://documents.worldbank.org/curated/en/2012/11/17097815/
        turn-down-heat-4%C2%B0c-warmer-world-must-avoided.

[4]   Intergovernmental Panel on Climate Change. Climate Change 2007:
        Synthesis Report. 2007. URL:
        http://www.ipcc.ch/publications_and_data/publications_ipcc_
        fourth_assessment_report_synthesis_report.htm.

[5]   Intergovernmental Panel on Climate Change. Climate Change 2014:
        Impacts, Adaptation, and Vulnerability. 2014. Summary for Policymakers.
        Fifth Assessment Report (AR5). URL: http://ipcc-wg2.gov/AR5/
        images/uploads/IPCC_WG2AR5_SPM_Approved.pdf.

[6]   Matt McGrath. Climate Inaction Catastrophic—US. 2014. BBC News.
        URL: http://www.bbc.com/news/science-environment-26824943.

[7]   Reuters. The Unequal State of America: Why America is More Unequal
        Than Most. 2012. URL: http://www.reuters.com/article/2012/12/
        20/us-equality-indiana-oecd-idUSBRE8BJ0J520121220.

[8]   Robert Frank. Billionaires Own as Much as the Bottom Half of Americans?.
        2011. Wall Street Journal. URL:
        http://blogs.wsj.com/wealth/search/billionaires%20own%20as%
        20much%20as%20the%20bottom%20half%20of%20americans/?s=
        billionaires+own+as+much+as+the+bottom+half+of+americans.

[9]   Oxfam International. Working for the Few: Political Capture and Economic
        Inequality. 2014. URL:
        http://www.oxfam.org/sites/www.oxfam.org/files/
        bp-working-for-few-political-capture-economic-inequality%
        2D200114-summ-en.pdf.

[10]   Jason DeParle, Robert Gebeloff, Sabrina Tavernise. Older, Suburban and
        Struggling, 'Near Poor' Startle the Census. 2011. New York Times. URL:
        http://www.nytimes.com/2011/11/19/us/
        census-measures-those-not-quite-in-poverty-but%
        2Dstruggling.html.

[11]   Associated Press. Census Shows 1 in 2 People are Poor or Low-Income.
        2011. USA Today. URL: http://usatoday30.usatoday.com/news/
        nation/story/2011-12-15/poor-census-low-income/51944034/1.

[12]   Byron Tau. Obama: Big Money Helps Cause Washington Gridlock. 2013.
        Politico. URL: http://www.politico.com/story/2013/10/
        obama-big-money-politics-washington-gridlock-97999.html.

[13]   Drew DeSilver. Congress Ends Least-Productive Year in Recent History.
        2013. Pew Research Center. URL:
        http://www.pewresearch.org/fact-tank/2013/12/23/
        congress-ends-least-productive-year-in-recent-history/.

[14]   Rasmussen Reports. 70% Say Big Government and Big Business on the
        Same Team. 2009. URL: http://www.rasmussenreports.com/public_
        content/business/general_business/april_2009/70_say_big_
        government_and_big_business_on_the_same_team.

[15]   Gallup. Confidence in Institutions. 2013. URL: http:
        //www.gallup.com/poll/1597/confidence-institutions.aspx.

[16]   John Christoffersen. Robert Shiller: Income Inequality Is 'Most Important
        Problem'. 2013. URL: http://www.huffingtonpost.com/2013/10/15/
        shiller-income-inequality-problem_n_4100509.html?ncid=
        txtlnkushpmg00000029.

[17]   Bruce Katz, Jennifer Bradley. How Cities Are Fixing America. 2013. The
        Daily Beast. URL: http://www.thedailybeast.com/articles/2013/
        06/17/how-cities-are-fixing-america.html.

[18]   William Darity. International Encyclopedia of the Social Sciences.
        Macmillan Reference USA/Thomson Gale. 2008. URL:
        http://www.encyclopedia.com/topic/economics.aspx#1.

[19] Henry George. The Science of Political Economy. Robert Schalkenbach Foundation. 2004. URL:
http://www.politicaleconomy.org/speindex.html.

[20] Office of Management and Budget. OMB Bulletin NO. 10-02, Update of Statistical Area Definitions and Guidance on Their Uses. 2009. URL:
http://www.whitehouse.gov/sites/default/files/omb/assets/bulletins/b10-02.pdf.

[21] John C. Boik. Can Local Currencies Help Advance Global Sustainability?. 2013. The Guardian. URL:
http://www.guardian.co.uk/sustainable-business/can-local-currencies-advance-global-sustainability.

[22] John C. Boik. Can Local Currencies Be the Foundation for the Sharing Economy?. 2013. Sharable. URL: http://www.shareable.net/blog/local-currencies-as-a-foundation-for-the-sharing-economy.

[23] John C. Boik. Weathering Climate Change: The Role of Local Currencies. 2013. Stanford Social Innovation Review. URL:
http://www.ssireview.org/blog/entry/weathering_climate_change_the_role_of_local_currencies.

[24] John C. Boik. First Microsimulation Model of a LEDDA Community Currency–Dollar Economy. 2014. Working Paper 0001, Principled Societies Project. URL: http://ideas.repec.org/p/psp/wpaper/0001.html.

[25] Dustin R. Rubenstein, James Kealey. Cooperation, Conflict, and the Evolution of Complex Animal Societies. 2012. Nature Education. URL:
http://www.nature.com/scitable/knowledge/library/cooperation-conflict-and-the-evolution-of-complex-13236526.

[26] J. E. Strassmann, O. M. Gilbert, D. C. Queller. Kin Discrimination and Cooperation in Microbes. Annual Review of Microbiology. 2011;65:349–367. URL:
http://www.ncbi.nlm.nih.gov/pubmed/21682642.

[27] A. Gardner, J. J. Welch. A Formal Theory of the Selfish Gene. Journal of Evolutionary Biology. 2011;24(8):1801–13. URL:
http://www.ncbi.nlm.nih.gov/pubmed/21605218.

[28] Kristin Ohlson. The Cooperation Instinct. 2012. Discover Magazine. URL:
http://discovermagazine.com/2012/dec/29-cooperation#.UZ5vDNdLHgU.

[29] University of California B. Social Scientists Build Case for 'Survival of The Kindest'. 2009. Science Daily. URL: http://www.sciencedaily.com/releases/2009/12/091208155309.htm.

[30] Elizabeth Svoboda. Hard-Wired for Giving. 2013. Wall Street Journal. URL: http://online.wsj.com/news/articles/ SB10001424127887324009304579041231971683854.

[31] JoAnna Wendel. Epigenetics Sheds New Light on Altruism. 2013. Genetic Literacy Project. URL: http://www.geneticliteracyproject.org/2013/09/10/ epigenetics-sheds-new-light-on-altruism/#.UrBgMkMlHiw.

[32] Louis Putterman. The Good, The Bad, and The Economy: Does Human Nature Rule Out a Better World? Langdon Street Press. 2012. URL: http: //www.amazon.com/The-Good-Bad-Economy-Nature/dp/193829601X.

[33] Adam Smith. The Theory of Moral Sentiments. London: A. Millar. 1759. URL: http://www.econlib.org/library/Smith/smMS.html.

[34] Adam Smith. An Inquiry Into the Nature and Causes of the Wealth of Nations. London: Methuen & Co., Ltd. 1776. URL: http://www.econlib.org/library/Smith/smWN.html.

[35] Joseph E. Stiglitz, Bruce C. Greenwald. Externalities in Economies With Imperfect Information and Incomplete Markets. Quarterly Journal of Economics. 1986;101:229–264. URL: https://academiccommons.columbia.edu/catalog/ac%3A148226.

[36] John Rawls. A Theory of Justice (revised edition). Belknap Press. 1999. URL: http: //www.amazon.com/A-Theory-Justice-John-Rawls/dp/0674000781.

[37] John Rawls. Political Liberalism (expanded edition). 2nd ed. Columbia University Press. 2005. URL: http://www.amazon.com/ Political-Liberalism-Expanded-Columbia-Philosophy/dp/ 0231130899.

[38] Amartya Sen. The Idea of Justice. Harvard University Press. 2009. URL: http://www.amazon.com/Development-as-Freedom-Amartya-Sen/ dp/0385720270.

[39] Kenneth Joseph Arrow. Social Choice and Individual Values. 3rd ed. Yale University Press. 2012. URL: http://www.amazon.com/ Social-Choice-Individual-Values-Foundation/dp/0300179316.

[40] United Nations Development Programme. Human Development Index (HDI). 2014. URL: http://hdr.undp.org/en/statistics/hdi.

[41] Elizabeth Dickinson. GDP: A Brief History. 2011. Foreign Policy. URL: http://www.foreignpolicy.com/articles/2011/01/02/gdp_a_ brief_history.

[42] Lorenzo Fioramonti. Gross Domestic Problem. Zed Books. 2013. URL: http://www.zedbooks.co.uk/paperback/gross-domestic-problem.

[43] Joseph E. Stiglitz, Amartya Sen, Jean-Paul Fitoussi. Report of the Commission on the Measurement of Economic Performance and Social Progress. 2009. URL: http://www.stiglitz-sen-fitoussi.fr/documents/rapport_anglais.pdf.

[44] Cedric Afsa, Didier Blanchet, Vincent Marcus, Pierre-Alain Pionnier, Laurence Rioux, Marco Mira d'Ercole, et al.. Survey of Existing Approaches to Measuring Socio-Economic Progress. 2008. Commission on the Measurement of Economic Performance and social Progress. URL: http://www.stiglitz-sen-fitoussi.fr/documents/Survey_of_Existing_Approaches_to_Measuring_Socio-Economic_Progress.pdf.

[45] Howard Silverman. Proxy Voting Platforms for Liquid Democracy. 2012. Solving for Pattern. URL: http://www.solvingforpattern.org/2012/10/02/proxy-voting-liquid-democracy/.

[46] Bryan Ford. Delegative Democracy. 2002. URL: http://www.brynosaurus.com/deleg/.

[47] Metagovernment. Homepage. 2014. URL: http://www.metagovernment.org/wiki/Main_Page.

[48] LiquidFeedback. Homepage. 2014. URL: http://liquidfeedback.org/.

[49] Fredreka Schouten, Gregory Korte, Christopher Schnaars. 25% of Super PAC Money Coming From Just 5 Rich Donors. 2012. USA Today. URL: http://www.usatoday.com/news/politics/story/2012-02-21/super-pac-donors/53196658/1.

[50] Eric Lipton, Ben Protess. Banks' Lobbyists Help in Drafting Financial Bills. 2013. New York Times. URL: http://dealbook.nytimes.com/2013/05/23/banks-lobbyists-help-in-drafting-financial-bills.

[51] Open Secrets. Washington Lobbying Grew to $3.2 Billion Last Year, Despite Economy. 2009. URL: http://www.opensecrets.org/news/2009/01/washington-lobbying-grew-to-32.html.

[52] Open Secrets. Where the Money Came From. 2011. URL: http://www.opensecrets.org/bigpicture/wherefrom.php?cycle=2010.

[53] Open Secrets. Revolving Door. 2013. URL: http://www.opensecrets.org/revolving/.

[54] Martin Gilens, Benjamin I. Page. Testing Theories of American Politics: Elites, Interest Groups, and Average Citizens. 2014. Perspectives on Politics, forthcoming Fall 2014. URL: http://www.princeton.edu/~mgilens/Gilens%20homepage%20materials/Gilens%20and%20Page/Gilens%20and%20Page%202014-Testing%20Theories%203-7-14.pdf.

[55] G. William Domhoff. Who Rules America? The Triumph of the Corporate Rich. 7th ed. McGraw-Hill Humanities/Social Sciences/Languages. 2013. URL: http://www.amazon.com/Rules-America-Triumph-Corporate-Rich/dp/0078026717.

[56] GovTrack US. Bills and Resolutions. 2012. URL: http://www.govtrack.us/congress/bills/.

[57] Deliberative Democracy Consortium. Homepage. 2014. URL: http://www.deliberative-democracy.net/.

[58] Open Plans. Home Page. 2014. URL: http://openplans.org/.

[59] Open Secrets. Homepage. 2014. URL: http://www.opensecrets.org/.

[60] Sunlight Foundation. Homepage. 2014. URL: http://sunlightfoundation.com/.

[61] Melissa Mark-Viverito. Participatory Budgeting in Year Two: Reinvigorating Local Democracy in NYC. 2013. Huffington Post. URL: http://www.huffingtonpost.com/melissa-markviverito/participatory-budgeting-nyc_b_2492156.html.

[62] Participatory Budgeting in New York City. Homepage. 2014. URL: http://pbnyc.org/.

[63] Rasmussen Reports. 60% Say Federal Government Does Not Have the Consent of the Governed. 2012. URL: http://www.rasmussenreports.com/public_content/politics/general_politics/october_2012/60_say_federal_government_does_not_have_the_consent_of_the_governed.

[64] Sean Di Somma. 2013 Proxy Season Preview: Key Shareholder Proposals. 2013. Harvard Law School. URL: http://blogs.law.harvard.edu/corpgov/2013/03/21/2013-proxy-season-preview-key-shareholder-proposals/.

[65] Andrew Behar. Record Number of Social and Environmental Shareholder Resolutions Filed in 2014. 2014. Tripple Pundit. URL: http://bit.ly/1hxRPBS.

[66] Clare O'Connor. New App Lets You Boycott Koch Brothers, Monsanto And More By Scanning Your Shopping Cart. 2013. Forbes. URL: http://www.forbes.com/sites/clareoconnor/2013/05/14/new-app-lets-you-boycott-koch-brothers-monsanto-and-more-by%2Dscanning-your-shopping-cart/.

[67] Joseph Rotella, Dennis Van Roekel. How Everyone Else Pays for Big Business's Tax Breaks. 2012. US News. URL: http://www.usnews.com/opinion/articles/2012/04/05/how-everyone-else-pays-for-big-businesss-tax-breaks.

[68] Paula Dutko, Michele Ver Ploeg, Tracey Farrigan. Characteristics and Influential Factors of Food Deserts. 2012. USDA Economic Research Report No. (ERR-140). URL: http://www.ers.usda.gov/publications/err-economic-research-report/err140.aspx#.Uz2LCfglHiw.

[69] U. S. Census. DP03: Selected Economic Characteristics, 2011 ACS. 2014. American Factfinder. URL: http://factfinder2.census.gov/faces/tableservices/jsf/pages/productview.xhtml?pid=ACS_11_1YR_DP03&prodType=table.

[70] Debbie Bocian, Delvin Davis, Sonia Garrison, Bill Sermons. The State of Lending in America & its Impact on U.S. Households. 2012. Center for Responsible Lending. URL: http://www.responsiblelending.org/state-of-lending/State-of-Lending-report-1.pdf.

[71] Phil Izzo. Nearly Half of Americans Are 'Financially Fragile'. 2011. URL: http://blogs.wsj.com/economics/2011/05/23/nearly-half-of-americans-are-financially-fragile/.

[72] Stacy Mitchell. 2014 Independent Business Survey. 2014. Institute for Local Self-Reliance. URL: http://www.ilsr.org/2014-survey/.

[73] John Tozzi. Investing in Main Street Instead of Just Wall Street. 2012. BusinessWeek. URL: http://www.businessweek.com/articles/2012-04-25/investing-in-main-street-instead-of-just-wall-street.

[74] Slow Money. Homepage. 2014. URL: http://slowmoney.org/.

[75] Eric Mack. Obama Crowdfunding Bill Signing. 2012. Crowdsourcing.org. URL: http://www.crowdsourcing.org/editorial/obama-crowdfunding-bill-signing-/13174.

[76] org C. ccDatabase. 2014. URL: http://www.complementarycurrency.org/ccDatabase/les_public.html.

[77] Bernard Lietaer, Jacqui Dunne. Rethinking Money: How New Currencies Turn Scarcity into Prosperity. Berrett-Koehler Publishers. 2013. URL: http://www.amazon.com/Rethinking-Money-Currencies-Scarcity-Prosperity/dp/1609942965.

[78] Georgina M. Gómez. Making Markets: The Institutional Rise and Decline of the Argentine Red de Trueque. 2008. Doctoral thesis, Institute of Social Studies: The Hague (NL). URL: http://78.46.126.155/Record/1612.

[79] De la Rosa JL, Stodder J. On the Velocity in Several Complementary Currencies. 2013. 2nd International Conference on Complementary and Community Currencies Systems, The Hague. URL: http://www.iss.nl/fileadmin/ASSETS/iss/Research_and_projects/Conferences/CCS_June_2013/Papers/Josep_Lluis_de_la_Rosa.pdf.

[80] Federal Reserve Bank of St. Louis. Loans and Leases in Bank Credit, All Commercial Banks (LOANSNSA). 2014. FRED Economic Data. URL: http://research.stlouisfed.org/fred2/series/LOANSNSA.

[81] American Society of Civil Engineers. 2013 Report Card for America's Infrastructure. 2013. URL: http://www.infrastructurereportcard.org/a/#p/grade-sheet/gpa.

[82] Alex Morales. Climate Protection May Cut World GDP 4% by 2030, UN Says. 2014. Bloomberg. URL: http://www.bloomberg.com/news/2014-01-16/climate-protection-may-cost-4-of-world-gdp-by-2030.html.

[83] Congressional Budget Office. The Distribution of Major Tax Expenditures in the Individual Income Tax System. 2013. URL: http://www.cbo.gov/sites/default/files/cbofiles/attachments/43768_DistributionTaxExpenditures.pdf.

[84] Federal Reserve. 2010 Survey of Consumer Finances. 2013. URL: http://www.federalreserve.gov/econresdata/scf/scf_2010.htm.

[85] Michael I. Norton, Dan Ariely. Building a Better America—One Wealth Quintile at a Time. 2010. URL: http://www.people.hbs.edu/mnorton/norton%20ariely%20in%20press.pdf.

[86] John Talberth. Report: Closing the Inequality Divide. 2013. Center for Sustainable Economy. URL: http://www.ips-dc.org/reports/closing_the_inequality_divide.

[87] Internal Revenue Service. SOI-Tax Stats-Top 400 Individual Income Tax Returns With the Largest Adjusted Gross Incomes. 2013. URL: http://www.irs.gov/uac/SOI-Tax-Stats-Top-400-Individual-Income-Tax-Returns-with%2Dthe-Largest-Adjusted-Gross-Incomes.

[88] Central Intelligence Agency. World Factbook. Distribution of Family Income–Gini Index. 2011. URL: https://www.cia.gov/library/publications/the-world-factbook/fields/2172.html.

[89] Safa Motesharrei, Jorge Rivas, Eugenia Kalnay. Human and Nature Dynamics (HANDY): Modeling Inequality and Use of Resources in the Collapse Or Sustainability of Societies. Ecological Economics. 2014;URL: http://www.sciencedirect.com/science/article/pii/S0921800914000615.

[90] Julianne Pepitone. Forbes 400: The Super-Rich Get Richer. 2010. CNNMoney. URL: http://money.cnn.com/2010/09/22/news/companies/forbes_400/.

[91]   Matthew C. Murray, Carole Pateman. Basic Income Worldwide: Horizons of Reform. International Political Economy. 2012. URL: http://www.amazon.com/Basic-Income-Worldwide-International-Political/dp/0230285422.

[92]   Annie Lowrey. Switzerland's Proposal to Pay People For Being Alive. 2013. New York Times. URL: http://www.nytimes.com/2013/11/17/magazine/switzerlands-proposal-to-pay-people-for-being-alive.html.

[93]   Jason DeParle. Harder for Americans to Rise From Lower Rungs. 2012. New York Times. URL: http://www.nytimes.com/2012/01/05/us/harder-for-americans-to-rise-from-lower-rungs.html.

[94]   Miles Corak. Income Inequality, Equality of Opportunity, and Intergenerational Mobility. Journal of Economic Perspectives. 2013;27(3):79–102. URL: http://www.aeaweb.org/articles.php?doi=10.1257/jep.27.3.79.

[95]   Corporation for National and Community Service. In Tough Times, Volunteering in America Remains Strong. 2009. URL: http://www.nationalservice.gov/about/newsroom/releases_detail.asp?tbl_pr_id=1426.

[96]   Masahiko Suzuki. "Would They Be Lazier or Work Harder Given Free Money?": The Namibia BIG Pilot Project and the Possibility of Basic Income as a Strategy of Social Cooperation. Journal of Political Science & Sociology. 2011;14:53–80. URL: http://koara.lib.keio.ac.jp/xoonips/modules/xoonips/download.php?file_id=50968.

[97]   Tomas Chamorro-Premuzic. Does Money Really Affect Motivation? A Review of the Research. 2013. Harvard Business Review. URL: http://blogs.hbr.org/2013/04/does-money-really-affect-motiv/.

[98]   Daniel H. Pink. Drive: The Surprising Truth About What Motivates Us. Riverhead Books. 2011. URL: http://www.amazon.com/Drive-Surprising-Truth-About-Motivates/dp/1594484805.

[99]   Ryan RM, Deci EL. Self-Determination Theory and the Facilitation of Intrinsic Motivation, Social Development, and Well-Being. American Psychologist. 2000;55:68–78. URL: http://psycnet.apa.org/index.cfm?fa=buy.optionToBuy&id=2000-13324-007.

[100]   Neel Burton. Our Hierarchy of Needs. Psychology Today. 2012;URL: http://www.psychologytoday.com/blog/hide-and-seek/201205/our-hierarchy-needs.

[101]   Daniel Kahneman, Angus Deaton. High Income Improves Evaluation of Life but Not Emotional Well-Being. PNAS. 2010;URL: http://www.pnas.org/content/early/2010/08/27/1011492107.abstract?sid=ab0a6073-400b-41b6-9a5d-e7384363ec75.

[102] Eugenio Proto, Aldo Rustichini. A Reassessment of the Relationship Between GDP and Life Satisfaction. PLoS ONE. 2013;8(11):e79358. URL: http://www.sciencedaily.com/releases/2013/11/131127225439.htm.

[103] John Bates Clark. The Distribution of Wealth: A Theory of Wages, Interest and Profits. The Macmillan Company. 1908. URL: http://www.econlib.org/library/Clark/clkDW0.html.

[104] Douglas Vickers. Economics and Ethics: An Introduction to Theory, Institutions, and Policy. Praeger. 1997. URL: http://www.amazon.com/Economics-Ethics-Introduction-Theory-Institutions/dp/0275959791.

[105] Frank Thompson. Morally Arbitrary Economic Advantage. 2013. Thomas Weisskopf Festschrift Conference Paper. URL: http://www.peri.umass.edu/236/hash/1316e5c326f174efa4ca748c76815953/publication/572/.

[106] AFL-CIO. Trends in CEO Pay. 2012. URL: http://www.aflcio.org/Corporate-Watch/CEO-Pay-and-the-99/Trends-in-CEO-Pay.

[107] Al Lewis. Fraud, Failure and Bankruptcy Pay Well for CEOs. 2013. Market Watch. URL: http://www.marketwatch.com/story/fraud-failure-and-bankruptcy-pay-well-for-ceos-2013-08-28.

[108] Bureau of Labor Statistics. May 2013 National Occupational Employment and Wage Estimates, United States. 2013. URL: http://www.bls.gov/oes/current/oes_nat.htm.

[109] Blake Ellis. Female Grads Earn $8,000 Less Than Men. 2012. CNN Money. URL: http://money.cnn.com/2012/10/23/pf/college/women-men-pay-gap/.

[110] Andrew G. Berg, Jonathan D. Ostry. Equality and Efficiency. 2011. Finance and Development. URL: http://www.imf.org/external/pubs/ft/fandd/2011/09/Berg.htm.

[111] Annie Lowrey. Income Inequality May Take Toll on Growth. 2012. New York Times. URL: http://www.nytimes.com/2012/10/17/business/economy/income-inequality-may-take-toll-on-growth.html.

[112] David Cooper, W. David McCausland, Ioannis Theodossiou. Income Inequality and Well-Being: The Plight of the Poor and the Curse of Permanent Inequality. Journal of Economic Issues. 2013;XLVII(4). URL: http://ideas.repec.org/a/mes/jeciss/v47y2013i4p939-958.html.

[113] Bureau of Labor Statistics. Table A-1. Employment Status of the Civilian Population by Sex and Age. 2014. URL: http://www.bls.gov/news.release/empsit.t01.htm.

[114] Bureau of Labor Statistics. Table A-15. Alternative Measures of Labor Underutilization. 2014. URL:
http://www.bls.gov/news.release/empsit.t15.htm.

[115] Depression Script. Homepage. 2014. URL:
http://www.depressionscrip.com/.

[116] Alex Von Muralt. The Worgel Experiment With Depreciating Money. 1934. Annals of Collective Economy. URL:
http://monetary-freedom.net/reinventingmoney/muralt-worgl_experiment_depreciating_money.html.

[117] Margrit Kennedy, Declan Kennedy. Interest and Inflation Free Money: Creating an Exchange Medium That Works for Everybody and Protects the Earth. Inbook. 1995. URL: http://www.amazon.com/Interest-Inflation-Free-Money-Everybody/dp/0964302500.

[118] Gwendolyn Hallsmith, Bernard Lietaer. Creating Wealth: Growing Local Economies With Local Currencies. New Society Publishers. 2011. URL:
http://www.amazon.com/Creating-Wealth-Growing-Economies-Currencies/dp/0865716676.

[119] Thomas H. Greco. The End of Money and the Future of Civilization. Chelsea Green Publishing. 2009. URL: http://www.amazon.com/End-Money-Future-Civilization/dp/1603580786.

[120] Charles Eisenstein. Sacred Economics: Money, Gift, and Society in the Age of Transition. Evolver Editions. 2011. URL: http://www.amazon.com/Sacred-Economics-Money-Society-Transition/dp/1583943978.

[121] Bernard Lietaer, Stephen Belgin. New Money for a New World. Qiterra Press. 2011. URL:
http://www.amazon.com/New-Money-World-ebook/dp/B006MXZBR6.

[122] Thomas H. Greco. Money: Understanding and Creating Alternatives to Legal Tender. Chelsea Green. 2001. URL: http://www.amazon.com/Money-Understanding-Creating-Alternatives-Tender/dp/1890132373.

[123] Sally J. Goerner, Bernard Lietaer, Robert E. Ulanowicz. Quantifying Economic Sustainability: Implications for Free-Enterprise Theory, Policy and Practice. 2009. Ecological Economics. URL: http://www.sciencedirect.com/science/article/pii/S0921800909003085.

[124] Stephen DeMeulenaere, Albert Flode. Online Database of Complementary Currencies Worldwide. 2014. ComplementaryCurrency.org. URL: http://www.complementarycurrency.org/ccDatabase/les_public.html.

[125] Jens Martignoni. A New Approach to a Typology of Complementary Currencies. International Journal of Community Currency Research. 2012;16:A1–A17. URL: http://ijccr.files.wordpress.com/2012/04/ijccr-2012-martignoni.pdf.

[126] Paul Glover. Creating Community Economics With Local Currency. 2011. URL: http://www.paulglover.org/hourintro.html.

[127] BerkShares. Homepage. 2014. URL: http://www.berkshares.org/.

[128] Lee Romney. Unified by the Coin of Their Realm. 2012. Los Angles Times. URL: http://articles.latimes.com/2012/feb/06/local/la-me-bernal-bucks-20120206.

[129] Bay Bucks. Homepage. 2014. URL: http://www.bay-bucks.com/.

[130] Bristol Pound. Homepage. 2014. URL: http://bristolpound.org/.

[131] Steven Morris. Mayor to Take Salary in Bristol Pounds. 2012. The Guardian. URL: http://www.theguardian.com/uk/2012/nov/20/mayor-salary-bristol-pounds.

[132] Elizabeth Fry. One Year On, Bristol Pound is Helping Put City on the Map. 2013. Bristol Post. URL: http://www.bristolpost.co.uk/year-Bristol-Pound-helping-city-map/story-19708463-detail/story.html.

[133] Mariana Colacelli, David J. H. Blackburn. Secondary Currency: An Empirical Analysis. Journal of Monetary Economics. 2009;53(3). URL: http://la-macro.vassar.edu/SecondaryCurrency.pdf.

[134] Bitcoin. Homepage. 2014. URL: http://bitcoin.org/.

[135] Peter J. Henning. For Bitcoin, Square Peg Meets Round Hole Under the Law. 2013. New York Times. URL: http://dealbook.nytimes.com/2013/12/09/for-bitcoin-square-peg-meets-round-hole-under-the-law/.

[136] Nicole Perlroth. Unlike Liberty Reserve, Bitcoin Is Not Anonymous—Yet. 2013. New York Times. URL: http://bits.blogs.nytimes.com/2013/05/29/bitcoin-is-not-anonymous-but-it-could-be/.

[137] Denver Nicks. The European Union Has Issued A Warning About Buying Bitcoin. 2013. Time: Business and Money. URL: http://business.time.com/2013/12/13/europe-warns-of-bitcoin-dangers/.

[138] Jon Matonis. Top 10 Bitcoin Merchant Sites. 2013. Forbes. URL: http://www.forbes.com/sites/jonmatonis/2013/05/24/top-10-bitcoin-merchant-sites/.

[139] Timothy B. Lee. This Senate Hearing is a Bitcoin Lovefest. 2013. The Washinton Post. URL: http://www.washingtonpost.com/blogs/the-switch/wp/2013/11/18/this-senate-hearing-is-a-bitcoin-lovefest/.

[140] Bernard Lietaer. Community Currency Guide. 2009. URL: http://www.lietaer.com/2009/12/community-currency-guide/.

[141] Smarter Travel. Best New Frequent Flyer Development. 2011. URL: http://www.smartertravel.com/travel-advice/editors-choice-awards-2011-best-new-frequent-flyer%2Ddevelopment.html?id=7680666.

[142] Economist. Frequent-Flyer Miles: In Terminal Decline?. 2005. Economist. URL: http://www.economist.com/node/3536178?story_id=E1_PVPGTSR.

[143] Public Banking Institute. Homepage. 2014;URL: http://publicbankinginstitute.org.

[144] National Credit Union Administration. Homepage. 2014;URL: http://www.ncua.gov/.

[145] Cyclos. Homepage. 2014. URL: http://www.cyclos.org/.

[146] Michael McLeay, Amar Radia, Ryland Thomas. Money Creation in the Modern Economy. 2014. Bank of England Quarterly Bulletin Q1. URL: http://www.bankofengland.co.uk/publications/Documents/quarterlybulletin/2014/qb14q1prereleasemoneycreation.pdf.

[147] Biz2Credit. Biz2Credit Small Business Lending Index Reports New High in Big Bank Loan Approvals in February 2013. 2013. URL: http://www.biz2credit.com/pressroom/small-business-lending-index-february-2013.html.

[148] Patrick Clark. Big Banks, Credit Cards, and Small Business Lending. 2013. Businessweek. URL: http://www.businessweek.com/articles/2013-06-04/big-banks-credit-cards-and-small-business-lending.

[149] Lewis D. Solomon. Rethinking Our Centralized Monetary System. Praeger Publishers. 1996. URL: http://www.amazon.com/Rethinking-our-Centralized-Monetary-System/dp/0275953769.

[150] KickStarter. 2011: The Stats. 2012. URL: http://www.kickstarter.com/blog/2011-the-stats.

[151] Eugene Steuerle. Blurring the Line Between Charities and Businesses. 2007. Washington Post. URL: http://www.washingtonpost.com/wp-dyn/content/article/2007/10/07/AR2007100701167.html.

[152] United Nations. International Year of Cooperatives 2012. 2012. URL:
http://social.un.org/coopsyear/.

[153] International Co-operative Alliance. Homepage. 2014. URL:
http://ica.coop/en.

[154] Kevin Zeese, Margaret Flowers. The Foundation of a New Democratic
Economy Is Worker Self-Directed Enterprises. 2013. TruthOut. URL:
http://truth-out.org/opinion/item/
13823-the-foundation-of-a-new-democratic-economy-is%
2Dworker-self-directed-enterprises.

[155] Robert Reich. Supercapitalism: The Transformation of Business,
Democracy, and Everyday Life. Vintage. 2008. URL:
http://www.amazon.com/
Supercapitalism-Transformation-Business-Democracy-Everyday/
dp/0307277992.

[156] Joseph Stiglitz. Making Globalization Work. W. W. Norton & Company.
2007. URL: http://www.amazon.com/
Making-Globalization-Work-Joseph-Stiglitz/dp/0393330281.

[157] National Philanthropy Trust. Philanthropy Statistics. 2013. URL:
http://www.nptrust.org/philanthropic-resources/
charitable-giving-statistics.

[158] William Domhoff. Wealth, Income, and Power. 2014. URL: http:
//sociology.ucsc.edu/whorulesamerica/power/wealth.html.

[159] Thomas Piketty. Capital in the Twenty-First Century. Belknap Press. 2014.
URL: http://www.amazon.com/
Capital-Twenty-First-Century-Thomas-Piketty/dp/067443000X.

[160] Bruce Upbin. The 147 Companies That Control Everything. 2011. Forbes.
URL: http://www.forbes.com/sites/bruceupbin/2011/10/22/
the-147-companies-that-control-everything/.

[161] Rasmussen Reports. 68% Believe Government and Big Business Work
Together Against the Rest of Us. 2011. URL:
http://www.rasmussenreports.com/public_content/politics/
general%5Fpolitics/february%5F2011/68_believe_government%
5Fand_big_business_work_together%5Fagainst_the_rest_of_us.

[162] Stephanie Strom. A Quest for Hybrid Companies That Profit, but Can Tap
Charity. 2011. New York Times. URL:
http://www.nytimes.com/2011/10/13/business/
a-quest-for-hybrid-companies-part-money-maker-part%
2Dnonprofit.html.

[163] Sheila Shayon. California Law Creates New "Flexible Purpose" Category of Positive Impact Corporation. 2011. BrandChannel. URL: http://www.brandchannel.com/home/post/2011/10/17/ California-Law-Creates-New-Category-of-Positive% 2DImpact-Corporation.aspx.

[164] Muhammad Yunus. Creating a World Without Poverty: Social Business and the Future of Capitalism. PublicAffairs. 2009. URL: http://www.amazon.com/ Creating-World-Without-Poverty-Capitalism/dp/1586486675.

[165] Grameen Creative Lab. Homepage. 2014. URL: http://www.grameencreativelab.com/.

[166] Muhammad Yunus. Building Social Business: The New Kind of Capitalism That Serves Humanity's Most Pressing Needs. PublicAffairs. 2010. URL: http://www.amazon.com/ Building-Social-Business-Capitalism-Humanitys/dp/ B004LQ0E7I.

[167] Urban Institute. Nonprofits. 2014;URL: http://www.urban.org/nonprofits/.

[168] Congressional Research Service. An Overview of the Nonprofit and Charitable Sector. 2009. URL: http://www.fas.org/sgp/crs/misc/R40919.pdf.

[169] P2Pfoundation. Homepage. 2014. URL: http://p2pfoundation.net/.

[170] Michel Bauwens. FLOK Project Research Plan. 2014. URL: http://en.wiki.floksociety.org/w/Research_Plan.

[171] Kiva. Latest Statistics. 2012. URL: http://www.kiva.org/about/stats.

[172] Craig McIntosh. Monitoring Repayment in Online Peer-to-Peer Lending. 2011. URL: http://irps.ucsd.edu/assets/037/11366.pdf.

[173] Michele Boldrin, David K. Levine. Against Intellectual Monopoly. Cambridge University Press. 2008. URL: http://www.amazon.com/ Against-Intellectual-Monopoly-Michele-Boldrin/dp/ 0521879280.

[174] Robin Feldman, Kris Nelson. Open Source, Open Access, and Open Transfer: Market Approaches to Research Bottlenecks. 2008. Northwestern Journal of Technology and Intellectual Property. URL: http://www.law.northwestern.edu/journals/njtip/v7/n1/2/.

[175] Josh Bivens, Lawrence Mishel. The Pay of Corporate Executives and Financial Professionals as Evidence of Rents in Top 1 Percent Incomes. Journal of Economic Perspectives. 2013;27(3). URL: http://www.aeaweb.org/articles.php?doi=10.1257/jep.27.3.57.

[176] Jason Schultz, Jennifer M. Urban. Protecting Open Innovation: The Defensive Patent License as a New Approach to Patent Threats, Transaction Costs, and Tactical Disarmament. Harvard Journal of Law & Technology. 2012;26. URL:
http://papers.ssrn.com/sol3/papers.cfm?abstract_id=2040945.

[177] Defensive Patent License. Homepage. 2014. URL:
http://www.defensivepatentlicense.com/.

[178] Robert A. Saunders. Intellectual Property Pools and the Disappearing Essentiality Requirement. 2010. Social Sciences Research Network. URL:
http://papers.ssrn.com/sol3/Delivery.cfm/SSRN_ID1884597_code1687637.pdf?abstractid=1884597&mirid=5.

[179] World Business Council for Sustainable Development. Eco-Patent Commons. 2013. URL: http://www.wbcsd.org/work-program/capacity-building/eco-patent-commons/overview.aspx.

[180] Federal Reserve Bank of St. Louis. Federal Reserve Economic Data (FRED). 2013. URL: http://research.stlouisfed.org/fred2/.

[181] Halah Touryalai. More Evidence On The Student Debt Crisis: Average Grad's Loan Jumps To $27,000. 2013. Forbes. URL:
http://www.forbes.com/sites/halahtouryalai/2013/01/29/more-evidence-on-the-student-debt-crisis-average-grads%2Dloan-jumps-to-27000/.

[182] Peter Schroeder. Holder's Remarks on Banks 'Too Large' to Prosecute Reignites Controversy. 2013. The Hill. URL: http://thehill.com/blogs/on-the-money/banking-financial-institutions/287115-holders-remarks-on-banks-too-large-to-prosecute%2Dreignites-controversy.

[183] Gretchen Morgenson, Louise Story. In Financial Crisis, No Prosecutions of Top Figures. 2011. New York Times. URL: http://www.nytimes.com/2011/04/14/business/14prosecute.html.

[184] Congressional Budget Office. The 2012 Long-Term Budget Outlook. 2012. URL: http://www.cbo.gov/publication/43288.

[185] Winston Gee. Debt, Deficits, and Modern Monetary Theory. 2011. Harvard International Review. URL: http://hir.harvard.edu/debt-deficits-and-modern-monetary-theory.

[186] Sidney Homer, Richard Sylla. A History of Interest Rates: Third Edition, Revised. Rutgers University Press. 1996. URL: http://www.amazon.com/History-Interest-Rates-Third-Revised/dp/0813522889.

[187] Rosa-Maria Gelpi, Francois Julien-Labruyere. The History of Consumer Credit: Doctrines and Practices. Palgrave Macmillan. 2000. URL: http://www.amazon.com/History-Consumer-Credit-Doctrines-Practice/dp/031222415X.

[188] Mara Bernstein. Change for the Church: Jews and Banking in Renaissance Italy. 2011. Hashta UMD. URL: http://sites.google.com/site/hashtaumd/contents-1/banking.

[189] Christopher Lewis Peterson. Truth, Understanding, and High-Cost Consumer Credit: The Historical Context of the Truth in Lending Act. Florida Law Review. 2003;55. URL: http://papers.ssrn.com/sol3/papers.cfm?abstract_id=878951.

[190] Ben Casselman, Justin Lahart. Companies Shun Investment, Hoard Cash. 2011. Wall Street Journal. URL: http://online.wsj.com/article/SB10001424053111903927204576574720017009568.html.

[191] Ben S. Bernanke. Inflation Expectations and Inflation Forecasting. 2007. Board of Governors of the Federal Reserve System; Monetary Economics Workshop of the National Bureau of Economic Research Summer Institute, Cambridge, Massachusetts. URL: http://www.federalreserve.gov/newsevents/speech/bernanke20070710a.htm.

[192] Jeff Korzenik. America's 15th Financial Panic. 2011. Chicago Tribune. URL: http://articles.chicagotribune.com/2011-07-04/news/ct-oped-0704-panic-20110704_1_panics-post-panic-lackluster-recovery.

[193] Civics Economics. Independent BC: Small Business and the British Columbia Economy. 2013. URL: http://www.civiceconomics.com/app/download/7114608204/Independent+BC+for+Screen.pdf.

[194] Civics Economics. The American Express OPEN Independent Retail Index. 2011. URL: http://www.civiceconomics.com/app/download/5841576504/American+Express+Open+Independent+Retail+Index.pdf.

[195] Robert J. Shiller. Prize Lecture: Speculative Asset Prices. 2013. Nobel Prize. URL: http://www.nobelprize.org/nobel_prizes/economic-sciences/laureates/2013/shiller-lecture.html.

[196] Bart Frijns, Willem F. C. Verschoor, Remco C. J. Zwinkels. Excess Stock Return Comovements and the Role of Investor Sentiment. Social Science Research Network. 2011;URL: http://papers.ssrn.com/sol3/papers.cfm?abstract_id=1881006.

[197] James Crotty. The Realism of Assumptions Does Matter: Why Keynes-Minsky Theory Must Replace Efficient Market Theory as the Guide to Financial Regulation Policy. 2011. Political Economy Research Institute:

Working Paper Series #255. URL: http://www.peri.umass.edu/236/
hash/ac5a9dafc1cc0e3fee23833db698f816/publication/452/.

[198] Drew DeSilver. U.S. Income Inequality, On Rise for Decades, Is Now
       Highest Since 1928. 2013. Pew Research. URL:
       http://www.pewresearch.org/fact-tank/2013/12/05/
       u-s-income-inequality-on-rise-for-decades-is-now-highest%
       2Dsince-1928/.

[199] U. S. Census Bureau. Table H-3. Mean Household Income Received by
       Each Fifth and Top 5 Percent, All Races: 1967 to 2011. 2013. URL:
       http://www.census.gov/hhes/www/income/data/historical/
       families/f03AR.xls.

[200] Don Lee. Fed Official: Job Gains Dominated by Lower-Paying Work. 2013.
       LA Times. URL: http://articles.latimes.com/2013/mar/22/
       business/la-fi-mo-fed-jobs-20130322.

[201] Andrew Hussey. Occupy Was Right: Capitalism Has Failed the World. 2014.
       The Guardian. URL: http://www.theguardian.com/books/2014/apr/
       13/occupy-right-capitalism-failed-world-french-economist%
       2Dthomas-piketty.

[202] Louis Johnston, Samuel H. Williamson. What Was the U.S. GDP Then?.
       2011. MeasuringWorth. URL:
       http://www.measuringworth.org/usgdp/.

[203] H. Goelzer, P. Huybrechts, S. C. B. Raper, M. F. Loutre, H. Goosse, T.
       Fichefet. Millennial Total Sea-Level Commitments Projected With the Earth
       Eystem Model of Intermediate Complexity LOVECLIM. Environmental
       Research Letters. 2012;7(4). URL: http:
       //www.sciencedaily.com/releases/2012/10/121001191531.htm.

[204] World Wildlife Federation. 2010 Living Planet Report. 2010. URL:
       http://assets.panda.org/downloads/lpr2010.pdf.

[205] Herman E. Daly, Joshua Farley. Ecological Economics, Second Edition:
       Principles and Applications. Island Press. 2010. URL:
       http://www.amazon.com/
       Ecological-Economics-Second-Principles-Applications/dp/
       1597266817.

[206] Gautam Naik. Vital Marine Plants in Steep Decline. 2010. Wall Street
       Journal. URL: http://online.wsj.com/article/
       SB20001424052748704895004575395273977526844.html.

[207] Louise Gray. World's Oceans Move Into 'Extinction Phase'. 2011. URL:
       http://www.telegraph.co.uk/earth/earthnews/8587354/
       Worlds-oceans-move-into-extinction-phase.html.

[208] Nick Collins. Oceans Acidifying at 'Unparalleled' Rate. 2012. The Telegraph. URL: http://www.telegraph.co.uk/earth/environment/climatechange/9115699/Oceans-acidifying-at-unparalleled-rate.html.

[209] Jerry M. Melillo, Terese Richmond, Gary W. Yohe. Climate Change Impacts in the United States: The Third National Climate Assessment. 2014. U.S. Global Change Research Program. URL: http://nca2014.globalchange.gov/.

[210] I. Joughin, B. E. Smith, B. Medley. Marine Ice Sheet Collapse Potentially Underway for the Thwaites Glacier Basin, West Antarctica. Science. 2014;URL: http://www.sciencedaily.com/releases/2014/05/140515090934.htm.

[211] Ben Strauss. What Does U.S. Look Like With 10 Feet of Sea Level Rise?. 2014. Climate Central. URL: http://www.climatecentral.org/news/u.s.-with-10-feet-of-sea-level-rise-17428.

[212] World Economic Forum. What If the World's Soil Runs Out?. 2012. Time. URL: http://world.time.com/2012/12/14/what-if-the-worlds-soil-runs-out/.

[213] Matthew Wilde. Study: Soil Eroding Faster Than Estimated. 2011. Cedar Valley Business. URL: http://wcfcourier.com/business/local/study-soil-eroding-faster-than-estimated/article_90a7f82c-8315-11e0-82f0-001cc4c03286.html.

[214] International Monetary Fund. Financial System Soundness. 2014. URL: https://www.imf.org/external/np/exr/facts/banking.htm.

[215] Davide Fiaschi, Imre Kondor, Matteo Marsili. The Interrupted Power Law and the Size of Shadow Banking. 2013. arXiv. URL: http://arxiv.org/abs/1309.2130.

[216] Emily Flitter. In Wake of JPMorgan Settlement, Big Banks Add to Defense Funds. 2014. Reuters. URL: http://www.reuters.com/article/2014/01/17/us-usa-banks-reserves-idUSBREA0G1PN20140117.

[217] Tracy Wilkinson, Ken Ellingwood. International Banks Have Aided Mexican Drug Gangs. 2011. Los Angles Times. URL: http://articles.latimes.com/2011/nov/27/world/la-fg-mexico-money-laundering-banks-20111128.

[218] François Lequiller, Derek Blades. Understanding National Accounts. 2006. Organisation for Economic Co-operation and Development. URL: http://www.oecd.org/std/na/38451313.pdf.

[219] Dennis Kuo, David Skeie, James Vickery, Thomas Youle. Identifying Term Interbank Loans From Fedwire Payments Data. 2013. Federal Reserve Bank of New York, Staff Report No. 603. URL: http://www.newyorkfed.org/research/staff_reports/sr603.pdf.

[220] James Manyika, Michael Chui, Diana Farrell, Steve Van Kuiken, Peter Groves, Elizabeth Almasi Doshi. Open Data: Unlocking Innovation and Performance with Liquid Information. 2013. McKinsey & Company. URL: http://www.mckinsey.com/insights/business_technology/open_data_unlocking_innovation_and_performance_with_liquid_information.

[221] Dirk Helbing. Globally Networked Risks and How to Respond. Nature. 2013;497:51–59. URL: http://www.nature.com/nature/journal/v497/n7447/full/nature12047.html.

[222] Geoffrey M. Hodgson. On the Limits of Rational Choice Theory. Economic Thought. 2012;1(94–108). URL: http://www.geoffrey-hodgson.info/user/image/limits-rational-choice.pdf.

[223] Oxfam. Haiti: The Slow Road to Reconstruction. 2012;URL: http://www.oxfam.org/en/policy/haiti-slow-road-reconstruction.

[224] Paul W. Glimcher, Ernst Fehr. Neuroeconomics: Decision Making and the Brain. 2nd ed. Elsevier: Academic Press. 2014. URL: http://www.sciencedirect.com/science/book/9780124160088.

[225] Jorge Moll, Frank Krueger, Roland Zahn, Matteo Pardini, Ricardo de Oliveira-Souza, Jordan Grafman. Human Fronto–Mesolimbic Networks Guide Decisions About Charitable Donation. PNAS. 2006;103(42):15623–15628. URL: http://www.pnas.org/content/103/42/15623.

[226] Elizabeth W. Dunn, Lara B. Aknin, Michael I. Norton. Prosocial Spending and Happiness: Using Money to Benefit Others Pays Off. Current Directions in Psychological Science. 2014;23(1):41–47. URL: http://cdp.sagepub.com/content/23/1/41.abstract.

[227] Robert H. Frank. The Theory That Self-Interest Is the Sole Motivator Is Self-Fulfilling. 2005. New York Times. URL: http://www.nytimes.com/2005/02/17/business/17scene.html.

[228] The Economist. New Model Army: Efforts Are Under Way to Improve Macroeconomic Models. 2013. URL: http://www.economist.com/news/finance-and-economics/21569752-efforts-are-under-way-improve-macroeconomic-models%2Dnew-model-army.

[229] Dirk J. Bezemer. Why Some Economists Could See the Crisis Coming. 2009. Financial Times. URL: http://www.ft.com/cms/s/0/452dc484-9bdc-11de-b214-00144feabdc0.html#axzz2ybN8PEae.

[230] Steve Keen. Debunking Economics. Zed Books. 2011. URL: http://www.amazon.com/Debunking-Economics-Revised-Expanded-Dethroned/dp/1848139926.

[231] J. D. Farmer, D. Foley. The Economy Needs Agent-Based Modelling. Nature. 2009;460(7256):685–686. URL: http://www.nature.com/nature/journal/v460/n7256/full/460685a.html.

[232] Christophe Deissenberg, Sander van der Hoog, Herbert Dawid. EURACE: A Massively Parallel Agent-Based Model of the European Economy. 2008. Applied Mathematics and Computation. URL: http://www.wiwi.uni-bielefeld.de/fileadmin/vpl1/EURACE-AMC.pdf.

[233] Netflix. Netflix Prize. 2012. URL: http://www.netflixprize.com/.

[234] Mogens Herman Hansen. The Athenian Democracy in the Age of Demosthenes: Structure, Principles, and Ideology. University of Oklahoma Press. 1999. URL: http://www.amazon.com/Athenian-Democracy-Age-Demosthenes-Principles/dp/0806131438.

[235] Marc Abrahams. Improbable Research: Why Random Selection of MPs May Be Best. 2012. The Guardian. URL: http://www.guardian.co.uk/education/2012/apr/16/improbable-research-politicians-random-selection.

[236] Rasmussen Reports. 43% Say Random Choices From Phone Book Better Than Current Congress. 2012. URL: http://www.rasmussenreports.com/public_content/politics/general_politics/february_2012/43_say_random_choices_from_phone_book_better_than_current_congress.

[237] Transparency in Europe. Liquid Friesland—Citizen Participation, 7 Days a Week, 24 Hours a Day?. 2013. URL: http://transparencyineurope.wordpress.com/tag/liquid-feedback/.

[238] Nicholas Kulish. Direct Democracy, 2.0. 2012. New York Times. URL: http://www.nytimes.com/2012/05/06/sunday-review/direct-democracy-2-0.html.

[239] Karl Fogel. Producing Open Source Software: How to Run a Successful Free Software Project. O'Reilly Media. 2010. URL: http://producingoss.com/.

[240] Adam Wyner, Tom van Engers. A Framework for Enriched, Controlled On-line Discussion Forums for E-government Policy-Making. 2010. Under review at eGOV 2010. URL: http://www.wyner.info/research/Papers/WynerVanEngersForum2010.pdf.

[241] Tom M. Van engers, Margherita R. Boekenoogen. Improving Legal Quality—A Knowledge Engineering Approach. International Review of Law, Computers & Technology. 2004;18(1):81–96. URL: http://www.tandfonline.com/doi/abs/10.1080/13600860410001674751#preview.

[242] Vjeran Strahonja. Modeling Legislation by Using UML State Machine Diagrams. Electrical and Computer Engineering, 2006 CCECE '06 Canadian Conference on. 2006;p. 624 – 627. URL: http://ieeexplore.ieee.org/xpl/freeabs_all.jsp?arnumber=4055070.

[243] ICAIL. ICAIL 2011: The Thirteenth International Conference on Artificial Intelligence and Law. 2011. URL: http://www.law.pitt.edu/events/2011/06/icail-2011-the-thirteenth-international-conference-on%2Dartificial-intelligence-and-law.

[244] Springer. Artificial Intelligence and Law. 2012. URL: http://www.springer.com/computer/ai/journal/10506.

[245] Anil Rupasingha. Locally Owned: Do Local Business Ownership and Size Matter for Local Economic Well-Being?. 2013. Federal Reserve Bank of Atlanta. URL: http://www.frbatlanta.org/documents/pubs/discussionpapers/dp1301.pdf.

[246] David A. Fleming, Stephan J. Goetz. Does Local Firm Ownership Matter?. 2011. Economic Development Quartely. URL: http://edq.sagepub.com/content/25/3/277.abstract.

[247] T. C. Blanchard, C. Tolbert, C. Mencken. The Health and Wealth of US Counties: How the Small Business Environment Impacts Alternative Measures of Development. 2011. Cambridge Journal of Regions, Economy and Society. URL: http://www.sciencedaily.com/releases/2012/02/120202201511.htm.

[248] Carl Bass. An Insider's View of the Myths and Truths of the 3-D Printing 'Phenomenon'. 2013. Wired. URL: http://www.wired.com/opinion/2013/05/an-insiders-view-of-the-hype-and-realities-of-3-d-printing/.

[249] David B. Kolesky, Ryan L. Truby, A. Sydney Gladman, Travis A. Busbee, Kimberly A. Homan, Jennifer A. Lewis. 3D Bioprinting of Vascularized, Heterogeneous Cell-Laden Tissue Constructs. Advanced Materials. 2014;URL: http://dx.doi.org/10.1002/adma.201305506.

[250] James Dornbrook. FabLab Helps Connect Budding Entrepreneurs, Tradespeople. 2011. Kansas City Business Journal. URL: http://www.bizjournals.com/kansascity/print-edition/2011/07/22/fablab-helps-connect-budding.html.

[251] Alexander George. 3-D Printed Car Is as Strong as Steel, Half the Weight, and Nearing Production. 2013. Wired. URL:
http://www.wired.com/autopia/2013/02/3d-printed-car/.

[252] Benjamin Tincq. From Henry Ford to Joe Justice: WikiSpeed, Manufacturing in the Age of Open Collaboration. 2012. OuiShare. URL:
http://ouishare.net/2012/10/wikispeed-agile-manufacturing/.

[253] Steve Denning. Wikispeed: How A 100 mpg Car Was Developed In 3 Months. Forbes. 2012;URL:
http://www.forbes.com/sites/stevedenning/2012/05/10/
wikispeed-how-a-100-mpg-car-was-developed-in-3-months/.

[254] Open Source Ecology. Distributive Enterprise. 2013. URL:
http://opensourceecology.org/wiki/Distributive_Enterprise.

[255] K. Kim, D. Chhajed, Y. Liu. Can Commonality Relieve Cannibalization in Product Line Design? Marketing Science. 2013;URL: http:
//www.sciencedaily.com/releases/2013/04/130429164921.htm.

[256] Bureau of Labor Statistics. Consumer Price Index Detailed Report. 2011. URL: http://www.bls.gov/cpi/cpid1109.pdf.

[257] Lisa Rathke. Local Food Index Ranks Vermont At Top, Florida At Bottom. 2012. Huffington Post. URL: http://www.huffingtonpost.com/2012/
05/08/local-food-index_n_1499379.html.

[258] Graham Bell. The Permaculture Way: Practical Steps to Create a Self-Sustaining World. Chelsea Green Publishing. 2005. URL:
http://www.amazon.com/
Permaculture-Way-Practical-Create-Self-Sustaining/dp/
1856230287.

[259] Intergovernmental Science-Policy Platform on Biodiversity and Ecosystem Services (IPBES). Even Farm Animal Diversity is Declining as Accelerating Species Loss Threatens Humanity. 2013. ScienceDaily. URL: http:
//www.sciencedaily.com/releases/2013/05/130527100624.htm.

[260] Nathan McClintock, Jenny Cooper. Cultivating the Commons: An Assessment of the Potential for Urban Agriculture on Oakland's Public Land. 2009. URL: https:
//d3gqux9s10z33u.cloudfront.net/AA/AD/oaklandfood-org/
downloads/27621/Cultivating_the_Commons_COMPLETE.pdf.

[261] Manuel Valdes. Seattle 'Food Forest' To Offer Pick-Your-Own Produce In Urban Environment. 2012. Huffington Post. URL:
http://www.huffingtonpost.com/2012/03/07/
seattle-food-forest_n_1327458.html.

[262] Beacon Food Forest Permaculture Project. Homepage. 2014. URL:
http://www.beaconfoodforest.org/.

[263] Nature Conservancy. Homepage. 2014. URL: http://www.nature.org/.

[264] U. S. Energy Information Administration. How Much Energy is Consumed in Residential and Commercial Buildings in the United States?. 2014. URL: http://www.eia.gov/tools/faqs/faq.cfm?id=86&t=1.

[265] Sandrine Dixson-Decleve. Concentrating on Building Efficiency is Europe's New Climate-Change Mantra. 2012. The Guardian. URL: http://www.guardian.co.uk/sustainable-business/building-energy-efficiency-europe.

[266] European Commission. Roadmap for Moving to a Low-Carbon Economy in 2050. 2011. URL: http://ec.europa.eu/clima/policies/roadmap/index_en.htm.

[267] Donald L. Elliott. A Better Way to Zone: Ten Principles to Create More Livable Cities. Island Press. 2008. URL: http://www.amazon.com/Better-Way-Zone-Principles-Livable/dp/1597261815.

[268] U. S. Department of Energy. Climate Change and Infrastructure, Urban Systems, and Vulnerabilities. 2012. URL: http://www.esd.ornl.gov/eess/esd_fact_sheets/Infrastructure022912.pdf.

[269] Rocky Mountain Institute. The Economics of Grid Defection. 2014. URL: http://www.rmi.org/electricity_grid_defection#economics_of_grid_defection.

[270] R. D. L. Smith, M. S. Prevot, R. D. Fagan, Z. Zhang, P. A. Sedach, M. K. J. Siu, et al. Photochemical Route for Accessing Amorphous Metal Oxide Materials for Water Oxidation Catalysis. Science. 2013;URL: http://www.sciencedaily.com/releases/2013/03/130328142356.htm.

[271] Chong Liu, Jinyao Tang, Hao Ming Chen, Bin Liu, Peidong Yang. A Fully Integrated Nanosystem of Semiconductor Nanowires for Direct Solar Water Splitting. Nano Letters. 2013;URL: http://www.sciencedaily.com/releases/2013/05/130516142654.htm.

[272] Alister Doyle. Window Closing on World's Ability to Meet Global Warming Targets: UN Study. 2014. The Globe and Mail. URL: http://www.theglobeandmail.com/news/world/window-closing-on-worlds-ability-to-meet-global-warming%2Dtargets-un-study/article17844804/.

[273] Jonathan M. Cullen, Julian M. Allwood, Edward H. Borgstein. Reducing Energy Demand: What Are the Practical Limits? Environmental Science and Technology. 2011;45(4):1711–1718. URL: http://pubs.acs.org/doi/abs/10.1021/es102641n.

[274] Jason Kane. Health Costs: How the U.S. Compares With Other Countries. 2012. PBS Newshour. URL:
http://www.pbs.org/newshour/rundown/2012/10/
health-costs-how-the-us-compares-with-other-countries.
html.

[275] Ewen MacAskill. US Health-Care Law Backed by OECD Days Before Supreme Court Decision. 2012. The Guardian. URL:
http://www.guardian.co.uk/world/2012/jun/26/
obama-healthcare-backed-oecd.

[276] Bloomberg. Most Efficient Health Care Countries. 2013. URL:
http://www.bloomberg.com/visual-data/best-and-worst/
most-efficient-health-care-countries.

[277] Organisation for Economic Co-operation and Development. Why is Health Spending in the United States So High?. 2011. URL:
http://www.oecd.org/unitedstates/49084355.pdf.

[278] U. S. Department of Health and Human Services. Highlights From the 2011 National Healthcare Quality and Disparities Report. 2011. URL: http:
//www.ahrq.gov/research/findings/nhqrdr/nhdr11/key.html.

[279] Bruce Japsen. Health Costs For Family Of Four Higher Than Year Of Groceries. 2013. Forbes. URL:
http://www.forbes.com/sites/brucejapsen/2013/05/22/
health-costs-for-family-of-four-higher-than-year-of-groceries/.

[280] Maggie Fox. U.S. Obesity Rates to Soar, Researchers Report. 2011. National Journal. URL: http://www.nationaljournal.com/healthcare/
u-s-obesity-rates-to-soar-researchers-report-20110826.

[281] Center for Disease Control and Prevention. Overweight and Obesity. 2013. URL: http://www.cdc.gov/obesity/adult/causes/index.html.

[282] Asheley Cockrell Skinner, Joseph A. Skelton. Prevalence and Trends In Obesity and Severe Obesity Among Children in the United States, 1999–2012. JAMA Pediatrics. 2014;URL: http:
//www.sciencedaily.com/releases/2014/04/140407164550.htm.

[283] Centers for Disease Control and Prevention. CDC Looks Ahead: 13 Public Health Issues in 2013. 2013. URL:
http://blogs.cdc.gov/cdcworksforyou24-7/2013/01/
cdc-looks-ahead-13-public-health-issues-in-2013/.

[284] I. Lenoir-Wijnkoop, P. J. Jones, R. Uauy, L. Segal, J. Milner. Nutrition Economics—Food as an Ally of Public Health. British Journal of Nutrition. 2013;109(5):777–784. URL:
http://www.ncbi.nlm.nih.gov/pmc/articles/PMC3583164/.

[285] Paula W. Yoon, Brigham Bastian, Robert N. Anderson, Janet L. Collins, Harold W. Jaffe. Potentially Preventable Deaths from the Five Leading Causes of Death—United States, 2008–2010. 2014. Centers for Disease Control and Prevention: Morbidity and Mortality Weekly Report. URL: http://www.cdc.gov/mmwr/preview/mmwrhtml/mm6317a1.htm?s_cid=mm6317a1_w.

[286] Gina Kolata. Mediterranean Diet Shown to Ward Off Heart Attack and Stroke. 2013. New York Times. URL: http://www.nytimes.com/2013/02/26/health/mediterranean-diet-can-cut-heart-disease-study-finds.html.

[287] John Carey. Do Cholesterol Drugs Do Any Good?. 2008. Businessweek. URL: http://www.businessweek.com/stories/2008-01-16/do-cholesterol-drugs-do-any-good.

[288] Michelle Roberts. Exercise 'Can Be as Good as Pills'. 2013. BBC News. URL: http://www.bbc.com/news/health-24335710.

[289] Adam D. M. Briggs, Anja Mizdrak, Peter Scarborough. A Statin a Day Keeps the Doctor Away: Comparative Proverb Assessment Modelling Study. British Medical Journal. 2013;347. URL: http://www.bmj.com/content/347/bmj.f7267.

[290] Preetha Anand, Ajaikumar B. Kunnumakara, Chitra Sundaram, Kuzhuvelil B. Harikumar, Sheeja T. Tharakan, Oiki S. Lai, et al. Cancer is a Preventable Disease that Requires Major Lifestyle Changes. Pharmaceutical Research. 2008;URL: http://www.ncbi.nlm.nih.gov/pmc/articles/PMC2515569/.

[291] Matt Sloane. A Workout a Day May Keep Cancer Away. 2013. CNN. URL: http://www.cnn.com/2013/05/16/health/cancer-research.

[292] Genevra Pittman. Vegetable Fats Tied to Less Prostate Cancer Spread. 2013. Reuters. URL: http://www.reuters.com/article/2013/06/10/us-health-vegetablefat-prostatecancer-idUSBRE95911X20130610.

[293] Cheri Cheng. More Evidence Confirms Healthy Lifestyle Changes Lead to Lower Death Rates. 2013. Counsel & Heal. URL: http://www.counselheal.com/articles/5620/20130603/more-evidence-confirms-healthy-lifestyle-changes-lead%2Dlower-death-rates.htm.

[294] Kim T. B. Knoops, Lisette de Groot, Daan Kromhout, Anne-Elisabeth Perrin, Olga Moreiras-Varela, Alessandro Menotti, et al. Mediterranean Diet, Lifestyle Factors, and 10-Year Mortality in Elderly European Men and Women. Journal of the American Medical Association. 2004;URL: http://www.ncbi.nlm.nih.gov/pubmed/15383513.

[295] Oyinlola Oyebode, Vanessa Gordon-Dseagu, Alice Walker, Jennifer S Mindell. Fruit and Vegetable Consumption and All-cause, Cancer and CVD Mortality: Analysis of Health Survey for England Data. Journal of Epidemiology & Community Health. 2014;31. URL: http://www.sciencedaily.com/releases/2014/03/140331194030.htm.

[296] Morgan E. Levine, Jorge A. Suarez, Sebastian Brandhorst, Priya Balasubramanian, Chia-Wei Cheng, Federica Madia, et al. Protein Intake Is Associated with a Major Reduction in IGF-1, Cancer, and Overall Mortality in the 65 and Younger But Not Older Population. Cell Metabolism. 2014;19(3):407–417. URL: http://www.sciencedaily.com/releases/2014/03/140304125639.htm.

[297] Frank Newport. In U.S., 5% Consider Themselves Vegetarians. 2012. Gallup. URL: http://www.gallup.com/poll/156215/consider-themselves-vegetarians.aspx.

[298] Orlich MJ, Singh PN, Fan J, Knutsen S, Beeson WL, Fraser GE. Vegetarian Dietary Patterns and Mortality in Adventist Health Study 2. JAMA Internal Medicine. 2013;173(13):1230–1238. URL: http://www.ncbi.nlm.nih.gov/pubmed/23836264.

[299] G. Fraser, S. Katuli, R. Anousheh, S. Knutsen, P. Herring, J. Fan. Vegetarian Diets and Cardiovascular Risk Factors in Black Members of the Adventist Health Study-2. Public Health and Nutrition. 2014;17:1–9. URL: http://www.ncbi.nlm.nih.gov/pubmed/24636393.

[300] U. Agarwal, S. Mishra, J. Xu, S. Levin, J. Gonzales, N. D. Barnard. A Multicenter Randomized Controlled Trial of a Nutrition Intervention Program in a Multiethnic Adult Population in the Corporate Setting Reduces Depression and Anxiety and Improves Quality of Life: The GEICO Study. American Journal of Health Promotion. 2014;URL: http://www.ncbi.nlm.nih.gov/pubmed/24524383.

[301] Raquel A Silva, J Jason West, Yuqiang Zhang, Susan C Anenberg, Jean-François Lamarque, Drew T Shindell, et al. Global Premature Mortality Due to Anthropogenic Outdoor Air Pollution and the Contribution of Past Climate Change. Environmental Research Letters. 2013;8(3). URL: http://www.sciencedaily.com/releases/2013/07/130712084455.htm.

[302] G. H. Donovan, D. T. Butry, Y. L. Michael, J. P. Prestemon, A. M. Liebhold, D. Gatziolis, et al. The Relationship Between Trees and Human Health: Evidence From the Spread of the Emerald Ash Borer. American Journal of Preventive Medicine. 2013;URL: http://www.ncbi.nlm.nih.gov/pubmed/23332329.

[303] David J. Nowak, Eric J. Greenfield, Robert E. Hoehn, Elizabeth Lapoint. Carbon Storage and Sequestration by Trees in Urban and Community Areas of the United States. Environmental Pollution. 2013;178(229). URL: http://www.sciencedaily.com/releases/2013/05/130507195815.htm.

[304] Jonathan Lemire. Anthony Weiner Rolls out New Health Care Plan. 2013. New York Daily News. URL: http://www.nydailynews.com/news/election/weiner-rolls-health-care-plan-article-1.1378589.

[305] Don McCanne. Friedman Analysis of HR 676: Medicare for All Would Save Billions. 2013. Physicians for a National Health Program. URL: http://bit.ly/1iWn2St.

[306] University of the People. Homepage. 2014. URL: http://uopeople.edu/.

[307] Tamar Lewin. Free Online University Receives Accreditation, In Time for Graduating Class of 7. 2014. New York Times. URL: http://www.nytimes.com/2014/02/14/education/free-online-university-receives-accreditation-in-time-for%2Dgraduating-class-of-7.html.

[308] edX. Homepage. 2014. URL: https://www.edx.org.

[309] Open edX. Homepage. 2014. URL: http://code.edx.org/.

[310] OpenCourseWare. Homepage. 2014. URL: http://www.ocwconsortium.org.

[311] Udacity. Homepage. 2014. URL: https://www.udacity.com/.

[312] Coursera. Homepage. 2014. URL: https://www.coursera.org/.

[313] Michael T. Klare. The Race for What's Left: The Global Scramble for the World's Last Resources. Metropolitan Books. 2012. URL: http://e360.yale.edu/feature/global_scarcity_scramble_for_dwindling_natural_resources/2531/.

[314] Gaia Vince. How the World's Oceans Could be Running Out of Fish. 2012. BBC. URL: http://www.bbc.com/future/story/20120920-are-we-running-out-of-fish.

[315] Steve Altaner. Mineral Resources: Formation, Mining, Environmental Impact. 2013. Connexions. URL: http://cnx.org/content/m41470/latest/?collection=col11325/latest.

[316] Katherine Seelye. Aquifer's Depletion Poses Sweeping Threat. 2011. New York Times. URL: http://green.blogs.nytimes.com/2011/05/04/aquifers-depletion-poses-sweeping-threat/.

[317] A. S. MacDougall, K. S. McCann, G. Gellner, R. Turkington. Diversity Loss With Persistent Human Disturbance Increases Vulnerability to Ecosystem Collapse. Nature. 2013;494(86-89). URL: http://www.nature.com/nature/journal/v494/n7435/full/nature11869.html.

[318] Christine Dell'Amore. Biggest Dead Zone Ever Forecast in Gulf of Mexico. 2013. National Geographic. URL: http://news.nationalgeographic.com/news/2013/06/130621-dead-zone-biggest-gulf-of-mexico-science-environment/.

[319] U. S. Fish and Wildlife Service. U.S. Fish and Wildlife Service Celebrates 25 Years of the Coastal Program. 2010. URL: http://www.fws.gov/pacific/news/news.cfm?id=2144374663.

[320] Dartmouth College. Mercury Releases Contaminate Ocean Fish: New Research Important to Discussion of International Mercury. 2012. Science Daily. URL: http://www.sciencedaily.com/releases/2012/12/121203150008.htm.

[321] U. S. Food and Drug Administration. What You Need to Know About Mercury in Fish and Shellfish. 2004. URL: http://www.fda.gov/food/foodborneillnesscontaminants/metals/ucm351781.htm.

[322] Juliette Jowit. Humans Driving Extinction Faster Than Species Can Evolve, Say Experts. 2010. The Guardian. URL: http://www.guardian.co.uk/environment/2010/mar/07/extinction-species-evolve.

[323] A. D. Barnosky, N. Matzke, S. Tomiya, G. O. Wogan, B. Swartz, T. B. Quental, et al. Has the Earth's Sixth Mass Extinction Already Arrived? Nature. 2011;471(7336):51–7. URL: http://www.nature.com/nature/journal/v471/n7336/full/nature09678.html.

[324] Tim Profeta. Report Warns of Sudden Climate Change Impacts. 2013. National Geographic. URL: http://newswatch.nationalgeographic.com/2013/12/05/report-warns-of-sudden-climate-change-impacts/.

[325] Drew T. Shindell. Inhomogeneous Forcing and Transient Climate Sensitivity. 2014. Nature Climate Change. URL: http://www.sciencedaily.com/releases/2014/03/140311184706.htm.

[326] Gail Whiteman, Chris Hope, Peter Wadhams. Climate Science: Vast Costs of Arctic Change. Nature. 2013;URL: http://www.sciencedaily.com/releases/2013/07/130724134256.htm.

[327] Dim Coumou, Alexander Robinson. Historic and Future Increase in the Global Land Area Affected by Monthly Heat Extremes. Environmental Research Letters. 2013;8(3). URL: http://www.sciencedaily.com/releases/2013/08/130815084845.htm.

[328] Hilary Russ. New York Lays Out $20 Billion Plan to Adapt to Climate Change. 2013. Reuters. URL: http://www.reuters.com/article/2013/06/11/us-climate-newyork-plan-idUSBRE95A10120130611.

[329] Stephane Hallegatte, Colin Green, Robert J. Nicholls, Jan Corfee-Morlot. Future Flood Losses in Major Coastal Cities. Nature Climate Change. 2013;URL: http: //www.sciencedaily.com/releases/2013/08/130819102601.htm.

[330] Yuval Rosenberg. The Coming Storm: Unsustainable Federal Disaster Costs. 2013. The Fiscal Times. URL: http://www.thefiscaltimes.com/Articles/2013/04/30/ The-Coming-Storm-Unsustainable-Federal-Disaster-Costs. aspx#page1.

[331] Rick Piltz. Cities Taking Initiative on Climate Change Preparedness. 2013. Climate Science Watch. URL: http://www.climatesciencewatch.org/2013/06/19/ cities-taking-initiative-on-climate-change-preparedness/.

[332] Institute for Local Government. Climate Action Plans. 2014. URL: http://www.ca-ilg.org/climate-action-plans.

[333] org C. Homepage. 2014. URL: http://www.c40.org/.

[334] Mike Scott. Cities Bypass Slow Government to Lead the Way on Climate Change. 2013. The Guardian. URL: http://www.theguardian.com/sustainable-business/ cities-bypass-government-climate-change.

[335] Intergovernmental Panel on Climate Change. Climate Change 2014: Mitigation of Climate Change. 2014. URL: http://report.mitigation2014.org/spm/ipcc_wg3_ar5_ summary-for-policymakers_approved.pdf.

[336] Thomas Powell, Tim Lenton. Future Carbon Dioxide Removal Via Biomass Energy Constrained by Agricultural Efficiency and Dietary Trends. Energy and Environmental Science. 2012;URL: http: //www.sciencedaily.com/releases/2012/06/120619225934.htm.

[337] Natural Resources Defense Council. Facts about Pollution from Livestock Farms. 2013. URL: http://www.nrdc.org/water/pollution/ffarms.asp.

[338] Robert Goodland. FAO Yields to Meat Industry Pressure on Climate Change. 2012. New York Times. URL: http://bittman.blogs.nytimes.com/2012/07/11/ fao-yields-to-meat-industry-pressure-on-climate-change.

[339] Robert Goodland. Hidden Cost of Hamburgers is Greater Than Reported. 2012. Earth Island Journal. URL: http: //www.earthisland.org/journal/index.php/elist/eListRead/ hidden_cost_of_hamburgers_is_greater_than_reported/.

[340] Fredrik Hedenus, Stefan Wirsenius, Daniel J. A. Johansson. The Importance of Reduced Meat and Dairy Consumption for Meeting Stringent Climate Change Targets. Climatic Change. 2014;URL: http://link.springer.com/article/10.1007%2Fs10584-014-1104-5.

[341] Juliette Jowit. UN Says Eat Less Meat to Curb Global Warming. The Guardian. 2008;URL: http://www.theguardian.com/environment/2008/sep/07/food.foodanddrink.

[342] Susan Brink. Fatal Superbugs: Antibiotics Losing Effectiveness, WHO Says. 2014. National Geographic. URL: http://news.nationalgeographic.com/news/2014/05/140501-superbugs-antibiotics-resistance-disease-medicine/#close-modal.

[343] World Health Orgainization. Antimicrobial Resistance: Global Report on Surveillance 2014. 2014. URL: http://www.who.int/drugresistance/documents/surveillancereport/en/.

[344] Natural Resources Defense Council. Saving Antibiotics: What You Need to Know About Antibiotics Abuse on Farms. 2014. URL: http://www.nrdc.org/food/saving-antibiotics.asp.

[345] Dave R. Simon. Meatonomics: How the Rigged Economics of Meat and Dairy Make You Consume Too Much, and How to Eat Better, Live Longer, and Spend Smarter. Conari Press. 2013. URL: http://meatonomics.com/.

[346] World Business Council for Sustainable Development. Vision 2050: The New Agenda for Business. 2011. URL: http://www.wbcsd.org/pages/edocument/edocumentdetails.aspx?id=219&nosearchcontextkey=true.